Essential New York

Essential New York

A Guide to the History and Architecture of Manhattan's Important Buildings, Parks, and Bridges

John Tauranac

Photographs by Dave Sagarin

Holt, Rinehart and Winston · New York

For Liza

Published by Holt, Rinehart and Winston, 383 Madison Avenue, New York, New York 10017.

Published simultaneously in Canada by Holt, Rinehart and Winston of Canada, Limited.

Maps by Dean McChesney

Library of Congress Cataloging in Publication Data

Tauranac, John, 1939–
Essential New York.

    Bibliography: p.
    Includes index.
    1.   Manhattan (Borough)—Buildings.
2.   New York (City)—Buildings.   3.   Historic
buildings—New York (City)   4.   Architecture—
New York (City)   I.   Title.
F128.37.T36   974.7′1   78-12413
ISBN Hardbound: 0-03-042621-9
ISBN Paperback: 0-03-042626-X

First Edition

Designer: Kathy Peck
Printed in the United States of America
10 9 8 7 6 5 4 3 2 1

Contents

Acknowledgments

I wish to thank Columbia University for its generosity in making its libraries, especially Avery Library, open free to the university's graduates; the Local History Division of the Main Branch of the New York Public Library for, among other things, its scrapbooks; the Print Room of the New-York Historical Society for its arcanum; the Municipal Art Society for its collective support; Steve Miller of the Museum of the City of New York for his long-lived enthusiasms; Tom Bender of New York University for his insight; Bayrd Still, likewise of NYU, for putting so much of urban history into perspective; Michael George for his critical eye; Elliot Willensky for all the work he did and for encouraging me to do more; Margaret Latimer for all her questions; Tom Molloy for sharing the secrets of his building; Dean McChesney for his cartographic artistry; Judy and Dave Sagarin, Judy for untangling some seriously garbled sentences and Dave for taking some seriously wonderful pictures; and Jennifer Josephy for taking on the project at Holt and Susan Schulman for getting it to her.

Dave Sagarin wishes to thank his wife Judy for her support, and the Vivitar corporation for technical assistance.

Preface

Samuel Eliot Morison said that "America was discovered accidentally by a great seaman who was looking for something else; when discovered it was not wanted; and most of the exploration . . . was done in the hope of getting through it or around it." So it went with New York. The first European to sail into the harbor was Giovanni da Verrazano, who stumbled upon the harbor in 1524 in search of a western waterway to China. In 1609 Henry Hudson, also in search of the elusive passageway, sailed up the river that now bears his name. It was not until 1625 that the Dutch West India Company established a trading post on the southern tip of Manhattan, and with it, New Amsterdam. Business was good, and the temptation for getting in on the profits was great. In 1664 the British could resist no longer and sailed into the harbor to claim the town. Governor Peter Stuyvesant wisely gave up without a fight, and New Amsterdam became New York, a British colony.

The city continued to flourish under the British, and benefited from the royal favors that were bestowed upon it. Under the Dutch the city had been the colonies' leading exporter of beaver pelts. The British gave the city a monopoly on wheat milling and exporting. These symbols of New York's hegemony led the city fathers in 1686 to adopt the official seal showing the sails of a windmill, wheat barrels, and beavers flanked by a Dutch sailor with a sounding line and a "New York" Indian. (Within the seal was the date 1664, which the City Council recently changed to 1625 in a fit of revisionism.) A population that stood at about 300 in 1630 had grown tenfold to 3,200 by 1680. By 1775 the population had again increased almost tenfold, to 25,000. At that time New York City, which consisted only of Manhattan, was second in population to Philadelphia. The city's streets were lined by Georgian red-brick buildings or houses with Dutch gables in the older sections, and a smattering of impressive churches. Uptown were farms and country estates. It was a prosperous and neat provincial city.

This book, which is arranged chronologically, begins in the waning days of the British presence and includes only structures that are still standing in Manhattan today. The late starting date is explained by natural disasters and a never-ceasing restlessness that resulted in the survival of few buildings from Manhattan's pre–Revolutionary War days. In fact, there is very little from before 1835.

New York is still an ephemeral city, and what is here today just might be gone tomorrow. Fortunately, the city has had its Landmarks Preservation Commission since 1965, a group of city planners, architects, historians, and those interested in the quality of urban life, whose goal is to designate buildings of historic or architectural importance and see that they are preserved. In the entries that follow, designated New York City landmarks are indicated by (L) after their names.

I'm sure that questions will be raised about the inclusion of some buildings and the exclusion of others. I have tried to include at least one representative of each major style, as well as buildings that are the best or the worst of something, the first or the last, the most generous or the meanest. I have also included buildings that synthesize the history of an institution or an intellectual movement, and buildings that represent places of historical importance. Naturally, not every building in Manhattan is included, otherwise this one volume would grow to a wall of books, and its worth would be diminished in proportion to its bulk. If I have included what should have been excluded, or excluded what should have been included, please blame it on my ignorance or myopia.

Essential
New York

St. Paul's Chapel of Trinity Parish (L)   1766

Bounded by Broadway, Fulton, Church, and
Vesey streets
Thomas McBean, Architect; steeple, 1794, James
Crommelin Lawrence

St. Paul's is remarkable because it proved that a skillful,
sophisticated building could be erected in a provincial,
commercial city with a population of less than 25,000. It is
the only pre–Revolutionary War church still standing in
Manhattan.

By some accounts, St. Paul's was the grandest church in the
nation when it was built. It certainly was the most substantial
church edifice in the city, far grander than its mother church,
Trinity, which at the time was built entirely of wood. If New
York's St. Paul's reminds you of London's St. Martin's in the
Fields, it's probably because the architect of St. Paul's,
Thomas McBean, was once a student of James Gibbs, architect
of St. Martin's.

As late as 1750 this site was a wheatfield. The chapel
was erected here on the southern end of Trinity Church's
extensive land holdings that spread north to Greenwich Village only because a "more convenient place" (meaning further downtown) could not be found. Stones that were quarried from the site were used for the body of the chapel (the
stone is Manhattan schist, the stuff that Manhattan's great-
ness is made of, since most of the city's skyscrapers stand on
it); the tower is sheathed in brownstone; and the steeple,
which was not added until 1794, is made of wood, although
it certainly looks like stone.

The chapel's main entrance is under the tower and
through the small portico overlooking the graveyard, which
rolled down to the bank of the Hudson River before landfill.
The Ionic portico on Broadway with the Palladian altar
screen (the screen was designed by Major Pierre Charles
L'Enfant, and added in 1787) is really the rear entrance.

The interior, with its fluted Corinthian columns, its
Waterford crystal chandeliers, and its balcony, adds up to
New York's finest Georgian interior. The gilded Prince of
Wales feathers were placed above the pulpit in obeisance to
the crown, since this was the established church in the Prov-
ince of New York.

1

St. Paul's was one of the few churches in the area to survive the Great Fire of 1776, and it was to St. Paul's that George Washington retired to pray after taking the presidential oath at Federal Hall. As president, he regularly came here, and his pew is clearly marked on the north side, as is Governor DeWitt Clinton's on the south side.

Today St. Paul's is the only pre–Revolutionary War church still standing in the city. The sculpturally rectilinear twin towers of the World Trade Center could not be a better foil for St. Paul's steeple, a gentle and civilized statement that lifts itself off its tower in a series of diminishing *jetés* until it reaches the sky.

Morris-Jumel Mansion (L)   1768

Between 160th and 162nd streets on Edgecombe Avenue
Ascribed to Edward Pryor

This fine Georgian Colonial mansion, exquisitely formed and detailed, was the summer home of Colonel and Mrs. Roger Morris.

This Georgian Colonial house makes a statement about the quality of life achieved by some of the colonists before the Revolution. By 1765 there was enough money in the provincial city that a few New Yorkers, like Colonel and Mrs. Roger Morris, could afford to build both a town house on Whitehall Street for their winters and a country residence in upper Manhattan for their summers. (She had been Mary Philipse, of Philipse Manor in Yonkers, and had married Colonel Morris, an aide to General Braddock, after having spurned the hand of George Washington.)

Their uptown property was on one of the highest sites in the city, commanding "the finest prospect in the whole country." Since their 100 acres ran from the Hudson to the Harlem rivers, they had fishing, clamming, and oystering at either end. They had an orchard with quince trees that bore "extraordinarily well" (according to the advertisement for the property, at least), and three gardens, with the produce "sent to the York markets daily."

The Morris mansion, a fine Georgian Colonial country residence of exquisite scale and detailing, was built of brick (cooler than wood) with a wooden facade. It is believed to have been designed by Edward Pryor, who also designed Morven, the governor's mansion in Princeton, New Jersey. Typical of Georgian houses is the portico, supported by four Doric columns, which impart a stately air. Adding to the stateliness are the fanlight and side windows at the front door, and the second-story balcony tucked under the portico with the Palladian window behind it. The cornices are denticulated, the corners have quoins, and the whole is neatly crowned by a rooftop balustrade.

Eight years after he moved in, the Tory Morris moved out, fleeing the hazards of the Revolution for the safety of England. The house was used consecutively as headquarters for George Washington, General Sir Henry Clinton, and Baron Wilhelm von Knyphausen. After the Revolution the house was sold by the Commissioners of Forfeiture for £2,250 and became a tavern called Calumet Hall, a stopping-off point for the New York–Boston coaches.

In 1810, Mr. and Mrs. Stephen Jumel bought the house. Jumel soon died and his widow, Betsy, married Aaron Burr. She proceded to redecorate the interior in the style of the French Empire. After Burr's death Betsy lived on in the house, sometimes in seclusion, until she died in 1865. The house finally came under the auspices of the Washington Headquarters Association in 1904. Volunteers maintain it and its herb and rose garden, lovely reminders of the way it was for the very few.

Dyckman House (L)   Circa 1783

Broadway and 204th Street, northwest corner
Architect unknown

This is not just the only farmhouse in Manhattan of the Dutch Colonial style, it is the only remaining farmhouse in Manhattan of any style.

Perched on a hill in the Inwood section of Manhattan is Dyckman House, a startling reminder of New York's recent rural past and of its rapid rate of urbanization. This was the hub of the Dyckman farm, at one time comprising 300 acres, and still active as a farm until after the Civil War. The land sloped down to the Harlem River, its fields lush with apple, peach, and cherry trees. As late as 1904 there were still apple trees thriving on what is today the line of the IRT subway.

The first Dyckman in New Amsterdam, and the man who started the farm, was Jan Dyckman, who came from Westphalia via Holland in 1661. In large part his success was due to the large tracts of land he bought and rented to laborers for farms. The rent was set as low as one or two hens a year for as long as seven years, with the provision that the lessees plant fifty fruit trees for the benefit of the Dyckmans. At the end of seven years Dyckman could charge whatever the traffic would bear for his farms, and be assured of a thriving fruit business as well.

This house, with its low-pitched gambrel roof, was built by one of Jan Dyckman's descendants. The retreating British burned down the original Dyckman house (on the same site), which had been built in 1748, and it is widely believed that parts of the older house were salvaged and incorporated into this sturdily built fieldstone, brick, and wood house. The fieldstone walls are 20 inches thick, and the clapboards that rise to the peak of the gambrel roof cover hand-hewn, white-oak beams. A cutaway in the wall of the main hall shows a detail of its interior construction—hand-hewn stud river laths are held together with homemade nails and fillings of mud and marsh grass.

The house is still here because in 1915 two Dyckman descendants learned that an apartment-house developer planned to demolish the building. They restored the house, filled it with Dyckman family and period furniture, and promptly donated it and the little park around it to the City. As in the Morris-Jumel Mansion, there is a lovely formal garden in the rear. On summer afternoons the hill is alive with the sound of buzzing, as bees make their way from flower to flower.

18 Bowery (L)   1789

(Originally Edward Mooney House)
Southwest corner of Pell Street
Architect unknown

This is probably the oldest row house in Manhattan, built in the first blush of the Federal period and still adhering to the Georgian tradition.

New York City suffered great hardship between 1776 and 1783. About a thousand houses, or 25 percent of the city, were consumed in the Great Fire of 1776, and in 1783 another three thousand houses went up in smoke. During the Revolutionary War the British bivouacked and had their headquarters here, and they did not leave until November 25, 1783. By the end of the occupation the city's population had declined from a prewar high of about 25,000 to roughly 12,000. Even with the decline in population, overcrowding

and privation were horrendous. Wood for heating was impossible to come by, and new housing starts were at a standstill.

One reason for the postwar drop in population was the number of Tories who had fled the country. James DeLancey was one of them, and this site, part of his forfeited land, was bought in 1785 from the Commissioners of Forfeiture by Edward Mooney, a merchant in the wholesale meat business. By 1789 Mooney had built this substantial red-brick building. The year it was finished was the year George Washington took his oath of office less than a mile away. Chronologically, the building is Federal, but architecturally it is Georgian in its proportions and attention to classical detail. The Georgian style was derived from the great Italian architect Palladio, and modified by generations of Englishmen. The doorcase of the Mooney house, for instance, could have been lifted from *The Designs of Inigo Jones*, published in 1727.

The house is a full three stories high, with a finished garret beneath a gambrel roof. Glass had only begun to be manufactured in any quantity in the middle colonies in 1740, yet here are windows that are especially generous, broad, and neatly topped by splayed lintels. Framing the roof are hand-hewn timbers, an elaborate and costly process that would disappear with the coming of the machine age.

Mooney's house is indicative of the tremendous resurgence the city would make after the Revolution. By 1789 visitors were talking about the city's grand houses, ships were beginning to fill the harbor again, and the population had practically doubled from its wartime low, reaching 23,614. By the turn of the nineteenth century the city would be gaining on Philadelphia as the nation's most populous city, and building would begin to match that growth. It would make fortunes for some, like John Jacob Astor, and hell for others, when some of the elegant Knickerbocker houses like Edward Mooney's were left behind in the northward movement and broken up into multifamily dwelling units that quickly deteriorated into slums.

Gracie Mansion (L)   1799

In Carl Schurz Park, at Eighty-eighth Street east
of East End Avenue
Architect unknown (some attribute it to Major
Pierre Charles L'Enfant); additions, 1966, Mott B.
Schmidt

*Originally a country home for a wealthy merchant, Gracie
Mansion has been the official residence of New York City's
mayors since 1943.*

In 1799 the East River at Eighty-eighth Street—although
Eighty-eighth Street would not even appear on maps until
twelve years later—seemed far enough away from the counting houses of Whitehall Street for merchant Archibald Gracie
to build a sixteen-room country home there. The site, on a
promontory, was ideal, and the house, with verandas surrounding it, would catch the summer breezes off the river.

The house was built for a man of taste and fortune, and
its Federal detailing—the main doorway with its lead-glass
sidelights and semicircular lunette above, the balconies with
their intricate latticework—makes it a glorious reminder of
the turn of the nineteenth century. Here the Gracie family
entertained the likes of Louis Philippe, later king of France,
President John Quincy Adams, and writers James Fenimore
Cooper and Washington Irving. (Irving was also a frequent
guest of John Jacob Astor, whose summer house was just up
the hill on what is today the south side of Eighty-seventh
Street between York and East End avenues.)

Gracie's fleet of ships, with their red and white signals,
called on ports around the world and poured their profits
into New York. Unfortunately, Napoleonic France seized two
of his ships in 1807 and Gracie lost over a million dollars,
finally leading his company into insolvency. What happened
between 1823, when the Gracie family sold the house to Joseph Foulke, and 1893, when the City bought it, is a little
unclear, and what the City did with it at first is also unclear.
In 1923 it was being used as a comfort station in Carl Schurz
Park. In 1924 it was made available to the newly created
Museum of the City of New York. But the house was not

fireproof, and in 1930 the museum moved its precious collection to its present home on Fifth Avenue at 103rd Street.

At the time, it was decided that the mayors of New York ought to be provided with an official residence. By 1942 the odds were on the purchase of the seventy-five-room neo–French Gothic château belonging to Charles Schwab on Riverside Drive at Seventy-third Street. When Mayor Fiorello La Guardia heard of the scheme, he said "What! Me in that!" and settled on Gracie Mansion as more appropriate, and a lot cheaper. Today Gracie Mansion is the only inhabited house of its era on Manhattan Island. In recent times public rooms were added, but so artfully that you would hardly realize it from the facade, nor from within.

Stuyvesant-Fish House (L)
1804

21 Stuyvesant Street, between Third and Second avenues
Architect unknown

This house has all the hallmarks of a classic Federal-style residence, except that its 28⅓-foot width and its height make it outsized.

If an aristocracy holds rank and wealth as a result of the actions of its forebears, then this house was built by New York's oldest, most venerable aristocratic family. It is on a piece of land which the Dutch West India Company granted in 1651 to Peter Stuyvesant, New Amsterdam's last director-general. His farm, which in Dutch is *bouwerij*, was bounded by today's Sixth Street, Third Avenue, Eighteenth Street, and the East River. The Dutch said that the road that led to his farm was the "road to the *bouwerij*," which in time came to be the Bowery. The irregularly angled Stuyvesant Street led from the confluence of the Bowery with Third and Fourth avenues to the home of Pegleg Peter.

The street was later developed by Stuyvesant's descendants, many of whom had vast wealth as a result of their inherited lands. For instance, when Peter G. Stuyvesant, a childless descendant, died in 1847, he bequeathed half a million dollars apiece to Hamilton Fish, Gerard Stuyvesant, and the son of his ward. To his widow was bequeathed $12,000 a year and their house, which diarist Philip Hone (who later became New York's mayor) described as "splendid." The remainder of his estate was divided among his nieces and nephews, and it was estimated that each of them would receive $100,000. With this kind of money in the family, it is no wonder that when the City wanted to knock down the houses on Stuyvesant Street and straighten the street to make it conform to the gridiron pattern, the city fathers realized that they simply could not afford to condemn the land and indemnify the owners.

This house was built by Peter Stuyvesant's great-grandson, not for himself but as a wedding gift for his daughter Elizabeth and her husband, Nicholas Fish. It was in this house that Hamilton Fish, legatee of half a million dollars, was born; he went on to become a governor, senator, and progenitor of other Fishes, among them, Stuyvesant. The house is a full three stories high, with a half-basement and, peaking out from the pitched roof, a pair of dormer windows indicating the fourth floor. The fanlight window above the entrance, the side windows that flank the entrance, the wrought-iron railing with the neo-classical motif, the splayed lintels, and the Flemish bond brickwork are all hallmarks of the Federal style. Unlike the Mooney house, this was not built as a row house. Its side windows once overlooked eastern vistas.

The Rectory of the Church of Our Lady of the Rosary (L)   1806

(Originally home of James Watson)
7 State Street, between Pearl and Whitehall streets
Eastern portion, 1793
Ascribed to John McComb, Jr.; architect of eastern portion unknown; restored by Shanley & Sturges, 1965.

This Federal row house is set back from the street with an Ionic porch in front to continue the building line and make a good thing of a bad angle.

This is a prime waterfront site, and businesses were attracted to it early. But by the 1790s, in one of the few examples of a southward flow of residential population in New York, first-class homes were being established here. With only a promenade along the waterfront and no major obstructions between the house and the harbor, the view was unexcelled. Just down the block, on the site of the U. S. Custom House, was Government House, designed as the official residence of the president, and new houses were arriving in its wake. In 1793 James Watson, who later ran for the office of lieutenant-governor on the Federalist ticket, built the eastern half of this pair of houses flush with the street in the restrained manner of the American Georgian style. Watson then had an extension added in 1806. Its design is ascribed to John McComb, Jr., the first American-born architect.

The new house was set back from the street and a porch with a double colonnade was incorporated. The columns—gracefully attenuated Ionic on top, stolid square Doric on the bottom—are not marble but wood. (Some sources say they were originally ships' masts.)

Because the wall of the extension was set back and curved at a greater angle than the street itself, it brilliantly resolved the problem of light. Row houses always suffer from too little light, since ordinarily light can enter only from the front or the rear. In addition to the usual exposures, the architect provided a southern exposure to the old house by setting back the extension. And by setting back the new house at an acute angle, he likewise gave it a southern exposure.

The house is in the Federal style, a period when the Georgian tradition was groping toward the classical revival that would blossom in the 1830s. Unlike the ersatz Federal houses that abound in American suburbs, there are no American Federal eagles over the doors.

In 1834 the *New York Daily Mirror* said that the row of houses on State Street had "an aristocratic and stately look. . . . Their proportions majestic . . . their construction solid and substantial." The Watson house is the last of the row, and although the brownstone lintels and windowsills have been replaced by white pressed stone, and although the free-standing dormers stand free no more, the house typifies the excellence and elegance of Federal architecture.

City Hall (L)   1811

City Hall Park, Broadway at Murray Street
Mangin & McComb, Architects

When this elegant city hall was being built, Mayor DeWitt Clinton decided to save money by using inferior stone on its uptown side. After all, he reasoned, hardly anybody lives north of Chambers Street, so hardly anyone will notice.

This small, neo-classical palace, combining the style of Louis XVI in its massing and the Georgian tradition in its detailing, is without peer in New York City.

You will find elements of this building in many other neo-classical buildings—egg-and-dart moldings, dentils, a balustrade, square-headed windows alternating with arched, keystoned windows—but nowhere else in New York City will you find these elements assembled so gracefully.

An Ionic portico sets the stage for it all. The central pavilion, divided vertically into three parts, is flanked by two wings, creating a tripartite theme horizontally. This theme is repeated vertically by the use of cornices, which divide but also act as the unifying bond.

Many people are stunned when they see City Hall for the first time. They find it hard to believe that this graceful, delicate building is the seat of a municipal government representing 7.5 million city residents. In fact, even many long-time residents mistakenly believe that the Municipal Building, not this small gem, is New York's city hall.

It was started as a show of confidence in the city. By the turn of the nineteenth century, New York City was no longer the federal or the state capital. Nevertheless, New York's population was over 60,000, it was a cosmopolitan place, and its burgher kings were prophesying a great future for the city.

It was a time when the new republic was constructing buildings of grandeur—James Hoban's White House was started in 1792, the cornerstone for the United States Capitol was laid in 1793, and Charles Bulfinch's State House in Boston was finished in 1798. New York's City Hall, then on Wall at Broad, had been built in 1700, and although remodeled by Major Pierre L'Enfant in 1789, it seemed neither large enough nor grand enough. In 1802 a competition was held for a new city hall, and Joseph François Mangin and John McComb, Jr., teamed up to win the $350 prize.

Architect Benjamin Latrobe, who had submitted his own design, was horrified. He described their design as a "vile heterogeneous composition . . . the invention of a New York bricklayer and a St. Domingo Frenchman in partnership." But contemporary newspapers agreed with the City's decision, calling Mangin and McComb's elevation "elegant," and a "credit to the taste and talents of the architects and . . . the judgement of the Corporation."

McComb, the "bricklayer," was the son of John McComb, Sr., architect of the Brick Church, and he was the first native-born architect in New York. Mangin, the "St. Domingo Frenchman," was an émigré from the French Revolution, who presumably traveled to New York via Santo Domingo. As an engineer, he had already surveyed the city streets.

Mangin was the chief designer of the facade, while McComb designed the interiors and oversaw the details of construction, for which he was paid the princely sum of $6 a day. When a cost overrun began, Mayor DeWitt Clinton decided that Newark brownstone should be substituted for the Massachusetts marble in the rear. At the time, hardly anyone lived north of Chambers Street, and the usually far-sighted Clinton believed that it would be many years before anyone would live far enough uptown to notice. (In 1954 the marble and sandstone were stripped off and replaced by veined Alabama limestone and red Minnesota granite, both front and back.)

The building has had its ups and downs. In 1833, when the Greek Revival was just beginning, the aldermen considered selling City Hall to the federal government for $500,000 and erecting a new city hall in Union Square. In 1858, in celebration of the laying of the Atlantic Cable, fireworks set off from its roof set fire to the entire upper story and cupola, causing the statue to crash through the roof. Some people urged that a new cast-iron city hall be built. In 1893 the City wanted to sell the building to the New-York Historical Society as the society's new home on Central Park West. And the Tilden Trust wanted it removed to Reservoir Square (now Bryant Park) and re-erected there as a library.

Lately there have been no such rumblings, because finally the building is appreciated both for its inherent worth as a thing of beauty and for its historical associations. It is the place where mileage from New York City was traditionally measured; where Abraham Lincoln lay in state while 500,000 mourners paid homage; where heroes like Charles Lindbergh, Gertrude Ederle, and John Glenn have been officially received. And because it is where the mayor has his office, and where the City Council and the Board of Estimate meet, it is where New Yorkers come when they want to fight City Hall.

Castle Clinton (L) 1811

(Originally the West Battery; subsequently Castle Garden, the Emigrant Landing Depot, and the New York City Aquarium)
Battery Park, at the southern tip of Manhattan Island
John McComb, Jr., Architect

Now a mere shell, the masonry walls, the embrasures, and the sturdy doors are about all that remain of this integral part of the port of New York's defenses.

From 1693 until 1823 a battery of cannon defended the toe of Manhattan Island. The first battery was placed on the narrow beach at about State and Bridge streets. In 1625 Fort Amsterdam, later Fort George, was built on what is now the site of the U.S. Custom House. And by 1807 work had begun on an impregnable defense that would sit on an island about 200 feet off the southern tip of Manhattan.

It was called the West Battery, and its intent was to command the Hudson River and the upper harbor, and to catch ships in the East River in a crossfire with Castle Williams across the water to the east, on Governors Island. To do the job, John McComb, Jr., designed a fort that bristled with twenty-eight 32-pounders set into embrasures in the 8-foot-thick walls. By 1811 the West Battery would be finished and in 1815 renamed Castle Clinton, in honor of DeWitt Clinton. It was all academic, since no enemy ships sailed into the harbor during the War of 1812—perhaps because of this formidable presence—and in 1823 the federal government decommissioned the fort and presented it to the City.

Castle Clinton became Castle Garden, a "place of resort." With a domed roof on top and a seating capacity of about six thousand, it was perhaps the largest assembly hall in the United States at the time, the place to go for lectures and concerts and political celebrations. A true hero's welcome had to start from Castle Clinton and continue up Broadway. It was here at a welcoming celebration for President Andrew Jackson in 1833 that the connecting bridge collapsed, dumping the revelers and two toll houses—but not Old Hickory—into the drink. And it was in a sold-out Castle Garden that P. T. Barnum introduced New Yorkers to singer Jenny Lind, the "Swedish Nightingale." And since demand exceeded supply, something else was introduced here—ticket scalping.

Another new life began for Castle Clinton in 1855 when it became the Emigrant Landing Depot, the first formal port of entry for immigrants in New York. This was the first time that the government—in this case, the City of New York—undertook any responsibility for formally processing immigrants. Much of that responsibility was protection for the lambs from the wolves that were lying in wait to fleece them, selling them tickets on trains that did not exist, renting them apartments in houses that were already full, taking every penny of hard-earned savings that could be snared. Instead, clerks would dispense information on train schedules and rates and would elicit the immigrants' immediate means of support and ultimate destinations, and physicians would give physical examinations. By 1892, when Ellis Island first opened, about 7.5 million immigrants had been processed through this building. In 1870 landfill was used to create Battery Park, ending the old fort's insularity.

With the departure of the immigration station to Ellis Island, Castle Clinton's role again changed, this time to the New York City Aquarium in 1896. McKim, Mead & White remodeled the building, adding two floors and installing gigantic tanks in which the public could easily view the different specimens. The Battery seemed a logical place for an aquarium, since it could use the water directly from the harbor—the filtering plant was in the fort's former ammunition vault. But it was soon apparent that the Hudson River, even then, was too filled with the effluvia of upriver cities and towns, and clean salt water was brought in from the ocean and stored in a 100,000-gallon tank under the lawn. By 1941 the aquarium had moved out, and the fort was again declared redundant.

Slated for demolition, and in the way of Robert Moses's proposed Brooklyn–Battery Bridge, the fort was saved by the federal government when it was declared a national historic monument in 1950. Now it is only a shell of its former self, but go down into it, stand behind one of the embrasures, look out over the vastness of New York Harbor and the total command that this fort held over it, and you will begin to feel the power that was once this island fortress.

Schermerhorn Row (L)   1812

2–18 Fulton Street, between South and Front streets
Architect unknown

There's not much left of the lower floors, nor of the high-pitched roof, but overall this is one of the best remaining Federal warehouse groupings in the United States.

In the mid-nineteenth century this area was the center for the coffee and tea trade with the Far East, the hemp trade with Java, the pelt trade with Canada, New York's part of the cotton triangle between the South and England, and a relay point for produce from the Midwest shipped via the Erie Canal. Exotic goods were sent here, put up for sale, inspected, bid on, haggled over, and sold amid a crowd of sea captains and merchants, seamen and teamsters, wheelers and dealers, and the mildly curious. Cape Horn traders, barks, and clipper ships all tied up on the East River, some alongside Burling or Peck Slip, others with their bowsprits pointed inland and overhanging South Street, the "Street of Ships." They docked on the East River because, unlike the Hudson, it seldom froze.

In 1800, however, none of this activity existed here. Nor did Schermerhorn Row, or the land it stands on. These commercial buildings were built for Peter Schermerhorn, a merchant. In 1795 he started buying land along Water Street, which at that time fronted on the East River. Then he bought lots that extended 230 feet underwater into the river. By 1811 land had appeared, created by landfill that contained so much filth it was said to have caused sickness in the area. Within a year the row was completed.

It was fortuitous timing. The Fulton Ferry to Brooklyn

opened in 1814, and the Fulton Market in 1822, both just across the street. And two events would shape the rise of the New York port, which by 1812 had already eclipsed Boston and Philadelphia as America's leading port, events that would leave those rivals in New York's wake: in 1818 the Black Ball line instituted the first regularly scheduled packet service between the United States and England, and in 1825 the Erie Canal linked New York City with the Great Lakes.

This row of warehouses is one of the few surviving rows of Federal commercial architecture in New York, one of the last rows to reflect all this excitement. Although it has been modified, it is overall the best remaining Federal grouping in New York and one of the finest in the United States.

The row was originally uniform, one idea architecturally, one idea stylistically, all reflecting one ideal—classic simplicity, scale, and harmony. Each of the row's eight central buildings was two bays wide, with a round-arched door alternating with a square-headed window on the main floor. (The only surviving arched doorway is found at No. 2, and its door is Victorian.) The corner buildings had greater frontage on Fulton Street, each being three windows wide. Above the main floor were three floors with sash windows. Each window was topped by a splayed brownstone lintel, with a brownstone sill below, and flanked by shutters. A cornice ran the length of the buildings, over which the slate-covered, high-pitched roof ran the length of the row. Unfortunately, the perfect symmetry was first broken when the Fulton Ferry Hotel added an additional floor which was topped by a mansard roof in 1868, then shattered when No. 12 was given a new facade and an extra floor in 1935.

The row was built to be commercial, and its tenants—merchants, commission merchants, and importers—were mostly tied to the tides of the East River. The main floors served as their offices, or "counting houses." Above were the warehouses, with three full floors of merchandise either stored to be sold from the premises, or awaiting transshipment. Hand-operated wooden hoists were used to get the merchandise up and down.

In the ebb and flow of urban life, many of the counting houses had become storefronts by the 1840s, with the Federal doorways and fenestration giving way to the Greek Revival ideal of a post-and-lintel system in granite; some cast iron even appears in the 1850s. Today it would require an urban archaeologist to sort out all of the pieces of Schermerhorn Row, but the South Street Seaport Museum and the New York State Maritime Museum are hard at it, and already some of the neighboring buildings are being brought back from architectural limbo.

21–29 Vandam Street (L)   1828–1834

Between the Avenue of the Americas and Varick Street
No. 19, 1828, Edgar Harriot, Builder; No. 23, 1833, Israel Clark, Builder; Nos. 25, 27, and 29, 1834, Daniel Turner, Builder

As fine a row of Federal-style "second-rate genteel" houses as New York has today, with dormer windows still peaking out from pitched roofs.

As recently as the 1900s, row after row of Federal-style row houses lined New York streets. Today only a few oases remain where rows of houses can be seen in any semblance of their original order, and this one on Vandam Street is about as good as any in New York. These houses were speculatively built for the middle class, whose places of business were within walking distance. The houses average 20 feet wide and are a full two stories high, with dormers peaking out from pitched roofs that show the third floor. Half-basements are below, and the service entrances are under the stoops. The trim is restrained, with plain or cap-molded lintels (No. 23's are slightly askew) and little decoration except the doorframes with their recessed Doric or Ionic columns supporting an architrave with a rectangular light above. The columns are wood.

The front of the basement almost always housed the family dining room, and the kitchen was in the rear. The first floor contained the formal dining and drawing rooms, the front and back parlors that were usually used only for company or major occasions. Upstairs were front and back bedrooms, with an unheated storeroom/attic under the pitched roof. As visiting William Ross said in 1834: "Such is the arrangement of one private house; the same description will apply to five hundred of them."

This property was originally owned by Trinity Church (the streets were not ceded to the City until 1808). By the 1760s there was an estate here called Richmond Hill, which by the turn of the nineteenth century had fallen into the hands of Aaron Burr. After his duel with Alexander Hamilton, Burr needed some quick cash, so he sold his property to John Jacob Astor. The property had already been platted (laid out in streets), and Astor, true to form, simply hung onto it until the pressure of a growing population had increased its value.

These homes were built in the same spirit. Their builders knew, as James Fenimore Cooper had pointed out in 1825, that "no American who is at all comfortable in life will share his dwelling with another. Each has his own roof, and his own little yard." By 1826 there was enough demand for Edgar Harriot to build No. 17 (not shown). By 1834 the row would be complete.

The plaques on Nos. 25 and 27 that say c 1823 were installed in an excess of wishful zeal, and are not official landmark plaques. The pedants are particularly enraged by them, not so much because the plaques show the wrong date but because they think "circa" is only supposed to be used to define dates that end in a zero or a five.

Northern Dispensary   Circa 1831

165 Waverly Place, at Christopher Street
Architect unknown

This red-brick building in the Federal vernacular style was New York's second free medical dispensary. By 1853 there would be four more.

This free-standing building has been dispensing free medical treatment and medication to the poor since it opened its doors in the early 1830s. Three stories high, it is straightforward and honest, the kind of building that would not intimidate the poor in need of medical help.

The dispensary is built on a triangular plot, bounded by the confluence of Grove with Christopher streets on one side, and by Waverly Place on two (Waverly Place splits here, continuing west to Grove as well as north to Bank). This peculiar geography has led people to describe the dispensary as having two sides on one street and two streets on one side.

By the time it was built the City had already been accepting some responsibility for the health of its citizens for almost a hundred years. It was in 1736 that an infirmary was first instituted, but that was only one room with six beds, and it was in the public workhouse (the infirmary ultimately became Bellevue Hospital).

In 1792 the City's first dispensary appeared, at the corner of White and Centre streets. In 1827, when the number of deaths in one year reached 5,181, the largest total recorded up to that time (it was not due to a plague, but to the increase in population), the City's second dispensary—the Northern, because it was so far uptown—was chartered.

Its exact opening date is imprecise, but if it was 1831 it could not have opened at a more propitious time. Since the

1790s, New York had been regularly visited by cholera and yellow-fever epidemics, and in 1832 more than 3,500 New Yorkers died of cholera. There was still no water delivery system, common sewers had not been installed, and pigs rooted around lower Broadway, acting as scavengers for garbage. When plagues did come, the City advocated resettlement of the population away from the pestilential quarters, barricaded the streets, spread quicklime, and set fires to purify the air.

But real progress was being made against disease. As early as 1816 free vaccinations for smallpox were given by the City Dispensary (the municipality contributed $1,000 for the effort), and by 1853 there would be six dispensaries in all, with responsibilities extending as far north as Eightieth Street on the West Side. That was the village of Bloomingdale, a village even further removed from the city to its south in 1853 than Greenwich Village was in 1831 when the Northern Dispensary was built.

Old Merchant's House (L) 1832

(Formerly home of Seabury Tredwell and family)
29 East Fourth Street, between Lafayette Street and the Bowery
Ascribed to Minard Lafever

A house that is still Federal but hints at the Greek Revival to come, built during one of the first great waves of real-estate speculation.

In 1807 a street commission was created whose goal was to bring order to the city's streets and provide a pattern for New York's growth. Four years later the commission's plan was promulgated. It called for a gridiron plan of right-angled streets, with numbered east-west streets progressing as far north as 155th Street, and numbered north-south avenues progressing west of First to Twelfth, and lettered avenues running east of First. The length of each block from building line to building line would measure 200 feet north and south, and range from 600 to 900 feet east and west. All streets above First Street would reflect this pattern, wiping out a major variation like Broadway and minor ones like Stuyvesant Street (it happened only on paper). Right-angled streets were selected because the commission believed that straight-sided and right-angled houses were the most economical to build, and that the street system should reflect building patterns. Building lots could be easily divided into 25-by-100-foot lots, or any variation on the width, and easily sold off. New York's real-estate market was made safe for speculation.

By the 1830s, this neighborhood had become the fashionable uptown quarter, thanks to Manhattan's relentless northward drift of population and the ease of subdivision. Merchant Peter Schermerhorn and mayor and diarist Philip Hone lived on Great Jones Street. The Samuel Ward Mansion, a two-story, porticoed house whose owner boasted the city's first private art gallery, was at Broadway and Bond Street. Down the block lived Samuel Ruggles, Gramercy Park's developer; and Albert Gallatin, Jefferson's secretary of the treasury and the founder of New York University. Most of the houses in the neighborhood were speculatively built, and their design features were borrowed from the style books of the day. The houses, however, were seldom stamped out of a mold, and there was tremendous diversity, even innovation.

This house, for instance, is either very late Federal or very early Greek Revival. Because of its elegant detailings, architectural historians believe that someone with a highly sophisticated eye had something to do with its design, perhaps Minard Lafever. Its doorway alone makes it different from earlier Federal houses. Here is a stone enframement with a round-arched doorway and a triple keystone. The columns are wood, and their straightforward approach to their Ionic design does more than provide a hint of the Greek Revival that would soon engulf architectural design. (The interior is Greek Revival, complete with Ionic columns separating the front and rear parlors.)

An English visitor to New York was stunned by the expanse of windows in the city's entranceways. In England there was a tax on windows, but in New York there was none, so each front door could boast a fanlight as well as sidelights, making the hall as well lighted as any room in the house. The stairway was set toward the rear of the house, so the landings themselves had natural light from windows in the rear, unlike later houses where stairways would rise in a central well. Fireplaces were the only source of heat in the house, and every room had its own, except the single-windowed bedrooms above the entrance.

The remarkable state of preservation of this house is not happenstance. It has had only three sets of owners. The man who bought it in 1832 was Joseph Brewster, a hat merchant. In 1835 he sold it to Seabury Tredwell, another merchant, and it was inhabited by Tredwell's descendants until 1933, a remarkable achievement in this otherwise ephemeral city. In 1935 the house was bought by a nonprofit corporation, which has been restoring it. The hollow urn newel-posts—elegant wrought-iron detailings that make this house distinctive—have already been replaced. More work is awaiting more money.

1–13 Washington Square North   Circa 1832

("The Row")
Between Fifth Avenue and University Place
Ascribed to Ithiel Town & A. J. Davis

In a break with the Federal concern for form came this row of red-brick houses with Greek Revival trim, a Romantic idea, the first of the eclecticisms.

The time had come to break away from the Federal concern for form and find a new ideal, a Romantic one which identified with a personal concern or a historical idea. In the 1820s the intellectual rage was for all things Greek. Shelley, Byron, and Keats had all become Grecophiles. Americans especially identified with Greece. It had been the first democracy, and it had begun its own war of independence in 1821. By the 1830s, American architecture was catching up with the intellectual movement, and the country was being swept by the first of many of the nineteenth century's eclectic movements, the Greek Revival.

This row of red-brick, Greek Revival houses is not only one of New York's earliest, it is also one of the city's finest. Built for the merchant aristocracy, the scale of these thirteen houses is far grander than the Federal houses that preceded them. Gone is the pitched roof of 18 Bowery, for instance.

Gone are the dormer windows of the Stuyvesant-Fish House. And gone are the fanlights of Seabury Tredwell's house. Here are three full floors for the family, with servants' quarters above and kitchen and family dining room in the half-basement. The entrances are free-standing neo-Greek porches, with Doric or Ionic columns topped by flat lintels. The cast-iron railings display standard Greek Revival trim, including anthemia (a stylized honeysuckle motif) and lyres.

An integral part of Greek Revival rows was a unified cornice line. The "improvement" to No. 3 that was made in the 1880s was the first to break it. Second were Nos. 7–13, seven houses that were gutted and made into one apartment building in 1939. The roofline was elevated to incorporate a full fifth floor. (Mercifully, the fronts were left pristine; the stoops today lead nowhere, since the real entrance is just around the corner, off Fifth Avenue.)

The original layouts and trim of these houses set the standard for first-class row houses in the nineteenth century. The parlor floor, which is the first floor reached by the stoop, was used for formal occasions. The front parlor was the sitting room, and the back parlor was the dining room. Each room could be closed off from the other by a pair of sliding doors, flanked in this case by columns that reiterated the Greek Revival theme. This was the floor with the richest woods, the most elaborately carved marble mantels, crystal chandeliers, and mirrors judiciously placed to catch as much light as possible. The basic layout of the houses was repeated on the two bedroom floors above, often with dressing rooms and closets separating the rooms.

For all the elegance of "The Row," remember that these houses had no running water, no plumbing, neither gaslight nor electricity, and the horses were kept stabled immediately behind in what is now Washington Mews.

Colonnade Row (L) 1833

(Originally LaGrange Terrace)
428–434 Lafayette Street, between Fourth Street and Astor Place
Ascribed to A. J. Davis

The first of New York's elegantly colonnaded rows of houses, and now, in its truncated and reduced circumstances, the last.

Nine sumptuously elegant houses originally comprised this row, a row that was conceived as a single entity, an urban space unified by twenty-seven Corinthian columns.

Unfortunately, five of the houses were torn down in 1911 to make way for a warehouse for the Wanamaker store. Gone too are the iron railing that ran across the front of the columns, making a balcony of the entire length of the first floor, and the Greek Revival railing that protected the parterre in front of the buildings. And gone as well are the stone slabs

topped by torchères that led up to the entrances. (These torchères, complete with their stone pedestals, have recently been discovered on the grounds of former Mayor Abram Hewitt's home, Ringwood Manor, in New Jersey.)

When these houses were being planned, wild blackberries were still growing here, and there were farms owned by families whose names like Bleecker and Brevoort are still recognized. By 1833 the area's bucolic aspect changed with the coming of a 100-foot-wide street that cut through to Astor Place, a street that speculative builders had petitioned to be as wide as any avenue. Named Lafayette Place (now Street), it honored the Revolutionary War hero, the Marquis de Lafayette, who only nine years earlier had returned to New York and a hero's welcome (they threw flowers at him, not ticker tape). No sooner had the street opened than Seth Geer, one of the petitioners, had these nine houses built with the help of Sing Sing prisoners who cut the Westchester marble. With the Lafayette Place address, the houses were named LaGrange Terrace, in honor of Lafayette's estate.

By the 1820s New York's fashionable residential district west of City Hall was beginning to be encroached on by the seemingly insatiable needs of commerce. When LaGrange Terrace opened, with houses costing $25,000 to $30,000, New York's wealthy stampeded uptown. The success of this urban paradise led to imitations. Within the year "Colonnade Houses" at 714 and 716 Broadway, buildings that backed onto LaGrange Terrace, were built with 25-foot-high Ionic columns. Underhill's Colonnade Buildings, overlooking New York Harbor from Brooklyn Heights, were erected in 1837. And in 1845 there appeared a row of houses designed by A. J. Davis that were set back on Twenty-third Street between Eighth and Ninth avenues, set off by uniform pilasters, and called London Terrace. All that remains of any of them is this truncated row, in reduced circumstances today, but a reminder of the halcyon days of the colonnaded house in New York.

Gramercy Park   1834

Between Twentieth and Twenty-first streets, at
the end of Irving Place and the beginning of
Lexington Avenue
Samuel B. Ruggles, Developer

*Speculator Ruggles realized that one way to enhance the
value of his lots was to place them around an urban amenity
like a private park, and so New York's most famous private
park was created.*

London is known for its residential squares, urban amenities
that make that city so civilized. Instead of creating vernal
oases in New York, by 1837 the City was selling off the land
that had comprised the only major park called for by the
Street Commissioners of 1807. Known as the Parade, it was
to have stretched from Twenty-third to Thirty-fourth streets,
between Third and Seventh avenues. But it was shortened
and renamed Madison Square. By the 1830s, however, both
Washington and Union squares had been rescued from their
role as potter's fields, and with the coming of Madison and
Stuyvesant squares, and Gramercy Park, the area between
Fourth and Twenty-eighth streets would have New York's
greatest concentration of London-like residential squares. All
of the city's parks, however, did not add up to 100 acres.

Gramercy Park started as a smart real-estate venture. In
1831 Samuel B. Ruggles bought a 20-acre farm from the heirs
of James Duane, New York's first mayor after the Revolution.
Ruggles realized that if he provided an urban amenity his

property value would be enhanced. One of the ways was to heed the words of the Rev. Dr. Hawks, the future minister of Calvary Church, who had said to him that "man makes buildings, but God makes space." Ruggles was already promoting Union Square and understood the values of light and air, so he laid out a formal square, a la London, and put up sixty-six lots for sale. Ruggles promptly sold his lots with the understanding that the lot owners would have the sole rights to the park providing they each paid $10 a year for its upkeep and maintenance. As the lot sales were consummated, the owners were presented with gold keys to the park. (Those who live on the periphery of Gramercy Park are still the only ones with keys, although the keys are no longer gold.)

The houses that were built around the park reflect the styles of the day. Gothic Revival drip-moldings are on the upper floors of The Players at No. 16; the lower floors were remodeled in 1888 by Stanford White after Edwin Booth had donated his home to The Players for a clubhouse (Booth's likeness in the role of Hamlet is the statue by Edwin T. Quinn that has stood in the center of the park since 1918).

Built in the waning days of the Greek Revival, 3 and 4 Gramercy Park West are glorious, their cast-iron railings, porches, and balconies, complete with the anthemion motif, adding a touch of New Orleans glamour. The "Mayor's Lamps" at No. 4 honor the home of James Harper, the Harper of *Harper's Weekly* and New York's mayor from 1844 to 1847. What is believed to be New York's first cooperative apartment house stands at 34 Gramercy Park East, and at 144 East Twentieth Street is the Brotherhood Synagogue, originally a Friends Meeting House.

This is New York's most formal and best-preserved park. It is the kind of formalism found in this park, with its feeling of an eighteenth-century garden, against which the Romantic movement would rebel a quarter of a century later.

St. Peter's Church (L)   1840

22 Barclay Street, southeast corner of Church Street
John R. Haggerty and Thomas Thomas, Architects

Although the Greek Revival might seem too austere for the liturgy of the Roman Catholic Church, even the Church succumbed to it.

The rage for all things Greek took a peculiar turn in the 1830s when even churches were designed in the style of the pagan Greeks. Most of the early churches were modest. Their side walls might be rubble stone or brick, their front walls a facade of brownstone often containing a pair of Doric columns flanked by pairs of antae, pilasters that set off walls. St. Peter's Church, however, is a great temple-church built with a front of gray granite. It has a full portico before it, with six impressive Ionic columns, each clearly three hunks of granite

supporting a perfectly austere pediment, with only a niche for a statue of St. Peter in it. The austerity of this St. Peter's is a far cry from Rome, and its Grecian purity was not even compromised by the cross atop its pediment until sometime after the 1890s.

Until 1785 there was no Roman Catholic church in the city, although Roman Catholics had been guaranteed freedom of religion under the Dongan Charter of 1686, and as early as 1687 services had been held in Fort James under Governor Thomas Dongan's rule. In 1785, with the aid of Hector St. John de Crevecoeur, consul-general of France, five lots were bought on "easy terms" from one of the city's wealthiest landlords, Trinity Church. (The local street names instantly identify the original owner of these lands—Trinity backed on Church Street, and the Reverend Henry Barclay was Trinity's second rector.) By 1786 the first St. Peter's on this site had been consecrated, and in 1808 it was estimated that of New York's 60,000 inhabitants, about 14,000 were Roman Catholic, though, according to one Jesuit, many had not seen the face of a priest since their arrival in the country. (New York's second Roman Catholic church was the first St. Patrick's Cathedral. Its cornerstone was laid on Mott and Prince streets in 1809.) By 1836 attendance was up and the old St. Peter's was torn down to make way for this imposing Greek temple-church.

Although St. Peter's might not look it, this building was an innovator in the construction and operation of high-rise buildings, not because of what it was, but because of what it got—in 1882 the steam it required for heating began to be delivered from a central plant via an elaborate distribution system. The New York Steam Company (now Con Ed) started in 1882 with sixty-two customers, with St. Peter's Church the fiftieth to sign up. With steam delivered as easily as water or electricity, the need for oil boilers and maintenance was abrogated. Today many of the city's offices and hotels and even some apartment houses are provided with steam from a central source.

Church of the Ascension (L) 1841

Fifth Avenue, northwest corner of Tenth Street
Richard Upjohn, Architect

Three firsts: the first Gothic Revival church in the city; the first church on Fifth Avenue; and the first church in the city with a brownstone facade.

By the late 1830s architects were beginning to chafe under the yoke of the Greek Revival. They believed that America was a Christian nation, and that its architecture, especially its church architecture, should reflect its Christianity. Greek was pagan. Gothic, they believed, was the true Christian style.

Europe was already experiencing a Gothic renaissance. Viollet-le-Duc was restoring the glories of Sainte-Chapelle and Notre-Dame. Victor Hugo had written his paean to the Middle Ages, *The Hunchback of Notre Dame.* Gothic had become the official style in England with Charles Barry and A. W. N. Pugin's Houses of Parliament in 1835. And Pugin's writings were popularizing the "Christian style."

The Gothic Revival first surfaced in New York in Richard Upjohn's Church of the Ascension, a symmetrically massed church in the English style. Five years later two churches would solidify the popularity of the Gothic Revival in New York: Upjohn's Trinity and Renwick's Grace.

The Church of the Ascension, the first church built on Fifth Avenue, was finished at a time when the avenue was just being developed. Within a few years, according to diarist George Templeton Strong, Fifth Avenue would be built up "without any great gaps" nearly to Twentieth Street.

The Church of the Ascension was also the first church with a facade of brownstone. Brownstone is a Triassic sandstone containing deposits of iron ore, and this gives the stone its distinctive chocolate color. Quarried in both Connecticut and New Jersey, it was delivered to New York city by barge. It was soft and easily worked, ideal for the nineteenth-century channeling machines to cut, but not so ideal for the New York climate, which weathers it. Until this church was built, brownstone had been used only sparingly—in the tower of St. Paul's, for instance, or as a substitute for more expensive materials for trim, but never to cover a building completely. Proper Victorian New Yorkers would grow to love brownstone because it had an air of propriety, of solidity, of quiet respectability, and soon row after row of houses was being covered by it. (One of the earliest, if not the first, is the Rectory at 7 West Tenth Street.)

In 1888 the chancel of the Church of the Ascension was remodeled under the direction of Stanford White, who gathered some of America's greatest talent for the job. John La Farge painted what many believed was the finest mural of the time, *The Ascension*, for which White provided the ideal setting with his reredos. Augustus Saint-Gaudens sculpted the angel figures. Charles Follen McKim designed the pulpit of Siena marble. And the stained-glass windows were created by John La Farge, D. Maitland Armstrong, and the Tiffany Studios, among others.

Federal Hall National Memorial (L)   1842

(Originally the Custom House)
28 Wall Street, running along Nassau Street from Wall to Pine streets
Ithiel Town & A. J. Davis and William Ross and John Frazee, Architects

This unadulterated, neo-Greek temple is one of the purest examples of the Greek Revival in New York, and marks the site where George Washington took his oath of office.

Town & Davis designed this elegant Doric temple for the federal government. Their original design called for a rooftop dome topped by a double-vaulted cupola, but in 1835, after the foundations for the 5-foot-thick walls had been laid, it was discovered that the interior columns that were intended to carry the weight of the dome could only carry the weight of their own entablature. The plan for the dome was scrapped, but the basic design was kept intact.

Work had begun in 1834, when the vogue for the Greek Revival was at its height, "as you may infer," said architect William Ross, "from the fact that everything is a Greek temple, from the privies in the back court, through various grades of prison, theatre, church, custom-house, and statehouse." But it would take until 1842 to finish, making this building one of the last of the neo-Greek temples, and, ironically, one of its purest examples.

The building assumes a forthright stand, with its eight, fluted, 32-foot-high Doric columns supporting an architrave of sixteen triglyphs, which in turn support a triangular pediment. Everything was so Greek, so pristine, that even Horatio Alger's Ragged Dick is told by his friend Frank that this custom house "looks like pictures I've seen of the Parthenon in Athens." Today people say the same thing.

The building is called Federal Hall National Memorial because the building that stood on this site from 1699 to 1812 was New York's second city hall. Mayor Richard Varick had lent that building to Congress as the seat of government while New York was the federal capital, making City Hall Federal Hall, the nation's first seat of Congress. On its balcony George Washington took his oath of office as the first president of the United States. Although Federal Hall had been remodeled for the occasion by Major Pierre Charles L'Enfant, it was torn down almost as soon as the plaster dried in the new city hall.

This building started life in 1842 as the Custom House, then became the U.S. Subtreasury in 1863, a branch of the Federal Reserve Bank in 1920, and finally a museum administered by the National Park Service in 1955. Inside are the suit of native homespun worn by Washington for his inauguration and part of the railing from the balcony on which the oath was taken.

Citibank (L)   1842

(Formerly the Merchants' Exchange and the Custom House)
55 Wall Street, bounded by William Street, Exchange Place, and Hanover Street
Isaiah Rogers, Architect; enlarged by McKim, Mead & White, 1908

Greek Revival in the lower colonnade. Greek Ersatz in the upper colonnade.

The building you see is only partly the building architect Isaiah Rogers designed. Rogers, who had designed both Boston's Tremont Hotel and New York's Astor House in the Greek Revival style, planned a three-story building for the Merchants' Exchange with one row of twelve Ionic columns, a small frieze above, and the whole topped by a dome. The building, erected to Rogers's plans, was built of blue Quincy granite (the 33-ton columns were the largest to come from the Quincy quarries), and its 124-foot-high dome became a prominent feature of the cityscape. Even then, Wall Street was a center for banking and commerce, and under that dome mercantile matters were transacted.

In 1863 the Custom Service moved out of Federal Hall and into this building, whose owners had gone bankrupt. After the Custom Service was safely installed came the heyday of political corruption during the 1870s. While the Tweed Ring was taking Manhattan, the Custom House officials were taking the harbor. New York was the largest port of entry in the United States. When the Custom House officials were not preying on importers, demanding kickbacks and threatening blackmail, they were stumping the backwaters of New York State on behalf of the Republican Party. (These were federal appointees, and Grant's appointee as Collector of the Port, Chester A. Arthur, made sure the patronage jobs paid off.)

By 1907 the new owner of the building was the National City Bank (now Citibank), and McKim, Mead & White was hired to enlarge the building. The dome was removed, much of the interior was gutted, and a three-story colonnade was superimposed atop Rogers's three-story Ionic colonnade. (Some cynics, knowing Wall Street real-estate values, are awaiting the arrival of the third order of classical architecture to be piled on.) The main trading hall retains some of its original power with a false domelike ceiling in the rotunda, but the sensation of standing under the original dome can never be recaptured.

The bank moved in one Saturday morning with military precision and heavy police protection. And no wonder, because crossing Wall Street that Saturday morning in 1908, going from the bank's old headquarters at 52 Wall Street to its new headquarters, was about $70 million in gold, silver, and bills, and about $450 million in bonds and securities. Today this building has been demoted from the bank's headquarters to merely a branch office.

Trinity Church (L)   1846

Broadway at Wall Street
Richard Upjohn, Architect

One of the great Gothic Revival churches; its brownstone facade set the tone for New York during the next fifty years.

Since 1699 there has been a Trinity Church on Broadway at the head of Wall Street, which in New York's relatively short

history means that Trinity Church has almost always been there. The first church burned down in the Great Fire of 1776; the second was torn down in 1839 because the wardens were afraid it would collapse from its own poor workmanship; the third, which architect Richard Upjohn virtually copied straight out of Pugin's *True Principals of Pointed or Christian Architecture*, cemented the Gothic Revival in New York. As in other Gothic Revival buildings, true Gothic building principles were ignored and contemporary building methods employed. The buttresses that flank the walls are there only for show and buttress nothing, since there is no lateral force to resist. The roof is of wood instead of stone, and the ceiling is made of plaster and suspended from trusses.

The church today might lead you to believe that its facade is "blackstone," but behind the layer of soot lies New Jersey's dark red sandstone, commonly called brownstone. Upjohn was inclined to a facing of gray limestone from Utica, New York, but Trinity's trustees overruled his wishes. Ironically, Upjohn is credited by many for using brownstone as Trinity's facade and popularizing it as a building material.

Set in the center line of Wall Street, the 284-foot tower still dominates the financial canyon when viewed from the east. When it was first constructed, however, it dominated the skyline of the entire city, and the spire was the thing to climb. From there the "eye can range over the entire city," wrote James D. McCabe, Jr., in 1872, "and take in Brooklyn and its suburban towns as well. . . . The people in the streets seem like pygmies, and the vehicles are like so many toys." What was then the tallest structure in New York—a steam engine was used to hoist the stones into place—is now dwarfed by the office buildings that surround it.

In 1894, Trinity's bronze doors were added, given by William Waldorf Astor and designed in bas-relief by Richard

Morris Hunt in the style of the Baptistry in Florence and the early Italian Renaissance. The work on the main entrance doors was executed by Karl Bitter, the sculptor of *Abundance* at Grand Army Plaza; the north doors by J. Massey Rhind; the south doors by Charles H. Niehaus. The south doors show Henry Hudson off Manhattan Island in 1609, Trinity's Dr. Barclay preaching to the Indians in 1739, and the consecration of the church itself in 1846.

Trinity was chartered by King William III in 1697. Since it was the Church of England, under British law it was the established church, which meant that it was supported by all New Yorkers, financially, at least, regardless of race, religion, or color. In 1705 Queen Anne gave Trinity a land grant that stretched west of Broadway from Fulton to Christopher streets, laying the groundwork for Trinity's enormous wealth. In 1709 the New York Protestant Episcopal Public School was started; today it is Trinity School. (New York's only older school is Collegiate, started in 1638 by the Dutch Reformed Church.) In 1754 King's College was started in one of the schoolrooms. Came the Revolution and King's College became Columbia College, and the Anglican Trinity Church became Episcopalian. Trinity is still one of the most powerful institutions in the city, with power that can be manifested in subtle ways. An obvious manifestation is in the street names around it: Trinity Place and Rector and Church streets are evident, but there are also Vesey Street, named for Trinity's first rector; Barclay Street, for its second rector; and Chambers Street, named for John Chambers, New York's first lawyer accepted to the bar in the Province of New York and an officer of the church. The churchyard is filled with the famous, including Alexander Hamilton, freshman at King's College, 1784.

Grace Church (L)   **1846**

800 Broadway, northeast corner of Tenth Street
James Renwick, Jr., Architect

With the lacelike quality of its tracery, the delicacy of its lines that lift your eyes heavenward, and its cool, correct Christian statement, Grace Church elevated the Gothic Revival to new heights.

The first Grace Church was on Broadway at Rector Street, but by the early 1840s all but two of its ten wardens and vestrymen lived within a half mile of Broadway and Tenth Street. The congregation decided to move uptown.

In 1843 a design competition was held for the new church. The winner was 25-year-old James Renwick, Jr., an engineer whose reputation rested solely on his Egyptian Revival design for the Croton Receiving Reservoir. He had read his Pugin and done his homework, and his cool, Christian design for Grace Church elevated the Gothic Revival to new heights. Built at a propitious site at the bend in Broadway, Grace Church can be seen from as far downtown as Wall Street.

Renwick insisted on white marble for the church, because he believed that it was beautiful, and although its original expense might be greater than sandstone, its durability made it economical in the long run. The wealthy yet frugal congregation agreed to the marble but insisted it be cut by convicts and that the church's steeple be built of wood. (When the wooden steeple was going to be replaced by marble, it was bruited that the tower could not sustain the added weight and would collapse in ignominy like Fonthill Abbey, but it has stood since 1884.)

New York's first choir school was started here in 1899, and a year later the chancel was extended to accommodate the boys' choir. Heins & La Farge designed the extension, the first work done on the church until then by anyone but Renwick, who had died in 1895.

The rectory, just to the north of the church, is another Renwick masterpiece. It is set behind the cast-iron fence and green lawn, and the total effect is of an open English quadrangle. Its gables and differently treated bow windows create a Romantic whole, a Gothic Revival grouping that is unsurpassed in New York.

From its opening day, Grace Church was a hit. Pews were sold at extravagant prices, some going for as much as $1,400, with an annual pew rent of 8 percent. To be a Grace Church-goer from christening to funeral became de rigueur for nineteenth-century New York Society, and to be married there was a must.

Sun Building   1846

(Originally A. T. Stewart's Store)
280 Broadway, east side between Chambers and Reade streets
John B. Snook and Joseph Trench, Architects

This was New York's biggest department store, and it created a sensation: its scale dominated the horizon, its facade was marble, its style Italianate.

It was called Stewart's Folly because New York's biggest department store was too expensive to build, too far uptown, and on the wrong side of Broadway. The east side of Broadway was the "shilling side," the west, the "dollar side," and all because the morning sun streamed onto the west side, lighting up the stores, making them more appealing and showing off their wares early in the day.

But then A. T. Stewart's Marble Emporium appeared, disproving the shilling side theory. The building did not look then the way it looks today. It would not be until 1851 that it would fill its Broadway frontage, later still until it filled so many lots on Chambers Street, and not until the 1880s, when it was no longer Stewart's, were the sixth and seventh floors added.

The building was constructed with 20-foot-high plate-glass windows set off by Corinthian pilasters on the main floor, providing more window space than anybody had ever seen. It was built of dazzling white Westchester marble, so it stood out sharply from its red-brick Federal and Greek Revival neighbors. And it was a full five stories high, so it towered over them as well. *Harper's* described the building as a "white marble cliff, sharply drawn against the sky." Diarist Philip Hone said there was "nothing in Paris or London to compare with this dry-goods palace." It was such an instant landmark that Stewart never even put his name on the building.

The style is Italianate, a "palace," as Hone said, and like an Italian palace it had a court in the middle, only it was covered by a skylight and ringed by selling floors. The building's outer wall is supported on the main floor by a post-and-lintel system, not of marble or granite but of cast iron. It is the strength of the cast iron that accommodates the huge expanse of windows and supports the weight of the building at the same time.

With Stewart's a shopper would never again have to go to a parasol shop for an umbrella, a fabric shop for a bolt of cloth, or a cutlery store for a knife. Everything could be bought under one roof, with the profits going to one man, Alexander T. Stewart. Stewart would become the richest man in America—during the Civil War his personal income for one year was $1,843,631. In 1862 he opened a store built of cast iron on Broadway at Tenth Street, and his Chambers Street store, so daringly far uptown when it opened in 1846, was relegated to the wholesale business. In this century the building was owned by the Sun Newspaper until the paper folded in 1952.

High Bridge (L)   1848

(Originally Aqueduct Bridge)
Across the Harlem River, from 174th Street
John B. Jervis, Engineer

Fifteen stone arches, eight of them spanning the Harlem River, brought Croton water into Manhattan as part of the City's greatest municipal undertaking of the nineteenth century.

With no water delivery system in the 1830s, Manhattan's fresh, potable water was becoming ever rarer and more expensive. Entrepreneurs were buying 130 gallons of the famous Tea Water Pump water for six cents and selling it for about a penny a bucketful. Compounding the problem were fires, and the need for water to extinguish them. Uppermost in people's minds was the Great Fire of 1835, when seventeen blocks of lower Manhattan were consumed. Almost seven hundred buildings, about five hundred of them stores, went up in smoke, ruining fire-insurance companies, closing banks, and precipitating the Panic of 1837.

A solution to the city's problems, and New York's most ambitious project of the nineteenth century, the Croton Water Delivery System entailed damming the Croton River in Westchester and building a 44½-mile aqueduct from Croton to City Hall, bridging rivers and valleys and tunneling through hills and mountains.

In 1842, after about $13 million had been spent, the clear, fresh, glorious water from the Croton Reservoir was first delivered, to the firing of cannon and the ringing of bells. Cofferdams, with built-in pipes, temporarily brought the water across the Harlem River. The Distributing Reservoir was erected on the future site of the Main Branch of the New York Public Library on Fifth Avenue, and two receiving reservoirs would be constructed in Central Park (the one between Eighty-sixth and Ninety-sixth streets is still there). Within the year New Yorkers like diarist George Templeton Strong were having bathrooms built, and leading "rather an amphibious life . . . paddling in the bathtub every night and constantly making new discoveries in the art and mystery of ablution."

How to carry the water in pipes across the Harlem River raised questions. The engineers had advocated a low bridge with only one pier in the river. The river was not then navigable, except by small vessels, but in the event it should later become so, a single-pier bridge would create the least obstruction to river traffic. Aesthetically, however, a high bridge with fifteen Roman arches, eight of them spanning the water, was preferred. In 1839 a contract for the high bridge, estimated to cost $737,755, was awarded. Nine years later, and about a quarter of a million dollars over budget, the 121-foot-high bridge was finished. It was New York's only stone bridge over a waterway, and at 1,460 feet, it was the nation's longest when it was completed. The bridge stood in its original form until 1923, when a single steel span replaced the piers in the riverbed. By then the river had been made navigable by the Corps of Engineers, and the War Department deemed that the piers were simply too close for easy navigation. Nevertheless, the glory of some of the original arches remains.

3–17 St. Luke's Place   1852–1853

Leroy Street, between Seventh Avenue South and Hudson Street
Architect unknown

A row of red-brick houses that leaves behind the Greek Revival and makes the transition to the Italianate tradition.

St. Luke's Place is one of New York's oases, tucked between the truck routes of Hudson Street and Seventh Avenue South. It is a virtually traffic-free enclave that seems unchanged from the day it was built, a row of three-story-plus-basement houses that reflects the scale and elegance of upper-crust mid-nineteenth-century housing. Ginkgo trees line the street, front gardens fill the air with springtime freshness, and iron fences with wreath motifs separate the buildings from the street yet act as a welcoming guide up the stoops.

The row marks the transition to the Italianate, an eclectic revival that would last in various degrees of sophistication throughout the rest of the nineteenth century. Gone are entrances with restrained Ionic porches, replaced by something a little more florid. Pediments are supported by grooved pilasters with scrollworked brackets, round-headed doorways within the frame repeat the pilaster-bracket theme, and rusticated basements act as a strong base. An unknown architect/builder clearly was tired of what was, and asked what might be, leading to something a little more Renaissance-ish. The builder was not entirely iconoclastic, however, rejecting the newly fashionable brownstone as a facade in favor of conservative red brick with brownstone trim.

The house numbering is peculiar. Leroy Street's numbering system begins at Bleecker Street and progresses to the south, with even numbers on its east side and odd numbers on its west side, as is the case with most New York side streets. At St. Luke's Place, the street bends west, and the system runs counter to the rest of the street, progressing from west to east, and the numbering progresses straight through, from 3 through 17, because a playground is on the south side of the street. There is no 13 St. Luke's Place, but there is a 12½.

It was into No. 6 that An Irish immigrant named William Walker moved his family in 1886. Billy Walker had risen from impoverished carpenter to lumber dealer and local Tammany Hall politician. His son, James, did not grow up to become the president of the United States, but for Billy Walker he became something better: the mayor of the City of New York, 1926–1933. Jimmy "Beau James" Walker lived here until 1934, and the "Lamps of Honor," the traditional symbol of a mayor's residence, still grace the newel-posts of this house.

Lutheran Church in America   1853

(Originally home of Isaac N. Phelps;
subsequently home of J. P. Morgan, Jr.)
231 Madison Avenue, southeast corner of Thirty-seventh Street
Addition, 1958
Architect unknown

A somber, dignified, free-standing home with a brownstone facade in the Italianate tradition. It was one of the earliest, is now one of the last, and will remain standing, God willing.

Sometimes a building that at first glance does not seem terribly important can weave together the threads of social, urban, and architectural history, illustrating within its walls the development of a city. This is one of those buildings.

By 1853 there were three free-standing buildings on the east side of Madison Avenue between Thirty-sixth and Thirty-seventh streets, all with substantial box stoops and Renaissance-style porches. They were three stories high (an additional floor has disturbed the scale and balance of No. 231), with three windows on the avenue and three on their sides (a wing was added to No. 231 in 1958). The houses had gardens between and behind them, and a service road at mid-block led to the stables in the rear. They were among the first domestic buildings in New York to bring together not just Italianate trim but form as well. And they created this feeling of the Italian Renaissance with brownstone facades, only twelve years after the first New York building had been completely sheathed in it.

They were in the vanguard of Manhattan's next wave of northward expansion and the first manifestations of the urbanization of Murray Hill. In 1848 Madison Avenue did not extend beyond Forty-second Street, and it was not until after the Civil War that the lots on the Park Avenue half of the block were even auctioned off for development.

Built by the Stokes family, founders of Phelps Dodge Corporation, the houses stood as an enclave of wealth (the mother of I. N. Phelps Stokes, author of *The Iconography of Manhattan Island,* grew up here). Frederick Lewis Allen described the houses as embodying the "undemonstrative grandeur of respectable prosperity," enough so that J. Pierpont Morgan, the nation's most famous banker, bought the one on the corner of Thirty-sixth Street for himself, ultimately buying the whole compound for his family. Two-thirty-one Madison was lived in by his son, J. P. Morgan, Jr., himself the head of the House of Morgan from 1913 until 1943. After Morgan's death in 1943, the Lutheran Church in America bought the house, the only remaining one of the three, for its national headquarters. In 1965 the building was designated a New York City landmark, much to the horror of the Lutherans, who wanted to demolish it to make way for an office building. In 1974, after years of litigation, the Lutherans got their way. The building was removed from the official landmark list, the only one to have fallen from that saving grace. If it means saving the building, maybe the City should remove the case from the courts and take it to a higher authority.

New York Shakespeare Festival (L)   1854

(Originally Astor Free Library)
425 Lafayette Street, between Fourth Street and
Astor Place
Alexander Saeltzer, Architect; center section,
1859, Griffith Thomas; north wing, 1881, Thomas
Stent; remodeled, 1966, Giorgio Cavaglieri

There was such local pride in the very idea of the Astor Free Library that four years before it opened it was illustrated in the border of a Manhattan map as a fait accompli.

New York has had libraries since 1698, but if you had wanted to read a book in one of them you would have had to pay for the privilege. By the 1840s John Jacob Astor, New York's wealthiest citizen, was being pressured into bequeathing some of his vast fortune to a library that would be free to all. He agreed, stipulating that of his $400,000 bequest, not more than $75,000 was to be spent on the building, and $120,000 put toward "books, charts, models, drawings, engravings, casts, statues," and other accouterments. The balance was to be invested to increase the library's holdings and defray expenses.

In 1849 thirty drawings were submitted for the design of the Astor Free Library, and although the committee found none "wholly satisfactory," Alexander Saeltzer took first place and the $300 prize. Although its opening was still four years off, by 1850 there was such local pride in the very idea of a free library that when M. Dripps published a map of Manhattan, he included a picture of the Astor Free Library in his illustrated border. The library finally did open in 1854, one year after the building itself was finished (to protect the books from any dampness in the walls), with about 90,000 volumes. Washington Irving was the library's first president.

The original building is the southern wing, five bays, or 65 feet wide, 67 feet high, and 120 feet deep. Descriptions of its design run the gamut from Florentine to Byzantine, but Italianate usually suffices. (The extensions are almost carbon copies.) The brick building with brownstone trim had an interior that was mainly of iron, with very little wood, making it a structure that was considered fireproof. Lecture and reading rooms were on the main floor, from which thirty-nine marble steps led to the 60-by-100-foot library hall, a two-story arcaded room topped by a skylight. Since the library was for reference only and had no artificial light (its hours were restricted to the daylight hours, 10 A.M. to 4 P.M., and abbreviated in the summer), if you worked you did not read.

Benefactions from the Astor family greatly expanded the library and its collection, until by 1881 it could boast of about 200,000 volumes and two additional wings. This vast collection, when merged with the Lenox Library, formed the nucleus of today's Main Branch of the New York Public Library, where you can still read books stamped "Astor Library." In 1965 the building was about to be demolished, but Joseph Papp's New York Shakespeare Festival found the money to buy it, and it has been a group of flourishing off-Broadway theaters ever since.

Haughwout Building (L) 1857

488–492 Broadway, northeast corner of Broome Street
John P. Gaynor, Architect

The dowager queen of cast-iron buildings had the first passenger elevator with a safety device.

As early as 1848 James Bogardus was using cast iron for buildings. What distinguishes these buildings and makes them important is that they are not merely facades of cast iron, but a building system using cast iron throughout. It meant posts and lintels of cast iron, and that meant a skeleton to support the building. The walls no longer had to bear the load, so they could hang there, like a curtain, heralding today's "curtain-wall" architecture.

Building with cast iron then was essentially the same as building with steel today. The elements were prefabricated at a factory and assembled at the site. First a cast-iron sill was set into a base of stone. Then a hollow, cylindrical column was bolted perpendicular to the sill. When two columns were up, a lintel was bolted into place to link them. This process continued, both horizontally and vertically, like a giant Erector set. Since there was no need for thick walls to support the load of the building, windows and delicate columns appeared. This created a rhythmic balance outside and a great deal of light inside. For retailers of crystal and cutlery, like the Haughwout store, this natural light was a boon.

Manufacturers of cast iron, like the Badger Iron Works, the supplier for the Haughwout Building, used to publish catalogs showing their wares. Architects could riffle through them, select the style they found interesting, and send away for it. Since classical forms could be repeated inexpensively, architects were free to pick and choose from the past. Gaynor modeled his design for the Haughwout store on the Sansovino Library of St. Mark's. He created a pleasing module—a keystoned arch flanked by a pair of colonnettes which are in turn flanked by Corinthian columns—and repeated it ninety-two times throughout the upper four floors of the building. For the horizontal treatment, he incorporated a cornice above each colonnade.

The problem of how to get people up and down the five-story building was neatly resolved by Elisha Graves Otis. He designed and installed the first passenger elevator with a safety device.

The perfection of a building system using a cast-iron skeleton and the arrival of the first practical elevator paved the way for skyscrapers. If there is one building in New York that should be preserved in aspic, this is the one. You will find cast-iron buildings in such disparate places as Galveston, Texas; Salt Lake City, Utah; and Glasgow, Scotland. But nowhere is there such a concentration of cast-iron buildings as right here in SoHo—the section of Manhattan south of Houston Street and north of Canal.

Cooper Union Foundation Building (L)   1859

At Cooper Square, bounded by Seventh Street,
the Bowery, Astor Place, and Fourth Avenue
Additions, 1890s; remodeled, 1973–1974
Frederick A. Peterson, Architect; additions,
Leopold Eidlitz; remodeling, John Hejduk

*The revolutionary wrought-iron beams that were rolled at
Peter Cooper's Trenton Iron Works and used in a light grid
were forerunners of today's steel I-beams.*

Peter Cooper's fortune, estimated by the 1850s at $2 million, was made in glue, iron, and locomotives. A modest, pragmatic man, Cooper understood that his wealth had come from the "cooperation of multitudes of men." To repay his debt to society he built a private college that "required no other credentials than a good moral character" and a passing grade on the entrance exams. His was the first college to offer adult-education courses, many given in the evenings to allow students to work and still attend classes. He spent $650,000 on Cooper Union, but he never endowed it, believing that rentals accruing from stores and offices on the first two floors would provide funding. During the Civil War, a tenant in an arcaded storefront was the Women's Central Association of Relief, a branch of the U.S. Sanitary Commission. In the 1890s the school received about $50,000 a year from rentals, but other sources still had to be tapped for funds.

The building was more of a unified whole in 1859 than it is today, more in the classical Italian tradition. Originally only five stories high, it was ringed by the arcade on the main floor, then four floors varied the fenestration theme, all topped by a balustrade running around the building and a pediment atop the Astor Place portico. A large building that took six years to erect, its conservative brownstone facade belied a radical breakthrough within—a light grid of 7-inch wrought-iron rail beams that transmitted their loads to the walls. The T-shaped beams had bulbs at the bottom of the vertical shaft, which, when fattened in later developments, evolved into a genuine flange and ultimately became an I-beam. Other revolutionary developments included an elevator and vents under each of the two thousand seats in the Great Hall in the basement through which fresh air was pumped by a huge fan. By 1893 the two top floors had been added to accommodate more classrooms and the collection of decorative arts that has since blossomed into the Cooper-Hewitt Museum. During 1973–1974 the entire building was gutted (it was propped up on the outside by steel towers and girdled by horizontal girders), with all the cast-iron columns and wrought-iron beams encased in fireproofing materials.

The Great Hall was the site of many of New York's most historic meetings in the last half of the nineteenth century. It was here one snowy February night in 1860 that Abraham Lincoln delivered an address that won him the support of the New York press and probably the presidential nomination. Mark Twain, William Jennings Bryan, Susan B. Anthony, Harriet Beecher Stowe, and her brother, Henry Ward Beecher, all spoke here. And the Committee of Seventy, created to investigate the alleged scandals of the Tweed Ring, started here, as did the American Red Cross, Volunteers of America, and the N.A.A.C.P.

312 and 314 East Fifty-third Street (L)   1866

Between First and Second avenues
Architect unknown

A pair of plain wood houses in the vernacular style with touches of the French Second Empire.

A wooden house built to conform to the grid system in midtown is a rare house indeed. The few that were built were erected when the area was neither suburban nor part of the city, and downtown there were no new wooden houses being built at all. The reason was fire. In developed areas a fire can spread quickly, with flames jumping from house to house and leaping streets until a fire becomes a conflagration. Wooden houses only feed the fire's combustibility. To regulate this obvious fire hazard, the City simply banned new construction of wooden houses in developed areas. As the population moved northward, the limits below which wooden houses could not be built kept abreast of development. In 1860 the line was placed at Fifty-second Street, one block south of these houses. In 1866, the year these houses were erected, the line was moved to Eighty-sixth Street, allowing them to sneak in under the wire.

Wood houses were inexpensive to build, thanks to the mass-produced nail that had been perfected by the 1820s and the balloon-frame house that had been perfected by the 1830s. The balloon-frame house was constructed with 2-by-4s that were nailed together instead of by the old-fashioned method of using heavy timbers mortised together and linked by wood pegs. With nails and 2-by-4s a house could be whacked together by one man working alone. (They were called balloon-frame houses not because they were blown up like balloons, but because originally it was feared they would blow away like balloons.)

When these houses were built, the French Second Empire style was *à la mode*, so the round-headed dormer windows were set into shingled mansard roofs. In an attempt to be even more Gallic, the sash windows were created to look like French doors, but anything more than a cursory glance will dispel the illusion. The only ornaments on the buildings are the cornices above the doorways and windows, with consoles supporting the cornices above the entrances. Otherwise, they are plain, vernacular architecture, the kind you might find on any Main Street in America. These buildings did not require an architect, yet fulfilled the function of providing attractive housing.

Unfortunately, air-conditioning units have been stuck into No. 314's facade. Virtually pristine, however, is No. 312. In 1968 a speculative builder offered $185,000 for the house. Instead of accepting it, the owner got the Landmarks Preservation Commission to assure its preservation by designating the house a landmark.

881 Broadway   1869

(Originally Arnold Constable & Co.)
Southwest corner of Nineteenth Street, extending
to Fifth Avenue
Extension, 1877
Griffith Thomas, Architect

*With its elaborate mansard roof, Arnold Constable was one of
the grandest stores on Ladies' Mile.*

Neighborhoods change. What was originally a residential
area becomes yesterday's first-class shopping center, today's
commercial district, and maybe the site of tomorrow's renaissance. By the 1870s this area was entering the second stage
of that urban progression. Moving into it were New York's
largest stores, stores that had started as small shops in lower
Manhattan. By 1900 this uptown migration would be complete, with New York's finest stores lining Broadway solidly
from Eighth to Twenty-third streets, and Sixth Avenue from
Fourteenth to Twenty-third streets. Since this was the cream
of New York's shopping, and since women were reputedly
the principal patrons, the stretches became known as Ladies'
Mile. Some of the buildings are gone, but many remain, and
if you peel back the years of neglect, the magic of palimpsest
will reveal their glories. Of them all, the building erected by
Arnold Constable & Co. is one of the best preserved and certainly one of the grandest.
  The business started in 1825, and by 1857 Arnold Constable was ensconced on Canal Street in a five-story building
with a marble front, designed by Griffith Thomas. By the end
of the Civil War enough profits had been made to move into
an even grander building in the vanguard of the uptown migration. Built in 1869, Thomas's second Arnold Constable
commission was a five-story building with a marble facade
on the corner of Nineteenth Street and Broadway. In 1873 its
two-story mansard roof was added, a roof that surely could
have been the inspiration for the best of cartoonist Charles

Addams's designs (its only serious competition left in New York is the old Gilsey House on Broadway at Twenty-ninth Street). By 1877 Thomas had re-created his Broadway facade on Fifth Avenue, but this time in cast iron instead of marble.

If post–Civil War society is described as the Gilded Age, this florid department store was its lily. Especially famous for its mourning clothes, it did a huge business in dry goods, carpets, and upholstery on its five selling floors. The cast-iron wing on Fifth Avenue housed the wholesale business, and the sixth and seventh floors were devoted to manufacturing.

In 1914, Arnold Constable continued its northward trek, joining the march to midtown and leaving behind this monumental pile. After 150 years in business, Arnold Constable closed its doors in 1975.

Criminal Court of the City of New York   1872

(Called the Tweed Ring Courthouse)
52 Chambers Street, between Broadway and
Centre Street
Unfinished
John Kellum, Architect; Leopold Eidlitz,
Architect, 1876

Given the chance to use the word "venal" just once in your life, if you use it to describe the goings-on at the Tweed Ring Courthouse you will have done justice to the word.

This building is the embodiment of post–Civil War urban and political history. Beginning with New York's first heavy wave of immigration in the 1840s, politicians began to realize that there were votes for the buying among immigrants. The politicians gave jobs to the immigrants, the immigrants gave their votes to the politicians. the politicians then gave jobs to the newly arrived relatives of the immigrants already on the payroll, and so on.

Many of the politicians wanted to hold office not to serve their city but to loot its treasury. William Marcy Tweed, a master of the art, rose through the Tammany Hall hierarchy to head a ring of corrupt politicians and equally corrupt con-

43

tractors. They all agreed that a 65/35 split on padded bills was a fair one, and soon the City was paying enormous sums for otherwise ordinary objects, like the $179,927.60 spent on three tables and forty chairs for this courthouse. Presumably those tables and chairs were delivered, which is more than can be said for other merchandise and material that was to go into the courthouse. Since the Legislature had authorized $250,000 for the courthouse, but it cost somewhere between $8 million and $13 million and still stands unfinished, somebody obviously made out like the proverbial bandit.

The courthouse, a rather awkward version of a Palladian-style villa, is built around a central well ringed by balconies. The marble for the interior walls was never applied, and the dome that was to act as the capstone to the building was never erected.

After John Kellum's death, Leopold Eidlitz was appointed architect of the courthouse in 1876. Kellum's widow took the City to court to recover what she claimed were unpaid fees. The City counter-claimed that the misuse of iron beams and of iron where other material could have been used to advantage had cost the City about $400,000. Mrs. Kellum lost.

If you can't figure out how to enter the building from Chambers Street and wonder why the Corinthian portico exists, stranded high above the sidewalk as it is, it is because the City removed the stairs leading up to the main entrance when Chambers Street was widened in 1960. Then the City had plans for the destruction of the courthouse to carry out a grandiose scheme for a municipal center, but in the summer of 1978 the plans were changed. Now the courthouse will be renovated—at the very least made safe from leaks—and perhaps the stained-glass dome that some architectural historians believe was suspended over the central well will turn up.

Central Synagogue (L)   1872

652 Lexington Avenue, southwest corner of Fifty-fifth Street
Henry Fernbach, Architect

The Moorish Revival style was a popular bit of eclecticism that filled an architectural void for Judaism.

Although the Gothic style was considered true Christian architecture, there has never been any true Jewish architecture. One of the glories of eclecticism, however, is that an educated person can look at a building in an eclectic style and relate to the building's function through the history associated with its style. A Moorish design alludes to the Near East and the roots of Judaism, so as a style it is a natural for a religion without an architectural heritage of its own. In fact, it became so popular for New York synagogues that by the 1890s "all of the finer Jewish synagogues of the city," according to one guidebook, were "Moorish in design and decoration."

This Moorish Revival synagogue was designed by Henry Fernbach, the first Jew to practice architecture in America

and a prolific designer of cast-iron buildings. Today his Central Synagogue is the finest example of the Moorish Revival in the city. One of the hallmarks of the style is its horseshoe arches, with their openings narrower than their greatest spans, and so called for their obvious likeness to equine footwear. The brownstone facade is brightened by the alternating shadings of the voussoirs within the arches, and by the stringcourses that link the arches. The minaretlike 122-foot towers start as squares but end as octagons, making the perfect transition for the copper melon domes. The minaret-tower theme is repeated in microcosm on the corners, complete with crenellations. The auditorium is ringed by a gallery that is neatly reflected in the side elevation. Each horseshoe arch has two sets of windows, the lower set with horseshoe arches, the upper set with Romanesque. It is the Romanesque window frames that light the gallery within.

Central Synagogue, one of the earliest Reform congregations in the city, was founded on Ludlow Street in 1846, when the Jewish population of New York was only about 12,000 out of a total of 500,000 residents. By 1872 the city's population had grown to about 900,000, with a Jewish population of about 120,000, and everyone was moving northward. By the 1880s there would be seven large synagogues between Nineteenth and Seventy-second streets. The largest was Temple Emanu-El, at Fifth Avenue and Forty-third Street, with a capacity of about 2,000. Central, with a capacity of about 1,300, was the second largest. Today it is not only the only synagogue of the seven still standing, it is the oldest Jewish house of worship in continuous use in New York State.

Central Park (L) 1873

59th to 110th streets, Fifth Avenue to Central
Park West (Eighth Avenue)
Frederick Law Olmsted and Calvert Vaux,
Landscape Architects; Jacob Wrey Mould,
Associate Architect

*America's first major urban park in a Romantic setting was a
break from the monotony of New York's right-angled streets
and a breakthrough in urban design.*

The Street Commissioners of 1807 stamped Manhattan with
a pattern of right-angled streets and avenues, a plan that ignored the island's natural topography and that they admitted
left few vacant spaces for parks and squares. The commissioners believed, however, that with New York's abundant
waterfront, New Yorkers could receive ample fresh air and
exercise. By the 1840s the city was experiencing its first
heavy influx of immigrants, and its first serious overcrowding. The few parks that did exist were small and inadequate,
and access to the waterfront in the built-up sections was already denied by commerce. Reformers began crying out for
a great park to act as lungs for the city, and in 1858 a competition was held for the Central Park—central not to the
population, most of whom lived south of Forty-second Street,
but to the island itself.

The winning design was "The Greensward," submitted
by a writer, Frederick Law Olmsted, and an architect, Calvert
Vaux. Theirs was the first major urban park design to break
away from the classical plans of eighteenth-century gardens
and initiate the Romantic tradition. Several cemeteries, including Cambridge's Mount Auburn (1831), Philadelphia's
Laurel Hill (1836), and Brooklyn's Green-Wood (1836), had
already broken from classicism. These seemingly naturally
rustic areas, with their meandering paths and pools flanked
by weeping willows, had become popular places for Sunday
excursions.

Like these cemeteries, every inch of Central Park would
be planned, with nothing left to nature, although it might
appear otherwise. Streams were diverted, pools were filled,
rocks were blasted, valleys were carved out, trees were
planted to frame vistas, and 10 million one-horse cartloads
of earth and stone were transported. Rustic arbors dotted the
landscape, graceful bridges arched over water or roads, and

everywhere was a feeling for nature. It still appears as if man has done little to these 840 acres, and many people mistakenly believe that this urban Eden is the way Manhattan was in the mid-nineteenth century.

Olmsted and Vaux wanted a balance in the park between "natural" areas for appreciating nature and formal areas for promenading, which explains the difference between such rural areas as the Ramble in the West Seventies, and formal ones like the Terrace, south of the rowboat lake, where architecture and statuary abound. One great Romantic vista is from the steps of the Terrace at Bethesda Fountain looking north to the Belvedere, a medieval-style castle intentionally created on a diminutive scale to appear even further off in the distance.

To discourage trotting races, the north-south roads were laid out with curves. To allow traffic and pedestrians to travel north and south without encountering the four transverse roads that carry crosstown traffic through the park's rolling topography, the roads were depressed—a revolutionary idea—and bushes and trees were planted so that strollers are hardly aware of the traffic. There was concern about how people would treat the park, so Olmsted insisted on some rules of decorum, including a ban on leashless dogs.

Central Park is the only municipal park that is a national historic landmark, and it is the City's first designated scenic landmark. But it is more than officialdom's recognition of the place that makes it great—it is New York's own backyard, touch-football stadium, ring-a-lievo field, and day in the country, all rolled into one.

National Arts Club (L) 1874

(Originally home of Samuel J. Tilden)
15 Gramercy Park South, Twentieth Street
between Park Avenue South and Irving Place
Calvert Vaux, Architect

The Revived Gothic of the 1840s becomes the Victorian Gothic of the Gilded Age.

The Gothic Revival of the 1840s seems a dreamy-eyed, naïve approach to architecture: first fabricate an ideal, then copy it.

By the 1870s architects were turning their ideals into buildings that reflected their own time. This was, after all, the beginning of the Gilded Age, with wealth and power the new by-products of industrialization. If the Victorian Gothic looks like the mass-produced furniture of Charles Eastlake, more gewgaws than substance, still it bore the stamp of individuality and made a statement.

Although the National Arts Club is a rather somber example of the Victorian Gothic, compare the exuberance of its facade with the restraint of the Gothic Revival drip moldings of the Players Club next door and you will see how the Gothic ideal changed in thirty years. Originally the one house was two houses, built in 1845. Samuel J. Tilden, breaker of the Tweed Ring, governor of the state, and presidential candidate in 1876, bought the two houses and hired Calvert Vaux to remodel them. (Tilden had a tunnel installed that led to Nineteenth Street in the event mobs proved unruly and he elected to escape unnoticed.) The style would not appeal to the merchant princes and industrialists of the 1880s and '90s, whose predilections led to the solidity and illusory safety offered by neo–Italian Renaissance facades. Everything is a little off balance and filled with surprises, like a medallion of Dante tucked into the facade and ponderous lancet windows set off by delicate crestings. The two bays, one squared off, the other trapezoidal, provide massing that gives unexpected depth to the facade.

Tilden, whose trust fund helped to establish the Main Branch of the New York Public Library, hired Donald McDonald of Boston in 1883 to create a dome of stained glass for his private library in this house. (Unlike Vaux's Victorian Gothic facade, the dome reflects the then-prevalent Islamic influence on Victorian decoration.) The ceiling is now backlit by electric lights, but in 1883 it was not, for the simple reason that electricity would not reach Gramercy Park until 1890.

The National Arts Club bought this building in 1906 and has used it as its clubhouse ever since. What was once Tilden's library is now the club's bar. If you can wangle an invitation for a drink, take it and run. Heaven's above.

670 Broadway   1874

(Originally Brooks Brothers)
Northeast corner of Bond Street
George E. Horner, Architect

48

Brooks Brothers had risen from a small store on the Lower East Side's Catherine and Cherry streets in 1818 to such prominence by the Civil War that during the Draft Riots the store was singled out by the mob and sacked. (Generals Grant, Sheridan, Sherman, and Hooker all wore Brooks Brothers uniforms, and their commander in chief was wearing a Brooks suit the night he was shot in Ford's Theater). Clearly no mob would dare sack this citadel of propriety, a seemingly impregnable fortress that was an adaptation of the Late Gothic from northern Italy. Just remove the showcase windows and substitute a wall with an easily defensible portal, add a good solid battlemented tower, and any decent Florentine would feel right at home. Unlike the Palazzo Vecchio, however, with its easily understood crests, Brooks Brothers' icons included clubs and diamonds and stars, with no sign of the golden fleece anywhere.

The building is a fascinating mix of materials, with brick walls, sandstone trim, and cast-iron columns on the first floor. Neither the columns' capitals nor their bases are pure anything, but an eccentric variation on something sort of Gothic, sort of Romanesque, sort of grotesque. You can ignore the date above the third floor (1873)—the store opened in April 1874. The front of the first floor was for ready-made clothing, with a special section for boys' and children's apparel. The front of the second floor was entirely devoted to military uniforms, with custom-made goods in the center of the floor. Since most of the manufacturing was done on the premises, the third floor housed the stock and receiving rooms, where cloth was examined prior to distribution. (The *Times* in 1877 lauded Brooks Brothers "both for its cheapness and excellence of materials.") The fourth floor was the cutting room, and when piecework was given out, it was from here. The top floor housed the workroom, where the sewing was actually done.

By this time the clothing industry had been revolutionized. During the 1840s Elias Howe had proved that one sewing-machine operator could sew five times faster than the fastest seamstress, and Brooks Brothers was making good use of the machines, as were others. By the 1870s New York's Bond Street would be comparable to London's, lined by men's clothiers of the highest quality. Brooks's stay was short-lived; in 1884 it joined the march uptown to the southeast corner of Broadway and Twenty-second Street.

655–671 Avenue of the Americas   1875

(Originally Hugh O'Neill's Store)
Between Twentieth and Twenty-first streets
Mortimer C. Merritt, Architect

What Arnold Constable was to the carriage trade on Ladies' Mile, Hugh O'Neill was to the hoi polloi.

Hugh O'Neill, called the Fighting Irishman of Sixth Avenue for his rough-and-tumble merchandising gimmicks, was the terror of the otherwise staid Ladies' Mile. He was described as not liking stuffiness and was accused of holding sales just to shake up his high-falutin' neighbors and pack in the hoi polloi to make his side of Sixth Avenue jump. Or so it seemed to the uninitiated. What O'Neill was really doing was practicing the art of the loss leader. He would practically give away sewing machines, for instance, knowing that a seamstress with a sewing machine but no material or notions is at a loss and that once a shopper was in the store, his or her sales resistance was down.

Although his company later merged with the Adams store next door and ultimately went out of business in 1915, for forty years O'Neill's store flourished in this huge cast-iron building. It is five stories high and measures 200 feet on the Avenue of the Americas, about 250 feet deep on Twentieth Street, and 75 feet on Twenty-first Street (the Third Cemetery of the Spanish and Portuguese Synagogue blocked his westward expansion). With three exceptions, the building is virtually unchanged today: gone is a pair of huge domes that sat atop the rounded corners; some rounded windowpanes have been replaced by flat panes; and the building is painted a drab gray instead of the shimmering white it once was.

The cast-iron construction allowed a great expanse of glass for picture windows on the street floor. Above, the building is carefully balanced, with two floors of bold fenestration topped by two floors of bold mullions, all flanked by the round towers. There's no missing the name of this store—placed within the pediment, the name HUGH O'NEILL can be clearly distinguished.

A 1901 photograph shows the Twentieth Street corner of O'Neill's, with a sign wrapped around the tower spelling out the name of the store in elaborate script. Set into the script were incandescent electric lights—one light for the dot over the i, two lights for the apostrophe, etc. Two years later the neighborhood, especially along Broadway, was described as "multi-colored bouquets of luminous advertising," the beginning of the Great White Way. As usual, Hugh O'Neill was in the vanguard.

Jefferson Market Library (L)   1876

(Originally Third Judicial District Courthouse,
and called the Jefferson Market Courthouse)
425 Avenue of the Americas, southwest corner of
Tenth Street
Withers & Vaux, Architects, 1876; remodeled,
1963, Giorgio Cavaglieri

*The last of a complex of municipal buildings on the site,
this is Victorian "Kitchen Sink" architecture at its most
extravagant.*

A raggle-taggle agglomeration of buildings, including a municipal market and a wooden fire tower, was torn down in
1873 to make way for a complex of three separate but architecturally similar buildings—a police court, a jail, and a municipal market. All that's left of the complex is what had been
the courthouse.

Its style is variously described as *Neuschwansteinian*,
Victorian Gothic, or Kitchen Sink, because it incorporates
everything but. Clearly, architects Frederick Clark Withers
and Calvert Vaux would have replaced Mies van der Rohe's
"less is more" with "more is not enough." There are bits of
French Romanesque and Venetian Gothic, whole gobs of
mansard, gabled, and pyramidal roofs, gargoyles here and
finials there, dormer windows and lancet windows and even
a trefoil window or two. The red brick is laid in the Flemish
bond style, and for added interest there are granite belt
courses and black-brick decorative details in geometric pat-

terns. And then there is the seal of the City of New York in relief.

The clock tower originally served as a fire tower. From it the fire watch could look over the neighboring roofs for a panoramic view of Greenwich Village, and the watchmen were only standing 92 feet above the sidewalk.

The style is not peculiar to Greenwich Village, although the courthouse is a Village landmark. In the wake of the neo-Gothic Houses of Parliament came Alfred Waterhouse's Town Hall in Manchester, England, for instance. Finished one year after the Jefferson Market Courthouse, the Mancunian version is almost its identical, but larger, twin.

For years this beauty stood empty, a sad pile that the City had decided to demolish by the late 1950s. But Greenwich Villagers made the long-broken clock run again and began paying more attention to the derelict, until by the early 1960s they were successfully fighting to have the building recycled, this time as a branch library. You will notice modern glass, metal roofing in place of the original polychromatic slate, and the bronze-colored aluminum door in the main entrance.

Maybe this building was saved because, as urban sociologist Jane Jacobs points out, it is an architectural focal point, and, in a city matrix, we need individual monumental focal points to get our bearings.

St. Patrick's Cathedral (L) 1878

Fifth Avenue, between Fiftieth and Fifty-first streets
Spires, 1888
James Renwick, Jr., Architect

To the Irish Catholic immigrant, St. Patrick's Cathedral was the symbol of collective success.

The plans of James Renwick, Jr., for the new seat of the Roman Catholic Archdiocese of New York began in 1850, making his plans relative latecomers amidst the field of Gothic Revival entries. When the cathedral opened twenty-eight years later, its style was almost an architectural anachronism,

52

and like other dinosaurs, it was a big one—at 306 feet long, and with spires that would reach 330 feet by 1888, it ranked eleventh in size among the world's churches. Its style is the decorated Gothic of the thirteenth century, almost a picture-book amalgam of the cathedrals of Rheims and Cologne, with some of the lacy quality that Renwick had brought to Grace Church. One of his brilliant strokes is in the transition from the square towers to the octagonal spires by the subtle use of finials, buttresses, and niches. Like so many other Gothic Revival churches, there are no flying buttresses, since with a roof of plaster instead of stone there is no need for them (the buttresses that do exist are ersatz).

The interior, with its tall, slender columns, is reminiscent of Amiens. With its bosses standing out in relief at the crossings of the ribs, with its cardinals' hats hanging suspended from the ceiling, with its sheer physicality, this cathedral is filled with all the mystery and power of the great medieval houses of worship.

The cathedral was built almost as an act of bravado. The Irish, who came to dominate the hierarchy of the Roman Catholic Church in New York, had arrived in a city with a society that was rigidly defined at the top, one with an established pecking order, and some rungs missing from the ladder of success. (Signs like NINA appeared regularly in store windows and job listings, meaning No Irish Need Apply.) By 1835 parts of New York were being described as if a slice of Cork or Dublin had been transferred to America. By 1860 about 50 percent of New York's population of 813,669 would be foreign born, and half of those, or 204,000, would be Irish. Many ultimately achieved the financial status they originally lacked either through the church or politics, finding in those two institutions an ideal form of upward mobility. When Archbishop John A. Hughes asked for $1,000 apiece from 150 wealthy Roman Catholics as a contribution to the building fund of St. Patrick's, he received the minimum contribution from 103 of them.

The cathedral's site had been purchased in 1828 as a burying ground, but even a cursory examination would have revealed the rocky terrain. At the time it was decided to use the site for the cathedral, the built-up portions of the city did not extend beyond Forty-second Street. But by the time it was finished, the cathedral was sitting smack dab in the middle of the coming residential enclave of New York's wealthiest, most exclusive district, where the Protestant establishment would otherwise have reigned supreme.

Brooklyn Bridge (L)
1883

From Frankfort Street and Park Row (City Hall Park) east across the East River to Brooklyn
John A. Roebling and Colonel Washington Roebling, Engineers

The greatest engineering triumph of the nineteenth century just might be the most majestic and inspiring bridge of all time.

During its construction it was called the East River Bridge. At its completion it was called the New York and Brooklyn Bridge. Today it is the Brooklyn Bridge, and the federal government calls it a national historic landmark.

Nothing in nineteenth-century New York caused more sustained excitement or symbolized America's manifest destiny better. In Manhattan, only the steeple of Trinity Church was higher (and just barely), and of the few successful suspension bridges of its time, none was longer—1,595 feet from tower to tower—nor spanned such an important body of water.

John Roebling, its chief engineer, conceived of the bridge as early as 1857. Like his peers, he was eclectic. For the towers he dallied with different styles, including the Florentine Renaissance, Romanesque, and Egyptian before finally settling on Gothic. To many his is the most beautiful bridge design in the world, but to others the design is secondary to his engineering breakthroughs. Roebling understood that stone in compression is unsurpassed, so he used granite for the towers. But he believed that there was a new and untested material with the tensile strength he wanted for the span—steel. Never before had steel been used for such a mammoth undertaking, either in a bridge or a building, but Roebling took a calculated risk and used it for the cables and stays that emanate fanlike from the towers and the decks below.

Work began on the great bridge in 1869. Fourteen years later, invitations on Tiffany stationery were sent to dignitaries asking them to attend the ceremonies celebrating the bridge's opening. The crowd heard speeches by Brooklyn's Mayor Seth Low and New York's Mayor Franklin Edson, among others; the Seventh and Twenty-third Regimental Bands played; President Chester A. Arthur marched across from New York to Brooklyn; peddlers hawked medals cele-

brating "The World's Eighth Wonder"; fireworks filled the night air; and 100,000 people walked across the bridge. Six days later, however, somebody said that the bridge was collapsing. Twelve people died in the panic to get off.

Despite the fears, voiced and unvoiced, the bridge was a huge success, resulting in the demise of many of the East River ferries linking the City of Brooklyn with the City of New York. Ironically, it was a ferry that caused John Roebling's death in 1869—one crushed his foot, and after its amputation he developed lockjaw and died. His son Colonel Washington Roebling, an expert in caisson disease, ironically contracted that disease and was confined to his home in Brooklyn Heights with the "bends." As he checked the progress on the bridge through binoculars, his wife Emily became fluent in engineering terms and acted as his liaison. Today's engineers maintain that given adequate maintenance this bridge, this majestic and inspiring presence, could last forever.

Potter Building   1883

38 Park Row, northeast corner of Beekman Street
N. G. Starkweather, Architect

Bigger, better, and, with an exterior of ornamental terra cotta and an interior of ironwork protected by hollow bricks, fireproof.

The Potter Building gives a hint of the scale of things to come. When it was built its eleven stories made it the tallest building in the neighborhood, and with frontages of 96, 145, and 90 feet, it was an imposing mass. It was built by Orlando B. Potter, a former congressman turned real-estate investor, and his offices were on the top floor.

It was the city's first office building with an ornamental facade of terra cotta. Until then the only mass-produced facades had been cast iron, but terra cotta (literally, baked

earth) facades also could be stamped out of molds and mass produced. It was also the city's first building with iron supports entirely sheathed by hollow bricks, providing protection from the heat of fire. By the 1870s many architects had become loath to use iron framing for fear that it would buckle in intense heat, but the introduction of protected iron beams reassured them. The combination of terra cotta and the protected iron led Mr. Potter to proclaim this masonry building fireproof.

It was a daring claim to make, not because it was necessarily untrue by contemporaneous standards, but because the Herald Building had gone up in flames on this very site the year before. One of the messages so dramatically conveyed by that blaze was the fire department's inability to extend ladders high enough to rescue victims.

In the 1890s Park Row was New York's Printing House Square. In the Potter Building alone were the *New York Press* (with a daily circulation of 111,812 it was New York's fifth largest newspaper) and the first and oldest religious newspaper, the *New-York Observer*. Allied businesses, including the Peter Adams Company and the Adams & Bishop Company, paper manufacturers, were also tenants. The *New York Daily News*, with both English and German editions, was at 32 Park Row; and at 3 Park Row was the *New York Mercury*, a Democratic paper that supported the "regular National, State and City nominations through thick and thin." Next door to the Potter Building, at 41 Park Row, was the *New York Times*, until it moved to Times Square in 1904. The Tribune Building stood on the northeast corner of Park Row and Spruce Street, and next door to it stood the Sun Building. Where there is now a ramp for the Brooklyn Bridge was Pulitzer's World Building. And around the corner, at 152 Nassau Street, were the offices of Currier & Ives, printers of the American scene.

The Dakota (L) 1884

1 West Seventy-second Street, between Seventy-
second and Seventy-third streets on Central Park
West
Henry J. Hardenbergh, Architect

*Until the mid-1880s and the advent of a few luxurious
apartment houses like the Dakota, if you were wealthy, you
lived in your own private home.*

The first apartment house in New York City for "respectable"
families was the Stuyvesant (now demolished), built in 1869
on Eighteenth Street near Third Avenue. But the idea of
apartment dwelling took a while to catch on. Blue-blooded
New Yorkers did not readily accept the idea that a common
roof and public stairs and hallways could be shared with
other families if one still desired to be considered respectable.
For a house to be a home, it had to be a private home. But
the Dakota—and other early luxurious apartment houses built
in the mid-1880s, such as the Osborne at 205 West Fifty-
seventh Street and 34 Gramercy Park East—helped to change
all that.

Seven of the Dakota's ten floors were originally devoted
to suites of apartments, with the eighth and ninth floors for
servants' quarters. These quarters, a hangover from pre-ele-
vator days, were in addition to the servants' quarters that
were standard in most apartments. Upstairs also housed laun-
dries, drying rooms, and a dormitory for transient servants.
The tenth floor housed a playroom and gymnasium for children.

The scale of these apartment houses was unknown before. The Dakota takes up a 200-foot frontage on Central Park
West. It was lavishly decorated inside and out, and cost
Singer Sewing Machine heir Edward Clark about a million
dollars to build. The sixty-five apartments ranged in size from
four to twenty rooms, with some parlors as big as 24 by 40
feet. The parlors, libraries, reception rooms, and dining

rooms were all paneled and wainscoted in mahogany, oak, or some other hardwood.

Eight elevators served the building. Four were for residents and their guests, and four were service elevators that went from the cellar, where wine could be stored, to the servants' quarters on the eighth and ninth floors.

The building was considered completely fireproof, and was built to last, with 6- to 12-inch rolled-iron beams set into the floors every 3 to 4 feet, and with load-bearing walls that are 28 inches thick at the bottom floors.

Architecturally, it is probably the most distinctive building on Central Park West. Its buff brick walls with terra cotta trim, its square- and round-headed windows, its mansard roof with peaks and gables and dormer windows, its seven-story bay windows on Seventy-second Street topped by their own pyramidal roofs all add up to a statement of solidity that overwhelms the viewer.

Although its promoters described the Dakota's neo–German Renaissance facade as having an "air of lightness and airiness," others find it "spooky," an idea no doubt reinforced by its use as the setting for the movie version of *Rosemary's Baby*.

The entrance to the building is on Seventy-second Street, past the gatehouse, through an arched carriage entrance, and into an I-shaped courtyard with a fountain. The passenger elevators and stairs are in the four corners.

When it was built, grounds stretching 175 feet west of the building were used for croquet and tennis courts and as private gardens. Below, safely sequestered from the Dakota itself, boilers and a dynamo supplied power for the building's own electricity. (Edison's company did not supply electricity north of Spruce Street when the Dakota was erected.)

And that brings us to why the building is called the Dakota. At the time of its construction, the Dakota stood practically alone in the midst of empty lots and run-down farms. Most of New York's population lived south of Fifty-ninth Street, and Seventy-second Street seemed as far away from "civilization" as the Dakota Territory. The name stuck.

The Dakota was built for the upper middle class, and it still attracts a wealthy clientele. A ten-room apartment in this cooperative apartment house was on the market in the summer of 1977 for $250,000, with monthy maintenance charges of $1,903.

Chelsea Hotel 1884

(Originally Chelsea Apartments)
222 West Twenty-third Street, between Seventh
and Eighth Avenues
Hubert, Pirsson & Company, Architects

*The first apartment house to rise twelve stories, and a
pioneer cooperative.*

Architect/builder Philip G. Hubert is one of the unsung heroes of apartment-house design in New York. He pioneered the ten- and twelve-story apartment house; he pioneered apartment houses whose apartments were sold by a joint

stock company and operated on a cooperative basis (it seems that 34 Gramercy Park East was New York's first coop, in 1883); and he was a pioneer in the creation of apartment houses that gave the feeling of private homes, introducing duplexes.

To make it all safe, he introduced sheathing of wood or steel beams with fireproof blocks or cement, a device that even today satisfies fire codes. His criterion for fireproofing would have made *The Towering Inferno* a one-reeler: the entire contents of a single apartment might burn to ashes, but the rest of the building would not be endangered or even disturbed. Clearly, Hubert hit upon something with his first-class, fireproof apartment houses—they were desirable enough to be the only houses in New York in which rents went up in 1884.

One of his most famous designs was the Navarro Apartments (now demolished), a group of eight buildings at Seventh Avenue and Fifty-ninth Street. His cooperative apartment houses include the ten-story Hawthorne, the ten-story Rembrandt, the ten-story and modestly named Hubert, and the city's largest, most luxurious and popular cooperative apartment/residential hotel when it opened, the Chelsea Apartments. There were spacious apartments with fireplaces in every room, painted ceilings in the parlors, and stained-glass transoms between the rooms. The facade is distinguished by its heavy, Ruskinian Gothic architecture, with its gables and window frames, some semi-elliptical, others lancet. The light cast-iron railings were ordered from the stock of D. D. Badger & Co., whose foundry and machine shop were crosstown on Fourteenth Street between Avenues B and C.

The prospectus for the Chelsea described the location as "very central," which it was, "near the shopping district [Ladies' Mile was only two blocks east], the theatres [they were clustered along Broadway from Union to Herald squares], and the churches." The Chelsea's one hundred suites were quickly sold, some at a premium, making it a highly successful business venture.

By 1905 the Chelsea Apartments had become the Chelsea Hotel, whose guest list has been distinguished by the likes of composers Virgil Thomson and George Kleinsinger, playwright Arthur Miller, poets Dylan Thomas and Edgar Lee Masters, writer Thomas Wolfe, and artist John Sloan.

Statue of Liberty Enlightening the World (L) 1885

Liberty (originally Bedloe's) Island, southwest of Manhattan Island in New York Harbor
Frédéric Auguste Bartholdi, Sculptor; Gustave Eiffel, Engineer; Richard Morris Hunt, Architect of the base

The modern world's greatest colossus, America's most famous statue, and Eiffel's other tower.

Sculptor Frédéric Auguste Bartholdi convinced the people of France to contribute the greatest colossus of modern times to the people of the United States in commemoration of the alliance between the two nations. The statue he envisioned would become the most famous, most recognized statue in the world, a woman clutching a tablet bearing the date July 4, 1776, with broken shackles at her feet, a woman with a benevolent countenance whose right arm holds high the torch of freedom. Bartholdi's *Statue of Liberty Enlightening the World* is 151 feet high (the *Colossus of Rhodes* was a mere 100 feet), standing on a 155-foot pedestal. The statue's skin is *repoussé* copper, sheets that were 3/32 of an inch thick, hammered into shape and riveted together. Without a framework, however, the statue would probably not stand up to the harbor's winds. Bartholdi went to Gustave Eiffel, France's great engineer, who designed a supporting iron tower as a skeleton. He supported the extended arm by running beams from the arm across the body to counterbalance the overhang. The statue was erected in Bartholdi's studio in suburban Paris, then disassembled and crated in 210 packing cases. And there it sat, with nowhere to go.

The statue had been given with the understanding that the American citizenry would pay for the construction of its base. Americans, however, were slow to come up with the funds. The hand bearing the torch was shown at Philadelphia's Centennial Exhibition, and erected in Madison Square in 1876 as a fund-raising gimmick. Little happened. In 1883 the Pedestal Fund Committee auctioned off a portfolio of original drawings and letters, including an occasional sonnet by Emma Lazarus:

> . . . Give me your tired, your poor,
> Your huddled masses yearning to breathe free,
> The wretched refuse of your teeming shore
> Send these, the homeless, tempest-tost to me,
> I lift my lamp beside the golden door.

The entire portfolio fetched $1,500. It took over eight years to collect less than half the funds needed. Then newspaperman Joseph Pulitzer started an editorial campaign. Within five months the World had collected $100,000 in pennies and nickels and dimes, and nine years after the fund-raising drive had started the three-masted warship Isère sailed into New York Harbor, bearing the statue in her hold.

To support the statue's enormous weight—the frame is 162,000 pounds, the copper 200,000—required a base of enormous strength. Under the direction of retired Engineer-in-Chief, U.S.A., General Charles P. Stone, the 65-foot foundation was created with the largest piece of concrete ever poured up to that time. The pedestal, designed by Richard Morris Hunt, is faced with granite.

On the day of the unveiling, tugs and pleasure boats and steamers and ironclads filled the harbor. During one of the orations, a false signal was given and the statue was prematurely unveiled. Steam whistles tooted, people cheered, yet Senator William M. Evarts went right on with his speech. President Cleveland, who was presiding, appeared to be paying strict attention, although it was impossible to hear a word of the speech. One statue, clearly, was worth a thousand words.

393–399 Lafayette Street (L)   1885

(Originally the DeVinne Press Building)
Northeast corner of Fourth Street
Babb, Cook, & Willard, Architects

The 40-inch-deep reveals on Lafayette Street show the depth of the load-bearing walls of this massive structure in the style of the Romanesque Utilitarian.

The first skyscraper, defined as a building supported by a steel skeleton construction with walls that did not bear the load, was Chicago's Home Insurance Building, designed by William LeBaron Jenney. The year was 1885. Buildings tall enough to be considered skyscrapers were being erected in

New York, but the city lagged in the true skyscraper race, continuing to erect buildings with load-bearing walls. In the same year that the Home Insurance Building appeared, the monumental DeVinne Press Building was erected. The girth of the building's load-bearing walls is shown in the 40-inch-deep reveals on the Lafayette Street side, walls that had to be thick because there was no skeleton of steel behind them to support the building itself as well as the presses and paper used to print such great American magazines as *Scribner's, St. Nicholas,* and *Century.*

The building was designed as a printing plant, and its facade discloses its role—there is no decoration, no delicate stonework, no sculpture, just an honest expression of strength. The only hint in the heavy facade that this was 1885 and the dawning of the age of the skyscraper is found within the reveals—a clearly delineated grid of steel and glass hangs in suspension, a common look in today's skyscrapers with their curtain walls.

The Romanesque Utilitarian is well suited to this kind of building. Its massive arches and bold massing take the place of ornamentation, the form carrying the building—the three-story arches on Lafayette Street are 16 feet wide and almost 50 feet high, and act as the basses in a chorus to the sopranos of the windows. Many New York factories and warehouses were built in this style, among them the playful Puck Building on Lafayette and Houston streets (Albert Wagner, 1885), 376 Lafayette Street (Henry J. Hardenbergh, 1888), and the U.S. Federal Building at 641 Washington Street (W. J. Edbrooke, 1899). They are all strong and massive, all red brick, and all have bearing walls.

This $200,000 edifice, the city's fifth most expensive building erected in 1885, was built by the great printer Theodore DeVinne. Fifty years earlier, when this area was first being developed, he would probably have bought a house here instead of building a printing plant, a shift explained by

Manhattan's relentless northward movement and its intensive land use. By 1899 DeVinne would be living in a house in the newly emerging Upper West Side. It, too, would be designed by Babb, Cook & Willard in the style of the Romanesque Revival.

Villard Houses (L)   1886

(Palace Hotel)
451–457 Madison Avenue, between Fiftieth and Fifty-first streets
McKim, Mead & White, Architects

New York's best grouping of brownstone mansions was yet another Romantic revival, this time in the style of the highly structured formalism of the Italian Renaissance.

Architects McKim, Mead & White, who until the Villard commission were practitioners of the Richardsonian Romanesque and the American Shingle style, were approached by Henry Villard to design six houses around a central carriage yard. Villard had made his fortune in West Coast railroads, and wanted a New York home that would be subdued and sedate, but which would announce to the world—here lives a prince. For his $587,134 he got his stately pleasure home amidst the finest grouping of brownstone houses in New York, houses that were urbane in scale and revolutionary in their high Italian Renaissance style. (In a complicated landmark deal, the houses are being incorporated as part of the new, fifty-one-story Palace Hotel, which is rising on their air rights behind them.)

The houses appear as one, but they were indeed six. Villard's house was in the south wing, built on a plot that measured 50 by 100 feet, his drawing room taking up the entire parlor floor on Madison Avenue. There were mosaics in ceilings and bas-reliefs over mantels, Tiffany glass and St. Gaudens clocks. Inscribed over his dining room's mantle was *Per Ardua ad Alia,* roughly "Through Hardship to Higher Things," a bit of irony since Villard lost his fortune almost within the year, and was forced to sell his house to another West Coast millionaire, Darius Ogden Mills. Mills gave it as an engagement present to his daughter, the future Mrs. Whitelaw Reid.

The five houses that comprise the balance of the complex

did not have such riches lavished on their interiors, since they were built speculatively by Villard. Their scale, nevertheless, was generous—the lots averaged about 30 by 50 feet and the house flanking Villard's measured about 45 by 50 feet. Altogether the five cost about $165,000 to build. Here were city houses in an urbane setting, houses that projected a unified whole while functioning as individual units. Four were reached by the courtyard—Villard's, No. 451, in the south; Harris C. Fahnestock's, No. 457, in the north; and Nos. 453 and 455 through the loggia. The other two houses had their entrances on Fifty-first Street.

It seems that the inspiration to produce a neo–Italian Renaissance facade based on Rome's Palace of the Chancellery, a Renaissance classic (1517), belongs to Joseph M. Wells. He inherited the assignment from the practicing partners, since both McKim and White were too busy for it. Gone was the picturesque tradition of Romanticism, replaced by yet another Romantic revival, the highly structured formalism of the Italian Renaissance. Wells's design set the firm's standard for the next twenty-five years, but he never did become a partner. One reason could be that when Stanford White claimed that one of his own drawings was, "in its way . . . as good as the Parthenon," Wells replied, "Yes, and so too, in its way, is a boiled egg."

20 West Seventy-first Street   1889

Between Central Park West and Columbus Avenue
Gilbert A. Schellenger, Architect

This five-story, 19-foot-wide house captures the essence of a "brownstone," both in its pristine look and its classic history.

A "brownstone" is a much misunderstood thing. Many people mistakenly use the word to describe indiscriminately any row house. Some even use the word to describe any small building that is old and built in a row with others, often confusing tenements with what used to be private homes. (Unscrupulous real-estate agents often lead impressionable young things into believing that an apartment is in a "charming, renovated brownstone," when in truth it is simply a remodeled tenement.) Many tenements do indeed have facades of brownstone, as did some free-standing mansions (J. P. Morgan's, for instance), and at least one bank (the Hanover, now India House).

A true brownstone, however, was always a single-family row house, seldom wider than three windows or 22 feet, usually with a high stoop on one side, generally four or five stories high, sometimes with a bay window, and always with a 6- or 8-inch facing of brownstone over common brick. Most were built in the last half of the nineteenth century, and they were built for the established upper middle class, or those aspiring to proper respectability. In fact, "brownstone respectability" was synonymous with New York's upper middle class in the last half of the nineteenth century.

Brownstone layouts were all basically alike, virtually unchanged from the layouts of the Greek Revival, brick-fronted houses on Washington Square North—half-basements with the kitchen, laundry room, and family dining room; the parlor floor with the front parlor for formal entertaining and the rear parlor for formal dining (a dumbwaiter linked the dining room with the kitchen below), often with a sitting room separating the parlors, and sometimes with a butler's pantry as an extension; two floors of front and back bedrooms, often separated by dressing rooms, sewing rooms, dens, etc.; and the top floor, with plank floors and basic accouterments for the servants. Rich woods predominated in the family quarters, with elegant newel-posts and balusters, wainscoting in the hallways, frames around doors and windows, and parquet floors. The parlor floor boasted massive fireplaces and marble mantels, with lesser variations in every room. The bathrooms contained the latest plumbing achievements, and some came with bathtubs encased in paneled woodwork. One row house on West Seventy-sixth Street even had a stained-glass ceiling, flooding the music room with roseate hues.

This brownstone is the only one of the original four (16–22 West Seventy-first Street) that were built by John and George Ruddell (they called themselves masons) that has not been modernized by the removal of the stoop among other renovations. Most builders ignored the services of an architect, erecting buildings by formula instead. But the Ruddells hired Gilbert A. Schellenger, a respected domestic architect, and got a splendid example of a classic brownstone for their $20,000 investment plus the cost of the lot (the going rate for a four-story brownstone on Seventy-fourth Street near Broadway was about $30,000 in the 1890s).

The brownstones were built in rows, not a whole block at a time but in clutches of three or four, clustered together and flanked by empty lots until the interstices were filled in.

They were built in multiples of the city lot, some 25 feet wide, most 20, which is a fifth of four lots, others diminishing to 18¾ feet, or a quarter of three lots, or 16⅔ feet, a third of two lots. Brownstones were built by speculators who realized that, with the advent of Central Park, uptown was ripe for development. History had shown that New York's population was increased by 25 percent every five years, and building lots on Manhattan were, after all, finite. While creating a market for building lots around it, Central Park itself had claimed about eight thousand lots. The pressure was on to snatch everything around the park before it was too late. The East Side, with better transportation and more direct access to downtown, developed first, but gradually the Upper West Side was taking on a new image. The shantytowns and squatters would not last. The air was too salubrious, the vistas too spiritually uplifting, and with horse cars and rapid transit in the offing, it was the area in which to invest.

This block was bought in January 1869, for $400,000. Less than forty-five days later it was sold for $505,000. But buildings failed to keep pace with the turnover in lots. Between 1870 and 1875 only 204 houses were erected on the whole of the Upper West Side, and as late as 1882, West Seventy-fourth Street was still a "paper" street, a mere trail leading to a vegetable garden. The coming of the elevated railroad to Ninth (Columbus) Avenue in 1880, with the reality of inexpensive and quick commutation, changed all this. Tenements sprang up along Columbus and Amsterdam avenues, and on many of the side streets between them.

The fashionable avenues—Central Park West, West End Avenue, and Riverside Drive—had their share of brownstones, but it was on the side streets that these private homes for the upper middle class are found in the greatest profusion. Most of them were lived in by single families until at least the Depression, but many were then broken up and some fell on hard times. By 1950, for instance, this building had a sprinkler system installed and was officially converted to a Class B dwelling, a boardinghouse with furnished rooms. However, by 1966 it had changed again, climbing back to a Class A rating, with eight apartments instead of a warren of furnished rooms.

Variations of the brownstone theme abound, but this house, nineteen feet wide, with its stoop intact, its half-basement, and its four stories, is about as classic an example of a brownstone home as exists in Manhattan today.

340 East Thirteenth Street   1889

Between First and Second avenues
Architect unknown

The infamous "dumbbell" tenement. It goes back 90 feet, and only one room in each of its twenty apartments received light and air from any source except a 5-foot air shaft.

The facts surrounding this dumbbell tenement house, and thousands like it, are abysmal. On a 25-by-100-foot lot a real-estate developer would erect a building that occupied the

front 25 by 90 feet, leaving ten feet in the rear for light and air. Because the Tenement House Law of 1879 stipulated that every bedroom had to have a window, 2½-foot-wide air shafts were cut into the flanks of each building at the midpoint, so that between each building there was a 5-foot air shaft, some as long as 60 feet. Because the buildings were pinched in at the middle, their configurations reminded people of dumb-bells, hence their name.

Unlike brownstones, whose stoops and entrances are on the side, tenement stoops and entrances are in the center of the building and lead directly to a hallway. Apartments could be placed on each side of the corridor, two in the front, two in the rear. The back apartments were usually three rooms; the front, four. Because one room led to another like a railroad car, the apartments were known as railroad flats. Only one room in each front apartment faced the street, with its light and air, and only one room in the rear apartment faced the 20 feet of space between it and the tenement on the next block. All of the other rooms looked out on the air shafts.

There was no heat, there was no hot water, there were no bathrooms, but there was a common toilet in the hallway for the use of the tenants on that floor. With rents at $10 to $20 a month, few tenement-dwelling families could afford to pay without assistance, so rooms were rented to lodgers. There might be as many as ten people to an apartment, forty to a floor, two hundred to a house. All tenements were walk-ups, some as high as seven stories. The walls were brick, often with a facing of brownstone, but the floors, stairs, door-frames, and doors were wood. When there was a fire, the houses burned with ferocity, the air shafts acting like flues, the drafts creating towers of flames. Often these homes doubled as factories: some families used their apartments to roll cigars; others turned out piece goods for the garment industry, the sewing machines operating from 6 A.M. to 10 P.M. By 1900 there were 42,700 tenement houses of all descriptions in New York, housing over 1.5 million people. In 1903 about 15 percent of the houses were still without fire escapes.

The irony is that the dumbbell tenement house was the product of a reform movement. As the middle and upper classes moved north along the spine of the island, the poor clung to the old areas, moving into the cast-off Knickerbocker homes. Soon rooms that might have once housed seldom-used front parlors were instead housing whole families. Real-estate manipulators quickly saw their opportunity. Only so many families could be crammed into the old homes, even after windowless rooms had been created in the middle of the houses. Instead of subdividing the old homes, new low-cost housing could be built, some of which would provide as much as a 40 percent annual return on their investment. One example, named Gotham Court, went up in 1853 at 36 Cherry Street. It was five stories high and 150 feet deep, and erected between a 9-foot alley on one side and 7-foot alley on the other. Twelve doors opened off the 9-foot alley, each door leading to a staircase, and each staircase leading to a landing with a pair of identical two-room apartments. One room measured 9 by 14 feet, the other 9 by 6. It adds up to 120 apartments. There was no plumbing, there was no heat, and only in 1863, when an estimated eight hundred dwellers inhabited the rooms, were privies installed in the basement.

Pioneer tenement legislation in 1867 (a law that was universally ignored) required adequate exits, lighting, and an occasional window. In 1879 the State Legislature went further and mandated that every bedroom had to have a window, which led a trade journal called *The Plumber and Sanitary Engineer* to hold a contest for a model tenement. First prize, called "Light, Air, and Health," was won by James E. Ware. He took the standard 25-by-100-foot lot and designed a house 90 feet deep and 25 feet wide, and in the center he stuck a narrow courtyard on each side. From his prototype in 1879 sprang variations, each meaner than the last, until in 1901 a new tenement house law was written, outlawing the dumb-bell tenement (this explains why some people call them old-law tenements). No window could look out on less than 12 feet of air, toilets and running water had to be installed in each apartment, and fire escapes had to be unobstructed.

This tenement house has an elaborate Victorian cornice and an entrance that could lead to a mansion. Otherwise, it's just like all the others that were made possible by greed and the 25-by-100-foot lot.

West Park Presbyterian Church   1890

(Originally Park Presbyterian Church)
Eighty-sixth Street and Amsterdam Avenue,
northeast corner
Henry F. Kilburn, Architect

In the tradition of the Richardsonian Romanesque:
asymmetrical massing that is close to the ground, with a
tower that soars.

The Village of Bloomingdale was centered at Eighty-sixth Street and Broadway, and by the 1880s it was in the throes of urbanization. Streets were displacing paths, row houses

were displacing farms, and congregations that had been gathering since the 1850s were becoming scattered. The Reverend Anson P. Atterbury wanted to keep his flock together, and, with an eye to the future, he hoped to attract new parishioners. In 1884 the chapel in the east end of this grouping was dedicated (architect unknown), and six years later this rough-hewn giant of a church was built.

The style is Richardsonian Romanesque, created by a follower of Henry Hobson Richardson. Richardson created bold masses of space, carving the forms first and dealing with the detailing, which was usually Romanesque, later. (Richardson became so infatuated with the Middle Ages that sometimes he wore monk's garb, his huge girth girdled by a rope.) Boston's Trinity Church is his, as is Pittsburgh's Allegheny County Courthouse (1888), a building to which this church bears an uncanny resemblance.

The church's facade is rough-hewn red sandstone, great hunks of stone that create an appearance of undeniable strength. Roman arches abound, great semicircular arches with wedge-shaped units that clearly play their role in the construction of the arches. Contrasting with the roughness of the stone and the strength of the arches is the delicate Byzantine leafwork that is carved in the capitals and over the three doors of the entrance. All this roughness and delicacy is reflected in macrocosm in the asymmetrical massing of the church and the soaring tower above.

The tower rises from the solid base of the church. Its slender, attenuated openings end in Roman arches. The tower then begins a series of artful terminations, first with horizontal bandings, then with three diminutive openings with Roman arches, more horizontal banding, and four miniturrets. The dome is an enlarged version of the corner finials.

The popularity of the Richardsonian Romanesque was, like many other eclectic revivals, short-lived. Nothing was ever copied verbatim from the past, but variations on old themes were created. The style was as adaptable for churches and courthouses as it was for row houses and apartment buildings (there's a good example at 101 West Eighty-fifth

Street on the northwest corner of Columbus Avenue). The church's facade was cleaned in 1976 at a cost of $50,000—about half what it originally cost to build the church.

29 East Thirty-second Street 1890

(Originally the Grolier Club)
Between Madison and Park avenues
Charles W. Romeyn & Company, Architects

A gentle Romanesque Revival statement which shows that the style was as much at home in a small clubhouse as in a huge printing plant.

Theodore DeVinne, who headed the DeVinne Press, was also the chairman of the building committee for the Grolier Club, whose object has been the "literary study and promotion of the arts pertaining to the production of books." DeVinne and his fellow clubmen were progressive, which is manifested in the choice of their design. It hints at things to come, like the design by Adler & Sullivan and Frank Lloyd Wright for Charnley House in Chicago.

Two solid Romanesque-style arches mark the base. A transition is made on the second floor, with a Romanesque window frame flanked by a pair of square-headed windows. (These windows are deceiving—the flanking windows open casement style, and the center square window within the Romanesque frame pivots.) The top floor is the logical conclusion, a loggia with four windows. The brickwork reinforces the massing. The pressed bricks are reminiscent of Norman bricks, only a little smaller, measuring 10 inches long and about an inch high. They provide detailing in the facade, as voussoirs around the second-floor arch, as keystones for the flanking windows, and as punctuation marks, signaling the end of a wall by curving into the window frames. The other decoration is pure Romanesque Revival in terra cotta.

The club had wanted to rent a clubhouse for $2,500 a year, but, as one club historian put it, due to the "antediluvian housing shortage," none could be found that was suitable. The club spent about $27,000 for this site, and about $21,000 for the building. Its walls are 12 inches thick above the basement, its floorbeams spruce. A luxury was steam heat, installed for $1,200.

The first floor almost entirely covers the 25-by-100-foot lot, with a reception hall and club office in the front, and a 25-by-50-foot lecture and exhibition hall in the rear. The skylit ceiling in this room is 16 feet high, and in the south wall a balcony was installed for musicians. The second floor housed the social, reading, and smoking rooms, with the library taking up the front of the third floor. The club moved out of this gem in 1917, when it moved into its present-day, Mayfair-style house at 47 East Sixtieth Street. There, amidst much of the original furniture, rest the ashes of the original mortgage on this building, carefully preserved in a glass urn.

Since the club moved out, this building has had a checkered career. Its interior has been remodeled for a cabaret, used as a furniture showroom and repair shop, and converted into an office/studio for graphic design artists. Most of the interior has been gutted, but a fireplace remains in the front room on the first floor. Amidst its Romanesque Revival trim is one jarring note—a bas-relief salamander, the symbol of Francis I and the beginnings of the French Renaissance. At first it seems a pointless anachronism, until the connection is made—Grolier de Servières, for whom the club was named, was the printer to Francis I, King of France.

Carnegie Hall (L)   1891

154 West Fifty-seventh Street, southeast corner of Seventh Avenue
With later additions
William B. Tuthill, Architect; Dankmar Adler and William Morris Hunt, Consultants

Built about a mile north of the theater district of the 1890s, Carnegie Hall became a whole performing-arts complex unto itself while keeping in touch with the mainstream of urban life.

Andrew Carnegie, president of Leopold Damrosch's Oratorio Society, became convinced that if he gave a new hall to the amateur singing group he could realize a decent return for his generosity. Since its beginnings in 1873 the peripatetic group had never had a hall to call its own, and no hall in New York ever seemed large enough to do justice to the full effects of the chorus.

In 1891 Carnegie presented the society with a $2 million gift—a 2,760-seat auditorium with superb acoustics. It was modestly and unpretentiously called the Music Hall.

At the time, this was an uptown residential neighborhood; the theater district, about a mile south, was huddled around Herald Square.

William B. Tuthill was the architect of the Renaissance-

style brick and terra cotta building, with Hunt and Adler, of Adler & Sullivan, as consultants. (To Adler go the laurels for the hall's acoustics.) The building they designed is only part of the building you see today—the original rose only six stories and did not stretch all the way to Fifty-sixth Street (you can see a break in the cornice line on Seventh Avenue). Within seven years, however, two additions had been added to it, one above and the other alongside.

The additions, which included apartments, studios, and offices, made this single building a major performing-arts center, one that does not segregate itself from the mainstream of urban life, but which contributes to its rich fabric.

The main body of the building is basically a series of Roman arches, set off by cornices. Two sets of five arches, one above the other, point out the entrance on Fifty-seventh Street, and one central set is incorporated on the Seventh Avenue facade for balance. (Originally there was no fire escape.) The statuary within the arches, complete with cupids, is a charming touch, as is the stained glass above the notice boards on Seventh Avenue.

Carnegie Hall has been the scene of some of America's most famous concerts, beginning with Tchaikovsky as guest conductor during its opening-week ceremonies, and including performances by Toscanini, Stokowski, Rubinstein, Horowitz, and Benny Goodman and his jazz concerts of 1937–1938.

The New York Philharmonic made Carnegie Hall its first home, and when the Philharmonic left for Lincoln Center, Carnegie Hall found itself without its major tenant and facing the specter of demolition. Fortunately, the fight put up by preservationists and performing artists like Isaac Stern won the day and saved Carnegie Hall. Today it is a steadily booked landmark. Ironically, it has never made anybody, not even Carnegie, any money.

American Museum of Natural History (L)   1892

Central facade, southern wing, in Manhattan
Square at Seventy-seventh Street, between
Central Park West and Columbus Avenue
J. Cleveland Cady & Co., Architects

*This vision of the Romanesque belies the reality behind its
facade of Canadian granite—the largest iron girders ever used
in the construction of a building went into supporting the
fireproof floors.*

Post–Civil War America witnessed the first great surge of
interest in natural history, and by 1869 the American Museum of Natural History was a temporary resident in Central
Park's Arsenal. Two years later the same legislation that gave
the Metropolitan Museum of Art a building and land in Central Park gave the Museum of Natural History a building (designed by Calvert Vaux and Jacob Wrey Mould) and its site
in Manhattan Square. The original building (1877) was soon
found to be too small, and by the turn of the century the
Legislature had passed over ten acts authorizing its enlarge-
ment.

The first of the extensions was the central facade of the
southern wing (the southeast and southwest corners would
not be finished until 1897). This 60-by-110-foot wing is a
romantic image of a Romanesque palace/fortress. If Kilburn's
Richardsonian Romanesque design for West Park Presbyterian Church was derived from the south of Europe, then
Cady's Romanesque was from the north, conjuring up images
of Norman keeps. Eight short polished columns support the
seven Roman arches that set the tone of the facade. An imposing stoop of Massachusetts granite curves up to meet the
arches, the central arches housing what was originally the
dignified entrance to the wing. A 1904 view of the proposed
museum in its entirety shows the same facade repeated on
all four sides, with transverse wings linking the four sides
and creating four interior courts. At the crossing was planned
a monumental Romanesque-style tower that would have been
over 200 feet high.

The building was erected of brick and iron, with a facing
of red granite from New Brunswick. The Legislature had stipulated that the building had to be fireproof, so its floors were
built of fire brick covered by concrete. And the museologists
had stipulated that unobstructed floor space was mandatory,
so to support the weight of the floors without interior pillars
the largest girders ever used in the construction of a building
up to that time were incorporated. Twenty-eight girders, each

measuring 62 feet and weighing 40,000 pounds, arrived by ship at the Hudson River at Fiftieth Street. Getting the girders from the docks to the building site was a problem. New York's largest wagons were hired, with one girder and twelve horses to a wagon. Between Fiftieth and Seventy-seventh streets two trucks collapsed under the weight, and a third sank to its hubs as soon as it left the pavement and drove into Manhattan Square. The contractor finally constructed a tramway to transport the girders across the square to the site.

Cathedral Church of St. John the Divine   Begun 1892

West 112th Street, between Morningside Drive
and Amsterdam Avenue
Unfinished
Architects: Heins & LaFarge, 1891–1911; Cram &
Ferguson, 1911–1942; Adams & Woodbridge,
1966–1974; Hoyle, Doran & Berry, 1974–

The world's largest Gothic-style church has a floor area greater than Notre Dame and Chartres combined, with walls 124 feet high and 601 feet long enclosing 16 million cubic feet of space.

The sixty entrants in the architectural competition for New York's Episcopal cathedral ran the gamut from Richardsonian exuberance to neo-classical pomp. The design that won, officially described as a "domical church in a Gothic shell," had interior walls covered with rich mosaics that made it more like St. Sophia than Salisbury, its Byzantine/Romanesque/Gothic mishmash a synthesis of the Great Age of the Eclectic.

Work began in 1892 and progressed as far as the crossing, where a dome under a monumental conical tower had been planned. From the outset, however, the foundation was problematic, and it was questioned whether the foundation would support the weight of the tower.

Until that problem could be resolved, it was decided to erect a temporary dome over the 100-square-foot crossing. For the dome, Rafael Guastavino & Co. designed and built an engineering landmark. The crossing was bridged with inch-thick tiles, starting with nine courses of tile at the base of the dome. The higher the dome the fewer the thicknesses of tiles, until just three thicknesses were used at its apex, making the apex only about 4½ inches thick. No falsework was used to support the dome from below. A scaffold for the masons was built on the dome as work progressed. When the dome was finished, Guastavino himself guaranteed it for ten years. That was in 1909.

In 1911 Heins & LaFarge's plan was thrown out and Cram & Ferguson's, a mixture of French and English Gothic, was adopted. Attitudes had changed, becoming more conservative and Anglican. The stylistic change was easily rationalized: in Europe, over the centuries, one style after another had been superimposed on some cathedrals, and so it would be in America in 1911, only telescoped in time.

Cram's design for the facade has every virtue, except excitement. Inside, however, is another story. It is the world's largest Gothic-style church, featuring one of the greatest interiors. It is 601 feet long and 146 feet wide, giving it a floor area greater than Notre-Dame and Chartres combined. It is 124 feet high at the nave and 162 feet high at the apex of the dome. With its long tapering lines lifting your eyes heavenward, its stained-glass windows suffusing it with roseate hues, its beauty and grace and awesome dimensions are humbling.

As ethereal as Cram's Gothic style is, his nave clashes with Heins & LaFarge's apse with its monolithic columns, but today's plans still call for a merging of the two styles. Work on the cathedral, discontinued since 1941, is beginning anew, but who knows when, if ever, the cathedral will be completed. Until then, many New Yorkers will still mockingly call it "St. John the Unfinished."

Washington Arch   1892

At the southern tip of Fifth Avenue, in
Washington Square
McKim, Mead & White, Architects

Stanford White's Washington Arch was in the vanguard of the City Beautiful Movement, which held that American cities could be beautiful if embellished by grand design and public sculpture in the neo-classical style.

New York is hardly a Baroque city, but to celebrate the centenary of George Washington's oath-taking in 1889, the city was treated to a bit of imperial pomp. It took the form of a temporary wood and plaster memorial arch that spanned Fifth Avenue at Washington Mews. Stanford White's design

for the temporary arch was such a hit that a cry went up for a permanent one in Washington Square itself. William Rhinelander Stewart, a local scion, formed another fund-raising committee (he believed that these were the first memorial arches erected by private subscription to mark an historic event; since he lived at 17 Washington Square North, a desire for a little neighborhood improvement might have prompted his enthusiastic altriuism). Ignace Paderewski staged a benefit concert at the Metropolitan Opera and donated the $4,500 gate to the fund. And architects McKim, Mead & White waived their fees, and builder David H. King, Jr., waived any profits.

The arch, with a single span 30 feet across and 47 feet high, is built of white marble from the quarries of Tuckahoe, New York. Finished in 1892, it was not officially given to the City of New York until 1895 when its entire cost of $133,500 had been completely paid off.

White was particularly proud of his memorial arch. Its single, 30-foot span beat any that a memorial arch of antiquity could boast. More importantly, he believed that the architectural treatment of the Washington Arch "differs from its classical predecessors in being generally lighter, in the prominence of the frieze, in the reduced height of the attic, and lastly and most important, in the absence of the Orders."

White could not have known that his arch was in the vanguard of the City Beautiful Movement. The movement consisted primarily of European-trained American architects who fought the concept that growth should be the only criterion for measuring the quality of a city—most Americans believed that if a city was bigger it was by definition better—arguing instead that a city should be a place of beauty embellished by neo-classical design and public sculpture. The notion flowered at the Columbian Exposition held in Chicago in 1893, resulting in the Roman style as the fair's predominant motif. The make-believe city in white plaster convinced Americans that their cities could indeed be beautiful, provided that neo-classical ideals and scale were adhered to. The movement spread until even the dinkiest towns in the Old West were sporting neo-Renaissance banks and post offices, and the country was awash in the American Renaissance.

Church Missions House   1893

281 Park Avenue South at Twenty-second Street
Robert W. Gibson and Edward J. N. Stent,
Architects

*Not Richardsonian Romanesque, but neo-Romanesque to the
point that if shrunk a little it could almost be a guildhall
somewhere in Belgium.*

This charming building is yet another anachronism from the
drawing boards of the eclectic architects of the nineteenth
century. There is no doubt about the secular purpose of this
building, but it has a Christian mission, as evidenced by the
cross at the apex of the central gable serving as the terminating finial, and the statuary in the tympanum (St. Augus-
tine preaching to the barbarians in England, representing the
Church of England, and Bishop Seabury preaching to the
barbarians in America, representing the Protestant Episcopal
Church).

American missionary work was in high gear during the
last half of the nineteenth century, a time when churches
were intent on "gaining the hearts and opening the minds of
the heathen," as one church yearbook put it. This building
was erected to serve as headquarters for the Protestant Episcopal missions, which were involved in work that spread
from neighboring tenement districts to the American South,
to India and China.

This is no Richardsonian Romanesque building, but
something less visceral, more intellectual. The porch sets its
neo-Romanesque tone and reflects the building in microcosm. Its semi-elliptical arch is harmoniously repeated in the
four spans of the second and third floors, complete with the
same intricate foliation. The sixth floor repeats the round-
headed windows on a small scale, and the seventh floor turns
the foliation into a central gable and pediments for the dor-

mer windows. To add further to the illusion of the Romanesque, Gibson and Stent added *chiens assis* to the roof, which in the Middle Ages were unglazed dormer windows that provided light and air to attics. The roof is topped by cresting, and the upper floors are flanked by bartizans, small overhanging structures for defense, only minus their lookouts. Just as the porch's tympanum is flanked by pinnacles, so is the building itself.

Something jars on the first floor. Cabinet windows, a nineteenth-century development, are set into square-headed spans that are as wide as the same spans above, which seemingly require arches for support. The truth is that behind the facade of marble and Romanesque doohickeys is a framework of steel, hardly Romanesque building material.

This stretch of Park Avenue South was filled with charitable institutions in the 1890s, an example of the concentration of industries in cities. The United Charities Building, on the northeast corner of Twenty-second Street, housed the New York Association for Improving the Condition of the Poor, and the Society for the Prevention of Cruelty to Children was on the southeast corner of Twenty-third Street.

Immaculate Conception Church (L)   1896

(Originally Grace Chapel and Mission buildings)
406–414 East Fourteenth Street, between First
Avenue and Avenue A
Barney & Chapman, Architects

A great ecclesiastical complex, like that of a medieval church, embracing institutions that were necessary for the physical, educational, and spiritual needs of the city.

In the patchwork quilt of ethnic neighborhoods that Jacob Riis described, the tenement district around Tompkins Square in the 1890s was filled with Germans, many of them Protestants living in a papist sea. Of the few churches to choose from, Grace Church (Protestant Episcopal) was within walking distance, but it classed itself beyond the means of the average working family by its policy on pew ownership.

Nevertheless, wealthy congregations like Grace Church were beginning to accept greater responsibility for the poor, and missionary work was encouraged.

The Grace Church congregation invested over a half million dollars in this neo-Loire Valley grouping in the style of the Late French Gothic. More than just another country church modeled after a romantic ideal and plunked down amidst Manhattan's grid of streets, it was a great urban complex in the medieval tradition.

Embraced within its walls on Fourteenth Street were the chapel itself and a hospital for the elderly and for children. The hospital and the morning chapel were set out to the building line, defining the space, with the chapel set back a few feet. Linking them is a bold campanile, two lancets wide and topped by a Francis I crown. Narrow-faced brown bricks and terra cotta are the building materials for the facade. There was no marble here, but the buildings were a strong contrast with the tenements around them.

On Thirteenth Street were the mission buildings, the central building almost a neo-Romanesque design, flanked by neo–Loire Valley designs. Here were the gym and swimming pool, the Sunday school classes, and the cooking classes to "teach the girls in the neighborhood how to prepare palatable food," as one magazine article put it. Within the complex, everything was connected by cloisters, arcades, and ramps.

It had been believed that no English-speaking, non–Roman Catholic church could survive in the neighborhood, but compared with its mother church, Grace Chapel did a land-office business in the 1890s. There were four times as many baptisms, almost three times as many confirmations, and more than twice as many burial services. The only sacrament that was performed more frequently at Grace Church was marriage. Ironically, Grace Chapel was sold to the Roman Catholic Archdiocese in 1944. The chapel became the Immaculate Conception Church, and the morning chapel became a grotto in honor of Our Lady of Lourdes.

Atrium Apartments   1896

(Originally Mills House No. 1)
160 Bleecker Street, between Sullivan and
Thompson streets
Ernest Flagg, Architect

What is now an apartment house was built by Darius Ogden Mills as Mills House No. 1, a clean and pleasant hotel for men where a room could be had for twenty cents a night.

Inspector Thomas Byrnes, chief of the New York detectives, wrote in 1892 that New York's cheap lodging houses were the breeding places for crime. For two bits the artful lodger could get a bed in a dormitory in the fanciest of them. For a little less he could fall prey to New York's own versions of Fagin. Mills House No. 1 must have been the answer to Inspector Byrnes's prayers. Built by millionaire Darius Ogden

Mills, who had made his fortune in the hills of California, the hotel was even better than a model lodging house. There wasn't just a bed in a dormitory for twenty cents a night, but a 5-by-7-foot room with a bedstead and a good horsehair mattress, a chair, a strip of carpet, an electric light, and a window facing either the street or a court. Granted, the partitions separating the rooms did not quite extend to the ceiling, but some privacy, if not quiet, was assured. The quarters were clean, pleasant, and comfortable, so much so that some men lived in the hotel for years.

With the price of the room came public parlors and sitting rooms with writing tables and inkwells, and a library to boot. For another thirty cents a day, meals could be had in the dining room where there were tablecloths on the tables. The all-male clientele was forthright and upstanding, with suits and derbies in evidence, as befitted gentlemen in an establishment where no liquor was dispensed nor credit given. It was a place for a decent male urban immigrant to hang his hat in comfort, without courting the dangers of the infamous lodging house.

This huge building (90 by 200 feet and ten stories high) was basically two separate buildings, each a hollow square built around its own center court and linked by elevators, stairs, and landings. Each fifty-foot-square court was glass covered and steam heated. The rooms that looked out on these atriums had wire mesh instead of glass-paned windows, so warm air could circulate from the courts (heat was also supplied by steam pipes suspended from the ceilings).

More than half of the 1,560 rooms faced outside, which led to some interesting fenestration. To avoid the jailhouse look, two tiers of three windows each were grouped together as one unit. The steel frame has a facade of white brick with Indiana limestone trim in the style of the Italian Renaissance; Florentine torchères, with six globes surrounding a lantern, originally flanked the entrance; a copper roof was supported by iron brackets; the corridors were marble and the whole place was fireproof. Mills House No. 1 (No. 2 was at Rivington and Chrystie streets, No. 3 on Seventh Avenue at Thirty-sixth Street) eventually became Greenwich House, a flophouse. In 1976 it was resurrected as Atrium Apartments, an apartment house. Under today's J-51 zoning law, nonresidential buildings that have been converted into housing units receive ninety-nine-year tax breaks, resulting in block after block of neglected old buildings being given new lives. With the "new/old" buildings have come new neighborhoods like SoHo (South of Houston) and TriBeCa (Triangle Below Canal).

9 East Seventy-second Street   1896

(Originally Henry T. Sloane House)
Between Fifth and Madison avenues
Carrère & Hastings, Architects

Designed by graduates of l'Ecole des Beaux Arts, this limestone mansion in the style of the late French Renaissance hints at the Beaux Arts designs to come.

Aspiring American architects in the last half of the nineteenth century flocked to Europe for the grand tour, formal training, or both. For formal education they preferred Paris's *l'Ecole des Beaux Arts* (School of Fine Arts), established by Napoleon I and described by Louis Sullivan as "the fountainhead of theory." There the students worked in studios with professional architects and immersed themselves in architectural design, composition, theory, and history. Soon the effects of Beaux Arts training began to be evident in America. At the Columbian Exposition, held in Chicago in 1893, the conservative Eastern architects, under the influence of Beaux Arts–trained Richard Morris Hunt, held sway over the avant-garde Chicago school. What resulted was the design of the fair in the Roman style, as well as the flowering of the Beaux Arts–trained architects.

The basic neo-classicism of Beaux Arts training, however, was not so much Roman as it was French, with all *la gloire* that goes with it. This house, in the style of the late French Renaissance, was designed by John M. Carrère and Thomas Hastings, both graduates of the school, and it hints at the Beaux Arts style to come. The addition of statuary as an integral part of the design would have made this adaptation of a late French Renaissance design a Beaux Arts building.

Gone is the Dutch stoop, replaced by a porte cochere topped by a Baroque doorhead, leading not to an interior court but to the reception and service areas on the first floor. This design heralded the "American basement" plan, with the social rooms on the floor above. The building is divided into three parts—horizontal, vertical, horizontal—with rustication on the lower floor, two stories of windows joined by florid Ionic columns, and the whole topped by a French roof with attic windows flanked by Renaissance consoles. The Indiana limestone facade is so heavily embellished with neo-classical trim that the third floor almost becomes an entablature, carved into brackets, dentils, volutes, escutcheons—trim that begins to confuse the eye instead of guiding it to a resolution. Restraint was not a Beaux Arts hallmark.

The French windows on the second floor give a hint of the scale of the house, a house that Henry T. Sloane spent about $100,000 to build. By any definition, it's a mansion.

616–632 Avenue of the Americas   1896

(Originally Siegel-Cooper Department Store)
Between Eighteenth and Nineteenth streets
De Lemos & Cordes, Architects

A massive confection from a recipe concocted at the Chicago World's Fair of 1893 that originally boasted a scaled-down version of Daniel Chester French's Republic.

In the wake of Chicago's Columbian Exposition and its espousal of the classical ideal came this bastardization of it all, a massive confection in white brick and terra cotta, with bronze columns on Sixth Avenue, marble columns on Eighteenth Street, and enough imperial trim to please a caesar.

"The Big Store—A City In Itself" was the way the Siegel-

Cooper Department Store billed itself when it opened in 1896 in the heart of Ladies' Mile. And what an opening. The crowd, estimated at 150,000, poured into the store to gape at its 15½ acres of selling space, its 17 elevators, its 3,100 employees, and its 18-foot-high replica of Daniel Chester French's statue, *The Republic* (the original was 65 feet high and had been a focal point of the Columbian Exposition). Its roof contained a pergola with glassed archways and a tropical garden that bloomed during the summer.

One of the most popular pastimes at the store was sipping ice-cream sodas while sitting around the splashing fountain that surrounded *The Republic*. Soon the slogan "Meet me at the fountain" became a byword for New York's favorite trysting place.

Business boomed, but by 1902 Macy's had already moved uptown to Thirty-fourth Street into another De Lemos & Cordes building, and in 1906 B. Altman boldly moved to Fifth Avenue. Ladies' Mile slid into a decline that was Siegel-Cooper's undoing. In 1914 the store closed, and Gimbels bought its stock. *The Republic* was rescued by French himself, but his daughter in turn sold it to Forest Lawn Cemetery in Los Angeles, where the statue is now with the loved ones.

With a floor that can safely bear 120 pounds per square foot, compared with the floor of an average office building that can bear 70 to 80 pounds, the old Siegel-Cooper Department Store makes an ideal commercial loft building and today is filled with printers and light-manufacturing firms in the garment trade.

Bishop's Crook
Lamppost   1896

Broadway at Wall Street
Richard Rodgers Bowker, Designer

*At least thirty of these cast-iron classics still remain—and
will remain—on the city's streets.*

Gaslight had been introduced to New York's streets by the
1820s, and by the 1860s nights were being made as bright as
days. By 1890 gaslight would be everywhere, with 27,114 gas
lamps lighting the city's streets and giving their name to the
era. But there would also be 801 electric lights illuminating
the streets in 1890, a number that would grow and eclipse all
gas lamps by 1910.

The first electric street lights had appeared in New York
as early as 1880. Inventor Charles Francis Brush had perfected electric arc lights, and one was placed at every intersection along Broadway from Fourteenth to Twenty-sixth
streets. Within the year, both Madison and Union squares
were bathed in Brush's 6,000-candlepower lamps, lighting
the entire area from atop 160-foot poles. The glare was so
great that people complained their complexions took on an
unnatural pallor.

By 1892 cast- and wrought-iron lamps were extending
their long arms over intersections, their incandescent light
bulbs giving off a more pleasing glow. In 1896 the classic
cast-iron bishop's crook lamppost—so called for the obvious

reason—had arrived, with tendrils and acanthus leaves and leaf-and-vine scrollwork and a charm that today's street furniture lacks.

Nothing that could compare to them in elegance ever appeared in any number on New York's streets except Fifth Avenue's traffic standards, commissioned by the Fifth Avenue Association in 1931. Designed by Joseph Freedlander, they were topped by bronze statuettes of Mercury that were cast by the Tiffany Studios. When Fifth Avenue's lighting was "upgraded," these charming traffic standards vanished.

Fortunately, Friends of Cast-Iron Architecture, under the direction of Margot Gayle, has arranged with the New York Department of Gas and Electricity to preserve *in situ*—these lampposts are tagged, like wild geese—at least thirty cast-iron beauties. One that has escaped official preservation stands before an art gallery on Tenth Street, east of Fourth Avenue, installed there by an enterprising entrepreneur.

Low Library (L)   1897

Columbia University, 116th Street between
Amsterdam Avenue and Broadway
McKim, Mead & White, Architects

Low Library, which came in the wake of the Columbian Exposition, is New York's best example of the American Renaissance.

By the 1890s subtle changes were creeping into the cityscape, wrought by architects trained at Paris's *l'Ecole des Beaux Arts*. Ideally, buildings should be grouped, they believed, and that meant planning on a grand scale. With most New York real estate bound by 25-by-100-foot lots, the grand design was virtually an impossible urban dream. However, it could be realized outside the everyday world of real estate in artificially created situations. One had been the Columbian Exposition of 1893. Another would be Columbia University, which moved to its new campus on Morningside Heights in the 1890s.

Columbia's style would be mandated by the Committee on Buildings, a group that had seen the future at the Columbian Exposition and believed it worked. They did not want traditional English Collegiate Gothic; they wanted something they described as "municipal classic." In Charles Follen McKim, Beaux Arts–trained and classically oriented, they got their man. In his design for the campus in general and Low Library in particular, they got their "municipal classic."

Built of Indiana limestone, Low Library was designed to be the unifying element around which the campus would be built. It set the tone and scale for the university, and all the buildings in the original complex are subject to it. All share in the neo-Renaissance trim, all have unified cornice lines, and all have limestone porticoes, window trim, and rustication.

The design for Low is deceptively simple: an Ionic portico before a building in the shape of a Greek cross topped by a saucer-shaped dome. Its scale is monumental, and its detailings, from the bands of neo-classical trim to the portico's coffered ceiling, are exquisite.

There is no doubt where the entrance to this building is. The way is paved by urns and fountains and terraces, and by steps that lead directly to the portico. McKim used Greek horizontal curves in the steps to counteract the apparent deflection in horizontal surfaces. The curves are arcs of circles, and their rise is barely perceptible, but indeed real. The lowest and widest set of steps, for instance, is 8 inches higher at its center than at its extremities. As the steps shorten, so the rise decreases.

With all these refinements, consider the placement of Low Library (as a library it was a failure; since the 1930s it has housed the university's administration). It was situated on its north-south axis with the idea that the city would nestle at its feet. If Low Library had simply been rotated 90 degrees to face the west, a grand approach from the Hudson River would have been created, with Columbia as the city on the hill.

Bayard Building (L)   1898

(Originally Condict Building)
65 Bleecker Street, between Broadway and
Lafayette Street, at the head of Crosby Street
Louis Sullivan, Architect

The form of a building without should follow its function within, and its decoration should be "of" it, not "on" it, ideas clearly articulated in Louis Sullivan's only New York building.

Debates were raging among the neo-classicists over the form an office building should follow: should it be an extruded Italian Renaissance *palazzo*, or classical orders piled atop each other, or should it look like a column, complete with

base, shaft, and capital? Architect Louis Sullivan, the only architect at the Chicago World's Fair to defy the dictate of neo-classicism, believed that predetermined ideas should not be taken from one form and applied willy-nilly to another. Instead, he sought natural resolutions. His iconoclasm led him to believe that an office building's form should follow its function, which is, after all, to house offices. Ideally, the building should be a soaring thing with a natural upward thrust, reflecting the frame of steel upon which the walls hang, and revealing the offices, all of which are about the same size and do about the same thing.

The lower floors should be set aside as service areas for banks, stores, restaurants, whatever is needed to serve the building. Then the building should rise as a shaft, with the openings for windows occurring at the necessary places, reflecting the nature of the structure. The top should house the machinery required for the building's operation. It is an idea to which people respond viscerally, because it fits the Aristotelian definition of a work of art—it has a beginning, a middle, and an end.

Unfortunately, New York City got only one of Sullivan's buildings, and not one of his best. Even so, the Bayard Building manifests his dictum that "form follows function" and that ornament should be "of," not "on," a building. Every other pier is load-bearing, which is clearly reflected in the Romanesque nave-arcade look of the facade. Since the building was supported by its frame of steel, the only function for its walls was to protect its inhabitants from the elements and to act as a fire retardant. For the facade, Sullivan used his favorite building material, terra cotta. With it he created the most flamboyantly plastic decoration—florid, convoluted capitals and his angelic caryatids—decoration that was his unique vision and easily stamped out of a mold. Unfortunately, the lower floor has been renovated, but the decoration above the entrance remains, as does the rest of the facade.

Ukrainian Institute of America   1899

(Originally home of Isaac D. Fletcher; then
Augustus Van Horne Stuyvesant)
2 East Seventy-ninth Street, southeast corner of
Fifth Avenue
Charles P. H. Gilbert, Architect

*One of the last of Fifth Avenue's neo–Loire Valley châteaus
to be built, and one of the last surviving, moat and all.*

Richard Morris Hunt started the vogue for neo–Loire Valley
châteaus when he designed a Fifth Avenue mansion for William K. Vanderbilt in the style of Francis I, a transitional
period between the Gothic and the Renaissance. The year it
appeared was 1881, and it created a *bouleversement*. No
longer would the *nouveaux riches*, or even the *nouveaux
hautes bourgeoises*, content themselves with the sobriety of
brownstone as a facade for their houses. Most, like Isaac D.
Fletcher, would opt for limestone, but a few would spring for
marble. No longer would there be high stoops to climb and
the proper parlors to go with them, but moats to cross and
Renaissance-style doors to swing wide, revealing grand foy-
ers and drawing rooms. The vogue would last about twenty-
five years. By the end of it, Fifth Avenue would boast fake
châteaus from Fifty-second Street to Seventy-ninth and beyond, and the avenue would be lined for two solid miles by
millionaires' mansions.

Like all Fifth Avenue mansions, Fletcher's was categor-
ized as a "one-family dwelling," and a fairly modest one,
compared to others. Its estimated price tag was $200,000, and
its frontage is only 32 feet on Fifth Avenue and 100 feet on
Seventy-ninth Street. If you don't count the service rooms,
this house had only about a dozen rooms, but those in the
west end ran the full width of the house.

Some rooms are easy to spot by their windows. On the
first floor, beyond the entrance, was the foyer. The drawing
room overlooked Fifth Avenue, and in the east end were the
conservatory, dining room, and butler's pantry (a dumbwaiter
linked the butler's pantry with the kitchen below). Overlooking the avenue on the second floor was the library; in the
center, the music room; and in the east end, Mrs. Fletcher's

bedroom. Mr. Fletcher's bedroom was directly above, on the third floor. Separating his room and the den were a sewing room and a guest room.

The house is set back, with a moat and a fence separating it from the street. French Renaissance detailing abounds, from the portal to the turrets and the mansard roof. Of course, it is all sham; here are employed modern building techniques like cleverly masked cast-iron lintels at the windows and amenities—including an elevator and steam heat—never dreamed of at Chenonceaux and Chambord. Considering the abundance of château-style mansions that New York once boasted, it is amazing that this one, moat and all, is one of the few remaining—and certainly the best preserved—of the lot.

University Club (L)   1899

1 West Fifty-fourth Street, northwest corner of
Fifth Avenue
McKim, Mead & White, Architects

A clubhouse in the style of an Italian Renaissance palace/ fortress could not have suited turn-of-the century clubmen better. It was imperious, it was imposing, it was impregnable.

About three hundred clubs were flourishing in New York City in the 1890s, making the Gilded Age the Great Age of the Club. Some clubmen, like Cornelius Vanderbilt, belonged to as many as sixteen at a time. With initiation fees hovering at $300 and annual dues averaging $100, these clubmen spent on their dues for one club about what the average working man earned in a year.

Many clubhouses were grand, but few were as grand as the University Club, and few as true to the Italian Renaissance. It was the ideal style for a rich man's club. After all, its members were the Medici princes of their day. They wanted to insulate themselves from the lower classes, and they wanted a building that was intimidating. What could be more appropriate than a palace/fortress in the style of a Renaissance *palazzo*?

The clubhouse that Charles Follen McKim designed for the university men was considered, even with the excesses of the Gilded Age, a bit of conspicuous consumption and decadent splendor. In the lounging room, which is the room that can be glimpsed from Fifth Avenue, panels of velvet crimson are flanked by pilasters of Italian walnut. The Corinthian capitals are gilded, and there is gold in the flutings as well. All the public hallways are paved with marble. The library is lined in English oak, with Alps-green marble trim, and the ceilings are painted by H. Siddons Mowbray. The ceiling in the main dining room, modeled after the Doge's Palace in Venice, was described by contemporaries as the city's most elaborate.

The facade is not limestone, as you might think, but pink Milford granite from Maine. There is a slight batter, or receding upward slope to the walls, adding to its austere majesty. Set into the walls are the crests of major U.S. universities, with the Ivy League schools predominating.

The whole is divided into three parts by cornices. Within each part is a set of tall, round-arched windows, indicating the major public rooms. Each round-arched window has its own keystone-grotesque. Each center window in the top row boasts, of all things beastly, elephants. The square-headed windows, tucked under each minor cornice, reflect the bedroom floors.

The club seal, with the statue of Athena modeled after a statuette owned by Stanford White, is above the entrance on Fifty-fourth Street. And what an entrance—the columns are a series of reeded and foliated drums, with the pilasters behind repeating the patterns. Aside from the elephants, the only funny thing in the facade is found in the entablature. Acting as the metopes to the triglyphs are mortarboards.

Park Row Building   1899

15 Park Row, between Ann and Beekman streets
R. H. Robertson, Architect

*Now forgotten or considered just another middle-aged
medium-sized building, at 390 feet the Park Row Building
was the world's tallest when it was built in 1899.*

The first building in New York to be constructed with a skeleton of steel and a curtain wall of brick, stone, and glass was the Tower Building at 50 Broadway, completed in 1889 and now demolished. Although it was only twelve stories high, and although there were taller buildings with load-bearing walls, it was considered New York's first true skyscraper because of its construction.

A scant ten years later the thirty-one story Park Row Building was finished. At 390 feet, it was the world's highest building, and in an age of hyperbole and superlatives, this was indeed a gargantuan undertaking. It took four thousand

piles driven through 40 feet of sand to hit Manhattan schist,
the bedrock upon which most New York skyscrapers are
firmly planted, before construction could even begin. (South
of Tenth Street, Manhattan's base of schist dips down until
at places it is below tide level.)

With its colossal caryatids on the lower floors, and the
whole topped by a pair of cupolas, architectural historians
John Burchard and Albert Bush-Brown described the Park
Row Building as rising "majestically from a throne of classic
bombast to end near the clouds in silly rabbit's-ear turrets."
Whatever we might think of its style today, they loved it in
the early 1900s. In the 1908 edition of *King's Views of New
York*, an artist's rendering shows Broadway lined with carbon copies of the Park Row Building. While walkways
bridged the enormous buildings, and dirigibles cast off for

places like the North Pole, the Panama Canal, and Japan, the caption asks: "What will posterity develop?"

By 1908 lower Manhattan already had more than 550 buildings over ten stories high, dozens over twenty stories high, and even the Singer Tower (now demolished), which rose 612 feet, or forty-seven stories. To describe the scene, the word "skyline" appeared.

City & Suburban Homes   1900

Between York Avenue and the FDR Drive,
Seventy-eighth to Seventy-ninth streets
Ernest Flagg, Architect

For wage-earners: model tenements, with light and air and toilets and bathtubs.

By 1900, reformers were demanding that a new tenement law be created, and once created, vigorously enforced. The dumbbell apartments were disasters, and everyone knew it. Needed now was a new model tenement.

Architect Flagg realized that an inherent problem with the basic design of dumbbell apartments was their inefficiency. Four buildings on a 100-by-100-foot lot, each taking up 25 by 90 feet, simply waste a tremendous amount of space in bends and angles and common walls and long corridors, to say nothing of the sociological problems that come with overcrowding and lack of privacy.

Flagg recommended that only two tenements be built on the same 100-by-100-foot lot. The number of rooms would remain the same (although they would be somewhat larger) so the quarters would remain cramped. However, the space saved by efficiency could be devoted to light and air, amenities that were glaringly absent in dumbbell tenements.

Flagg put his theories to work on the buildings commissioned by the City & Suburban Homes Company, whose goal was to offer a "safe and permanent 5 percent" return to investors, "while furnishing wage-earners wholesome homes at current prices." In 1901 many of the features that Flagg had designed into these buildings were written into a revised tenement law.

Instead of two 10-foot "back yards" separating the two rows of buildings, a block-long courtyard, about 27 feet wide, separates them. Instead of the 5-foot air shafts of the dumbbell apartments, there are rectangular courtyards that measure about 24 by 33 feet within the core of neighboring buildings. Although Flagg describes this as "but indifferent light," it was still light, and it was air. Instead of the toilet down the hall to be shared with all the other families on the floor, there was a private toilet in the apartment itself. Instead of a complete lack of bathing facilities, one-bedroom apartments had bathtubs in the kitchens, and in the smaller apartments, dwellers could use the baths on the first floors that were provided for them. And instead of having to lug the garbage down the stairs, tenants could use the building's dumbwaiter. Fire escapes were unobstructed, and all public halls were adequately lit.

To the otherwise plain, six-story, yellow-brick buildings, Flagg added a variety of trim. Some entrances resemble Doric temples, others are in the Gothic style, and still others are neo-Renaissance, complete with volutes, garlands, and keystones.

Ellis Island Immigration Station   1900

On Ellis Island, New York Harbor
Boring & Tilton, Architects

The symbol dreamed of by most immigrants was the Statue of Liberty. The reality dreaded by most steerage-class immigrants was Ellis Island.

Between 1890 and 1930 almost 16 million immigrants entered the United States via the port of New York. Between 1892 and 1925 over 12 million of them, all steerage-class immigrants hoping to become first-class Americans, were processed through the immigration station on Ellis Island. As the ships entered the harbor, the hopeful immigrants would jam the decks and stand gunwale to gunwale in eager anticipation of a glimpse of the Promised Land.

If the immigrants were traveling first or cabin class, their fears were minimized and their dignity was kept intact, because in the society where all men were created equal, first- and cabin-class immigrants were created a little more equal. Their papers were inspected and cursory medical examinations were given aboard the liners by inspectors who arrived and departed by cutters. The steerage-class immigrants were dumped on a dock and then taken by barge to Ellis Island, the "Isle of Tears," to await their fate.

The brick and iron buildings which replaced earlier wood structures that had burned down are a mishmash of neo-classicism with a hint of the Byzantine in the four 100-foot cupolas. Their walls bear outsized plaques of the stars and stripes topped by federal eagles and flanked by fruits flowing from upended cornucopias, representing to some the streets that were paved with gold. But with all their optimistic symbolism, these buildings are still authoritarian and intimidating.

The immigrants would deposit their luggage and belongings and be shepherded from room to room, cubicle to cubicle, tested for contagious diseases, given intelligence tests, questioned about their morality (prostitutes were not allowed in, and single women were suspect), and asked a litany of questions. Accustomed to overt corruption by petty officials, some immigrants clutched money, anticipating the need to bribe.

The main hall is ringed by the visitors' gallery, where welcoming relatives would seek out familiar faces. Screams of jubilation could be heard as fathers and mothers, sisters and brothers, sons and daughters, husbands and wives were found; but the real jubilation had to be tempered until the processing was over and the immigrant accepted. Once in the waiting rooms, the newly arrived and the already Americanized could finally embrace, giving the name "Kissing Post" to one of the pillars.

During Ellis Island's heyday (in 1907 over a million immigrants were processed, sometimes at a rate of as many as five thousand in a day), most of the immigrants were "new immigrants" from Southern and Eastern Europe. Some were victims of pogroms, others victims of more subtle persecutions. They were tired after a sea voyage that might have taken fifteen days. They were poor, many having invested their life savings in a one-way ticket. And they were yearning to breathe free, terrified of having the door to the Promised Land slammed shut in their faces.

Those who made it often received new names from the officials. Some were simply Anglicized versions of the original names, but some were entirely changed, often to reflect a place of origin—people from Bosnia-Herzegovina, for instance, might become Bosniaks or Hertzes.

For those who did not make it, for those who were turned back, the anguish could be overwhelming and many committed suicide a short ferry-ride away from their dream.

Appellate Division, New York State Supreme Court   1900

27 Madison Avenue, northeast corner of Twenty-fifth Street
James Brown Lord, Architect

One-third of this building's construction costs went into its decoration, making it a museum unto itself.

Today's goal is to have one percent of construction costs allocated for the arts, whether the building is a private or public undertaking, a goal that is aspired to but seldom met. Imagine the guffaws that would greet today's architect who advocated that one-third of the construction costs be spent on statuary and murals. Yet that is the amount that James Brown Lord allocated, almost to the penny, for the decorative aspects of this courthouse. Of the total $633,768 spent on its construction, statuary cost $157,000 and mural painting cost $54,300, a total of $211,300.

It is a federal building, however, and the federal government, beginning with Benjamin Latrobe's use of sculpture in the U.S. Capitol, has traditionally been the greatest patron of the arts in architecture. The sculpture is integral to the building's design. Without it, the building would be just another neo-classical courthouse, elegant, no doubt, but inconsequential. With it, the building is magnificent.

Sculpture is everywhere, from the front steps to the attic balustrade, where great lawgivers stand in heroic, Baroque majesty. The Madison Avenue facade has the easiest lawgivers to spot—Confucius and Moses. The Twenty-sixth Street facade gets a bit arcane, with (from left to right) Zoroaster (Persian law), Alfred the Great (Anglo-Saxon), Lycurgus (Spartan), Solon (Athenian), Saint Louis (French), Manu (Indian), and Justinian (Roman). Noticeably absent is Muhammad, but actually one statue is missing. Filling the gap was once a statue of Muhammad, but Muhammadan law forbids the likeness of man in sculpture or painting, and, with great embarrassment, the statue was removed. The central grouping on the Twenty-sixth Street roofline is *Justice*, flanked by *Power* and *Study*, sculpted by Daniel Chester French. The central grouping on Madison Avenue is *Peace*, flanked by *Wisdom* and *Strength*, by Karl Bitter. Although each piece of statue atop the balustrade was created by a different sculptor, there is a certain homogeneity to them, reflecting either iron-fisted control by Lord or a willing adherence to the Baroque tradition by the sculptors.

Like so many neo-classical·buildings, the entrance is unmistakable—a hexastyle crowned by a pediment showing a group representing the *Triumph of the Law* by Charles H. Niehaus, with steps flanked by *Wisdom* and *Force* by Frederick Wellington Ruckstuhl. The contemplative *Wisdom* (Michelangelo's *Moses*, anyone?) and dynamic *Force* emphasize the classical balance in the building and represent an abstraction of the scales of justice.

Cooper-Hewitt Museum (L) 1901

(Originally Andrew Carnegie Mansion)
2 East Ninety-first Street, at Fifth Avenue
Babb, Cook & Willard, Architects; remodeled,
1976, Hardy Holzman Pfeiffer Associates

Carnegie and his steel company gave New York three of its greatest free-standing mansions—Frick's, Schwab's (now demolished), and Carnegie's own.

A house built on an open lot is something you might expect to find in the suburbs, but to find one in Manhattan, and to find it built in the twentieth century, is rare indeed. But here it is, all sixty-four rooms of it, built and paid for by Andrew Carnegie, the Horatio Alger character whose rise from telegraph boy to multimillionaire was due more to pluck than luck.

When work began on this house in 1900, Fifth Avenue had only been surfaced in asphalt for two years. Nevertheless, Fifth Avenue's row of millionaires' mansions already stretched over two miles, from Murray Hill to Eightieth Street. The only man of fortune who already lived in this neighborhood was Jacob Ruppert, the brewer, whose house was up the avenue at Ninety-third Street. Otherwise, this was the edge of the city, with small farms operating between the streets that had been cut through, a rocky landscape dotted by squatters' shacks and goats. With Carnegie's purchase of the land it became known as Carnegie Hill, at 114 feet above sea level, Fifth Avenue's highest site.

So that his mansion would not be surrounded by the kind of saplings that are planted around the usual suburban development, Carnegie had full-grown trees transported from Westchester to adorn his grounds. He could easily afford this sort of luxury. In the early years of this century, Carnegie had an income that ranged between \$15 and \$30 million a year (that's income, not assets), at a time when the average annual income of an unskilled worker was \$460.

The rooms of this mansion, which now house the

96

Cooper-Hewitt Museum, are artfully masked behind three floors of solid, red-brick walls with limestone quoins and otherwise Renaissance-style trim, with an attic floor under a copper mansard roof tucked behind a balustrade. Neo-Georgian is the common adjective for describing this building's style, but it lacks the elegance, the refinement of eighteenth-century English, or even American, design, appearing almost bloated instead, like decadent royalty. Even the urns on the balustrade seem flatulent. A splendid stained-glass awning greets visitors, and in the southeast corner of the building is a delightful conservatory, a room that has been artfully incorporated within the museum's workings.

New York Yacht Club   1901

37 West Forty-fourth Street, between Fifth Avenue and Avenue of the Americas
Warren & Wetmore, Architects

A Beaux Arts design with a nautical motif that will leave you reeling like a drunken sailor.

Its scale and form are recognizably familiar as a side-street building erected at the turn of the century by a Beaux Arts–trained architect. It could almost be a private home like 9 East Seventy-second Street or a place of entertainment like the Lyceum Theatre or a gathering place for businessmen like the New York Chamber of Commerce (statues of famous New Yorkers were once displayed in what are now blank niches). In fact, if it did not have three windows fashioned after the sterns of eighteenth-century ships it would be like many other Beaux Arts buildings, but those windows make it unique.

The windows are there because this is, after all, the New York Yacht Club, built on land donated to the club by one of its members, J. P. Morgan, commodore of the club,1897–1899. It was built to house not only one of America's most exclusive clubs but also the America's Cup. (The cup, which was made of about $500 worth of silver in 1851, but which yachtsmen will spend millions to defend, was given by Queen Victoria. It sits in its own place of honor inside the club.)

Whitney Warren and Charles D. Wetmore, both members of the club, designed the building. The pilasters flanking the main entrance bear anchors that are so encumbered by ropes and pulleys and galleons and hooks as to become lost in all the trim. The keystone over the entrance is no ordinary grotesque, but Poseidon himself. If you wonder why there are free-standing, squared-off Ionic columns atop the balustrade, it is because the setback used to be a pergola, which must have been a charming place when the sun was over the yardarm.

Hidden behind the "stern windows" is the Model Room, and within are models of some of the world's most famous yachts, with half-models of still other great designs lining the walls. To describe this room as baronial is to demean it. To describe it as San Simeonesque is to underrate it.

If ever the United States should lose the America's Cup, let's hope the New York Yacht Club doesn't go with it.

Brown Building   1901

(Formerly the Asch Building)
29 Washington Place, northwest corner of Greene Street
Julius Franke, Architect

The City of New York considered this a fireproof building. After the Triangle Shirtwaist Fire had ravaged its top three floors, reform laws rose like a Phoenix from the ashes.

The fire burned less than fifteen minutes on the top three floors of the Triangle Shirtwaist Company before it was brought under control that Saturday afternoon, March 25, 1911. In that short time, 146 people died.

They died by jumping to the relative safety of the air to escape the certain death of the flames. They died because their bodies crashed through the life nets meant to save them, and continued crashing right through the deadlights that lit the basements below the pavement. They died because doors that should have been open were locked shut so that the management could make sure its employees weren't pilfering. They died because there was only one fire escape in the rear of the building, and it ended in midair. They died because the City said that floors in buildings that were not over 150 feet high could be constructed of wood instead of stone or concrete, and that window frames could be wood instead of metal. They died because the fire department's extension ladders only reached the sixth floor. Most of them were women, and most were in their teens or early twenties.

The horror of the corpses piled up on Greene Street, the shock in the Lower East Side where most of the garment workers' families and friends lived and mourned, the gruesomeness of the hastily arranged morgue for the identification of the bodies sent shockwaves through the city.

For years critics had pointed out the inevitability of a fire like this one, had raised their voices against the crowding in the sweatshops and the inadequacy of the safety precautions, but their voices had always been drowned out by the hum of the sewing machines. After this tragic blaze, however, reformers like Robert F. Wagner, Sr., Alfred E. Smith, Frances Perkins, Rose Schneiderman, Samuel Gompers, and others would ensure that adequate fire escapes were provided in buildings, that sprinklers were installed, that inspections were regularly made and fire drills regularly held.

Today the ironically named Asch Building is called the Brown Building, and it is part of New York University. If you walk inside you can see the courtyard where the workers fell or jumped from the fire escape that ended in midair. The goose bumps you experience will not come from the air conditioning in the summer nor from the cold of the winter, but from the sense that something awful happened here.

Soldiers' and Sailors' Monument   1902

Riverside Drive at Eighty-ninth Street
Charles W. Stoughton and Arthur A. Stoughton, Architects; Paul E. Duboy, Sculptor

A monument to the "Memory of the Brave Soldiers Who Saved the Union," and a monument to the City Beautiful Movement and its revival of classically correct structures.

City fathers seem to believe that if something is worth memorializing, it is worth memorializing in a park or square. As a result, many of New York's parks are cluttered with statues and exedras and colonnades and whatnots. Couple this proclivity for permanence with the City Beautiful Movement and tie it to the most popular dramatic subject in recent memory for those living in the 1890s, and a choragic monument dedicated "To the Memory of the Brave Soldiers Who Saved the Union" is a natural. Teddy Roosevelt laid the cornerstone for it in 1900, and at its unveiling on Memorial Day, 1902, Mayor Seth Low orated that "those who fought for the Union in the Civil War stand in need of no monument of stone or bronze. Our happy, prosperous, and reunited country is itself a monument greater than any sculptor can devise or that loving hands can set up." To those who had marched

to the monument, a custom that still continues on Memorial Day, the mayor's words surely sounded peculiar, especially since the architects and sculptor were in the audience and everyone was assembled for the dedication.

The world's largest American flag in its day, 74 feet long and 40 feet wide, veiled the monument, and at the given moment the release mechanism jammed. Only after a daring seaman had clambered up a jerry-built rig was the monument unveiled, with much applause for the seaman and cheers for the monument. New Yorkers had never seen such a memorial. The city had an obelisk for Major General Worth, an arch for George Washington, and a tomb for Ulysses S. Grant. Nothing seemed so pure, so elevated in taste, so sophisticated as this monument. It was made of gleaming white marble, with a circular canopy topped by a frieze of American eagles and supported by a peristyle of twelve Corinthian columns. It was modeled after the choragic monument of Lysicrates in Athens (334 B.C.), one of the small decorative structures erected to commemorate the victory of the leader of a chorus (hence, the word "choragic") in the competitive Dionysian choral dances.

The elaborate terraces and granite stairways with white marble balustrades are indicative of City Beautiful planning, the whole formal and grand, indicating that this was indeed a special place and should be approached reverentially. Nobody is entombed here, although a tomblike impression is created, and generations of West Side kids know what lurks behind that mystical door—a storeroom for Parks Department tools.

Yorkville Branch, New York Public Library   1902

222 East Seventy-ninth Street, between Second and Third Avenues
James Brown Lord, Architect

This neo-classical library was the first of the "Carnegie Libraries," so called because Andrew Carnegie gave the money for their construction—and it is as good an example of their style as there is.

Before sailing off to Europe in March 1901, Andrew Carnegie sent a letter to Dr. John S. Billings, director of the newly formed New York Public Library. His message was staggering: Carnegie offered to give $5.2 million to establish sixty-five branch libraries in New York City. Two strings were attached—that the City provide the land, and that it accept responsibility for upkeep and maintenance, just as it had agreed to do for the Main Branch (see p. 130). "Sixty-five libraries at one stroke probably beats the record," wrote Carnegie, "but this is the day of big operations and New York is soon to be the biggest of cities." The very next day, former Mayor Abram S. Hewitt offered to donate two library sites, one in the Bronx, the other in Brooklyn, because he believed that libraries were "great vice-preventing influences" and should be "poor men's clubs."

Carnegie's $5.2 million was arrived at by a casual computation that each building might cost about $80,000, and he simply asked if sixty or sixty-five circulating libraries would do the job. New York at the time was only beginning to cope with the concept of libraries that were open free to the public. Boston was already allocating more than fifty cents per resident on libraries and already had fifteen of them, but New York was spending less than nine cents per capita, and had hardly anything to show for it.

The original two strings that Carnegie had attached soon became three—he wanted an advisory board of architects to approve all library designs. What resulted is a look that is commonly described as "Carnegie Library," and the buildings are easy to spot, especially in the tenement districts, because they stand out so distinctively. The Yorkville Branch, the first of them, is indicative of the preferred architectural style: three stories plus a basement (a fourth story, originally intended for the janitor's use, is set back and not visible from the street), with a facade of Indiana limestone on a 40-by-90 foot plot, and all in the neo-classical, almost Palladian, mold. Its cost, with equipment, was $70,000, well under the original estimate. At its completion in December 1902, the City had bought only eight sites in all, and it was expected that the next library would not open until July 1903, more than six months later.

Just as the commission for this library had attracted James Brown Lord, so later commissions attracted architects of high quality, among them McKim, Mead & White, Carrère & Hastings, and Babb, Cook & Willard.

Metropolitan Museum of Art (L)   1902

Fifth Avenue at Eighty-second Street
Richard Morris Hunt and Richard Howland Hunt, Architects; George B. Post, Consulting Architect

The first of the great public buildings in the Beaux Arts style.

Richard Morris Hunt, who represented the standard of excellence among American architects in the last third of the nineteenth century, was a trustee of the Metropolitan Museum of Art. He was asked by the board to design not only a new Fifth Avenue facade for the museum, but a general scheme for all extensions as well. Calvert Vaux and Jacob Wrey Mould's original Ruskinian-Gothic building (1880) and later wings had all turned their backs on Fifth Avenue. Now the museum was to be reoriented, with a new facade on the avenue, a facade in the manner of the grand European palaces of culture.

Hunt had been one of the earliest Americans to study at Paris's *l'Ecole des Beaux Arts*, and could be as eclectic as they came, but he was especially partial to neo-classicism. When he drew up the original plans for the museum, he included an abundance of neo-classical statuary and trim, in the Beaux Arts tradition, but he died before the working drawings could be completed. His son, Richard Howland Hunt, took over the assignment. To most New Yorkers, the Hunt (*père et fils*) facade is *the* facade—three monumental

Roman arches flanked by pairs of colossal Corinthian columns. This porch is flanked by wings, each three windows wide. (The north and south neo-classical wings, added between 1911 and 1926, were designed by the firm of McKim, Mead & White.)

Four ziggurat-like piles of stone stand atop the attic story of the central pavilion, representing to some the fine Egyptian collection within. Actually they are there because Hunt had planned for the stone to be carved into four allegorical groups of statuary illustrating the great periods of civilization—Ancient, Medieval, Renaissance, and Modern. In the walls below each pile of stone are empty niches, which he had intended to fill with reproductions of statuary from each of the four eras. Unfortunately, the million dollars that the City had allocated for the facade seemingly ran out before the carvings could be made (some people claim that the trustees never wanted the statuary anyway).

Hunt had commissioned his protégé, sculptor Karl Bitter, to create the medallions for the central pavilion and the caryatids for the wings (*Painting, Sculpture, Architecture,* and *Music*). Bitter's caryatids are hardly the structural caryatids that tradition demands, but instead they are almost freestanding pieces of sculpture that relate to each other.

After this monumental facade had been completed to the extent it ever would be, postcards showing the museum still featured the old wings, with the Hunt facade mortised into the bottom left-hand corner. A message on one of the cards said: "Interested in art? This is full of nice things."

Flatiron Building (L) 1902

(Originally Fuller Building)
949 Broadway, at junction with Fifth Avenue at
Twenty-third Street
D. H. Burnham & Co., Architects

At 300 feet, this was a "triumph of steel-frame construction," according to a contemporaneous guidebook.

The Flatiron Building was one of the earliest buildings in New York City to be supported by a complete steel cage, and, steel cage or no, its twenty-one stories disturbed many New Yorkers. They were convinced that the wind would bring down the building, and only its heavy walls of rusticated limestone, which they mistakenly believed were supporting the building, reassured them.

Despite the technological breakthroughs that helped create buildings like this one, architects were loath to innovate with their wall treatments. Burnham made the lines of this building recognizably familiar; basically a column, with a base, shaft, and capital, its walls look like an Italian Renaissance *palazzo*. To create an undulating and rhythmic wall treatment, Burnham designed three eight-story hanging oriels on both the east and west facades, and for extra decoration he included terra cotta designs on the fourth and attic stories.

The Flatiron's distinctive triangular plan—it comes

down to a width of only 6 feet at Twenty-third Street—is derived from the confluence of Broadway with Fifth Avenue. Broadway is the major variation on the gridiron pattern of streets, and its diagonal line creates interesting angles from Tenth Street north to 106th. Because it is built on this peculiar triangular plot, the building has always reminded people of a flatiron, hence its name, despite the fact that it was officially named the Fuller Building, after its builder.

The wind that people were afraid would topple the building was certainly there. In 1907 John Sloan, the Ashcan artist, noticed "a high wind this morning and the pranks of the gusts about the Flatiron Building ... were interesting to watch. Women's skirts flapped over their heads and ankles were to be seen. And a funny thing, a policeman to keep men from loitering about the corner." And supposedly, what that policeman at the corner of Fifth and Twenty-third was saying was "Twenty-three skiddoo!"

But all the ogling and misgivings aside, the Flatiron Building was an instant success, and for years it served as the symbol of the dramatic new age of skyscrapers and as an inspiration to photographers like Edward Steichen.

New York Stock Exchange   1903

8 Broad Street, between Exchange Place and Wall Street
George B. Post, Architect; extension, 1923, Trowbridge & Livingston

A cool neo-classical facade for the tempestuous workings of the New York Stock Exchange.

In 1792 twenty-four brokers met under a buttonwood tree where 60 Wall Street now stands and fixed on a minimum commission of one-quarter of one percent on the sale of stock. Aside from that bit of price-fixing, the New York Stock Exchange has been the scene of fiercely competitive capitalism—the symbol, in fact, to most of the world—with its panics, recessions, depressions, and booms, some artificially created, others natural, and all weathered by the institution if not by some brokers and clients.

Before settling down, the oldest established permanent floating crap game in New York and its brokers did business out of their offices, in various taverns, the Tontine Building, and several merchants' exchanges, until finally in 1865 the New York Stock Exchange moved into its own quarters on this site. One observer, William Worthington Fowler, felt that the building reflected the pattern of investing in stocks. He said in 1870 that its "lofty facade on Broad Street . . . sinks into a modest two-story brick rear on New Street, emblematical of the stately fortunes which enter that stately front, and issue diminished from that diminished rear." In 1901 demolition began on the old building, and by 1903 the Stock Exchange moved into its new building (members spent the two years in the Produce Exchange).

George B. Post, whose career began with the iconoclastic design for the Long Island Historical Society, fell victim to the American Renaissance for his design of the Stock Exchange, creating a neo-classical temple for the facade. The

horizontal base neatly masks the entrance (which opening contains it?), then six 52½-foot Corinthian columns, flanked by Corinthian pilasters, provide the necessary shaft for the building, which is topped by a pediment created by J. Q. A. Ward and modeled by Paul W. Bartlett. The pediment contains eleven figures in various scales and stages of discomfort. The allegory is *Integrity Protecting the Works of Man*, a seemingly appropriate commercial theme for a stock exchange to bear. The twenty-two-story addition on the corner of Wall Street neatly carries the cornice line and balustrade along Broad Street, but for some reason, Trowbridge & Livingston ignored the lions that Post incorporated in his cornice.

More than 55 million shares have been bought and sold in a single day on "the floor" of the exchange. To witness the sometimes frantic wheeling and dealing, a visitors' gallery overlooks the "pit," where you will find the bulls and bears going at each other.

American Scandinavian Foundation 1903

(Originally Charles Dana Gibson's Residence)
127 East Seventy-third Street, between Park and Lexington avenues
McKim, Mead & White, Architects

No stoop leads up to a parlor floor, and there is not an ounce of brownstone to be seen. The haute bourgeoise town house had arrived with its "American-style basement."

By 1880, elevated railroads clattered up and down Second and Third avenues, and a tenement boom was started on the avenues and the side streets propinquant to the routes of the els. Safely sequestered by over 1,600 feet of real estate from the nearest el was Fifth Avenue, which by 1900 was rapidly becoming a gilded ghetto, an avenue almost entirely lined by the palaces of the rich. Filling the interstices between the newly rich and the newly Americanized and making the link between the rich and the poor were, as in society itself, the bourgeoisie, with the emphasis on the upper middle class on the blocks off Park Avenue.

By the turn of the century dozens of variations on the new theme of a "town house" were springing up. Some of the styles, like the Beaux Arts, would be short lived, petering out by 1910. Other styles, like the neo-Italian Renaissance and Colonial Revival, would flourish through the 1920s. One thing these town houses had in common was a facade of brick with marble or limestone trim, or complete facades of marble or limestone. Brownstone had become a facade of the past. Gone too were high stoops leading up to the parlor floors, with their entrances on the sides, replaced by centrally placed entrances with a few steps leading up to them. This "American-style basement" plan reflected a new standard of excellence and level of conspicuous consumption (one architect was given a dozen commissions in 1898 by homeowners eager to keep up with the Joneses—his task was to remove the high stoops from their homes).

It meant that the entire width of the building's first floor was devoted to a reception room in the front, creating a vast space, since town houses are, almost by definition, 25 feet wide. The kitchen was in the rear, with a pantry in the extension. No more was there a parlor floor, with a cramped entrance and a front parlor off it. Up a flight of stairs in a central hall were found the living and dining rooms. Up another flight in this house were the library and a bedroom with a dressing room and bathroom. Front and back rooms were on the fourth floor, with servants' quarters on the top floor. C. P. H. Gilbert advised the installation of an elevator in any house costing $25,000 or more (an elevator cost a minimum of $2,000), but none was installed in this house, even though it cost almost exactly twice Gilbert's "elevator criterion"—$49,734.

The style of the house is Colonial Revival, incorporating the hallmarks of eighteenth-century Georgian architecture—Flemish bond brickwork, an Adams-like panel in the balcony railing, smallish window panes, a restrained neo-classical porch with a rectangular toplight and side windows around the door, and everywhere, the feel of Palladio.

The Colonial style had not been considered grand enough for the *nouveaux riches* during the last half of the nineteenth century, their preferences leaning more toward the baronial. The City Beautiful Movement, however, taught scale, and with the increased sophistication in taste, the scale of Colonial-style buildings looked comfortable on New York side streets to the eyes of the middle class. As a result, the Colonial Revival would prove a durable bit of eclecticism.

This house was built for illustrator Charles Dana Gibson, who satirized New York Society with his acerbic wit, but who also glamorized it with his Gibson girls, his pre-Raphaelite beauties with their hourglass figures and upswept hair. The house was designed for him by his friend Stanford

White, and so it is one of those buildings that weaves together some threads of New York folklore. Gibson had used an artist's model who would come to symbolize the Gibson girls and the Floradora Sextette, a not-quite-fifteen-year-old named Evelyn Nesbit. Gibson painted her in profile, with her long hair forming a question mark, asking "The Eternal Question." It was the same Evelyn Nesbit with whom Stanford White would fall in love and on whose account he would be killed by Harry K. Thaw in 1906.

Lyceum Theatre (L) 1903

149 West Forty-fifth Street, between the Avenue of the Americas and Broadway
Herts & Tallant, Architects

An elegant neo-Renaissance facade theatrically masks this early comer to Times Square.

In 1890 there was not a single theater north of Fortieth Street. Sixteen years later and George M. Cohan was asking to be remembered to Herald Square (where the majority of the theaters remained), but also to "tell all the boys on Forty-second Street" (where the theaters were headed) that he would soon be there.

Seven theaters were already on Forty-second Street in 1906, seven more than in 1890. By 1930 almost eighty legitimate theaters would be built along the spine of Broadway from Thirty-eighth to Fifty-ninth streets, making the Times Square area the theater capital of New York then and now.

The reason for the sudden popularity of this new area is

that entertainment, like population, follows transportation. The transportation was the new subway that opened in 1904, making Times Square easily accessible—there was no stop at Herald Square—and starting a real-estate boom that stretched north for five miles along Broadway.

The Broadway theaters of the era were large, some easily accommodating over 2,500 spectators, and they gave rise to a specific kind of theatrical genre, the Broadway production. (Off-Broadway theaters are defined not by their geography but by their capaciousness—if a theater has fewer than 300 seats the unions allow smaller work crews, thus allowing experiments on limited budgets.)

Some of the theaters from the first wave have been torn down. Others, especially those on Forty-second Street, are now movie houses. Of the remaining legitimate theaters, the Lyceum is one of the grandest and best preserved.

The facade has all sorts of subtleties to it. One of the few hints that this is a theater is provided in the capitals. At the center of the Corinthian abacus, where you would normally find a fleuron, you find instead a lyre. Above each column is not the comedy/tragedy mask you might expect, but a theatrical mask nevertheless.

The only hint of the theater's name is given in the drums of the columns, where *LT*s are written in script. And what columns. They start at their capitals as classic Corinthian columns, alternating reeded flutings with foliated drums. But then stop-fluting with a buttercup pattern begins creeping in, first on only a few of the flutes, but increasing, gradually, until the buttercups completely dominate the columns. (The pattern is repeated in the pilasters as well.)

The Lyceum was built by one of the period's greatest producers, Daniel Frohman, who built in an apartment for his own use which overlooked the stage. What used to be his apartment is where the Shubert Organization, an old competitor, now keeps its archives.

Williamsburg Bridge   1903

From Clinton and Delancey streets across the
East River to Brooklyn
Leffert L. Buck, Engineer

The world's longest suspension bridge in its day and the East River's first all-steel bridge was a highway from the over-crowding of the Lower East Side to the wide open spaces of Brooklyn.

Until the coming of the Williamsburg Bridge there were only ferries and the Brooklyn Bridge linking Manhattan with Brooklyn. But two additional bridges were already planned for the East River, and all four had been officially named: the New York and Brooklyn Bridge was to become the Brooklyn Bridge; the new East River Bridge would be the Williamsburg Bridge; the third suspension bridge would be the Manhattan; the fourth bridge, a cantilever/truss linking Fifty-ninth Street

with the Borough of Queens, would be the Blackwell Island Bridge (now Queensboro).

The Williamsburg Bridge had a clearance of 135 feet, or 2 feet more than the Brooklyn Bridge, and its 1,600-foot span made it 5 feet longer than the Brooklyn Bridge, and the world's longest suspension bridge in its day. Unlike the Brooklyn Bridge, with its great masonry towers, the Williamsburg Bridge towers are riveted steel frames, and its piers and anchors are concrete, not masonry. These developments offered greater efficiency and economy, heralding the twentieth-century bridges to follow. Unfortunately, instead of something ethereal, we have something ungainly. The difference lies in the approach to bridge building. Roebling understood the impact that his bridge would have on the city, so he made it as graceful as he could. Buck concerned himself with engineering problems and their solutions. Roebling, for instance, had given his bridge fanlike stays and 17-foot-deep stiffening trusses for rigidity, whereas Buck gave his bridge stiffening trusses that are 40 feet deep. The trusses made it rigid, all right, but they also made it the ugly duckling of New York's bridges. Buck can be forgiven, however, because he was fighting the known perils of sway with the unknown qualities of steel. He simply overengineered the bridge.

It has done yeoman work. It originally had two roadways, two sidewalks, and six tracks for surface and elevated cars. In 1907 it carried 184 trolley cars an hour during rush hours, and by the 1930s it was carrying 50,000 vehicles a day. Today, the J and M subway lines offer one of the great views of the city from its deck.

The bridge's approaches required whole blocks of tenements on the Lower East Side to be torn down, bringing some light and air to the teeming neighborhood. The displaced residents, as well as others who wanted to escape the ghetto, fled across the *Naiye Brick*, Yiddish for New Bridge, to Williamsburg, a place where a tree could grow. So many made the journey to Brooklyn that the Williamsburg Bridge became known as "The Jew's Highway."

110

Seventy-second Street IRT Control House (L)

1904

Seventy-second Street and Broadway
Heins & LaFarge, Architects

This elegant little neo–Dutch Colonial control house is the only one of the original three that dotted Broadway when New York's first successful subway opened in 1904.

One of the city's most far-reaching events occurred when the Interborough Rapid Transit System (the IRT) opened on October 27, 1904. The route ran from City Hall up Centre and Lafayette streets to Astor Place, avoiding Broadway and its big buildings for fear that the blasting and tunneling would undermine their foundations. At Astor Place the route followed Fourth Avenue to Grand Central, where it zigged west to Times Square (today's shuttle) and zagged north on Broadway to 145th Street.

Control houses were built at three stations along Broadway—at 72nd, 103rd, and 116th streets (upon surrendering their tickets, passengers passed into the area "controlled" by the IRT; hence, "control houses"). The three were all basically the same style—variations on the neo–Dutch Colonial theme with Baroque trim, at the very least a fitting reminder of New Amsterdam. Of the original three, this is the only one still standing (a fourth was built at the Bowling Green station when the subway was extended to Brooklyn in 1908; it still stands). This is an elegant little building, with its Dutch gables, copper cresting (now unfortunately painted over), granite wainscoting, buff Norman brick, limestone quoins, terra cotta trim and finials, and, for the station name, polychromatic terra cotta in the shape of a Greek cross.

Serious talk of running a subway up the spine of Manhattan had been going on since at least the 1880s, and with electrification the possibilities seemed realistic (London had been operating steam-powered engines in its Underground since 1867). By 1900 August Belmont, Jr., son of the Rothschild representative in New York, had assembled a private railroad company called the Interborough Rapid Transit. On opening day, Mayor George B. McClellan, Jr., son of the Civil War general, used a silver controller bar to drive the train uptown, and he did it in just over the advertised time—26½ minutes instead of 24½. Everyone was impressed by the brightness of the stations. The walls were lined with white tiles, electric lights were set into sconces designed by Heins & LaFarge, and vault lights, thick pieces of glass the size of silver dollars, were set into the platform ceilings to admit natural light. Each station had a different color treatment, and some stations had decorative mosaics and bas-reliefs depicting local or national history. In 1908 the IRT was extended into Brooklyn, and by 1918 its Manhattan configuration changed from a Z to an H with extensions north of Forty-second Street on Lexington Avenue and south on Seventh Avenue.

Before the advent of public transportation, New York was a walking city, and most workers lived within a reasonable distance—an hour's walk, or about 3 miles—of their jobs. With the advent of the horse car, the distance doubled, increasing again with trolley cars and the elevated railroads. With the arrival of the subway, an 8-mile distance between home and work became a twenty-five minute ride, extending the boundaries of the commutable city one more time and setting off one more building boom along its route.

Ansonia Hotel (L)   1904

2107 Broadway, between Seventy-third and
Seventy-fourth streets
Paul E. M. Duboy, Architect

This great wedding cake of an apartment hotel was built on the avenue that was planned as the Champs Elysées of New York.

Today's Broadway from 59th to 155th Street was planned in 1866 as the Boulevard, a 160-foot-wide avenue with a planted median strip and a grand sweep to it. The Boulevard was designed to follow the old Bloomingdale Road and cut diagonally across New York's otherwise right-angled streets,

with open spaces for statuary in small parks and costly residences along its path, making it the Champs Elysées of New York. But Andrew Haswell Green's dream boulevard took about thirty years to develop, and it would not then be lined by private homes, but by some of the city's largest apartment houses.

If any building synthesizes the Baroque dream of Green and is an evocation of the Riviera or Paris of *la Belle Epoque*, it is the Ansonia, designed by a Frenchman in the full flowering of the purely decorative Beaux Arts style. A great wedding cake of a building, the Ansonia is situated at a propitious bend in Broadway, commanding it north to 106th Street, south to 59th.

The Ansonia was built by William Earl Dodge Stokes, a developer of the Upper West Side whose fortune was inherited from his father, a partner in the Phelps Dodge Corporation. Stokes oversaw every detail of design and construction, with some of his own diverse companies supplying the materials, like the terra cotta from his plant in New Jersey and the elevators from his firm in Worcester, Massachusetts.

Stokes built the Ansonia as an apartment hotel, and with over three hundred suites it was one of the largest in the world. Some apartments were huge, and few consisted of the usual rectangular rooms. The apartments at the corners have great round parlors with three windows bathing the rooms in light. Other apartments have a decorative diversity that is undreamed of today—ellipsoidal parlors, oval reception rooms, leaded windows, even sculpture niches. Over the years, some of its elegance has faded. No longer do Oriental carpets line the halls, nor does the Hungarian String Orchestra play in the cafe, nor do symphony orchestras play on the roof garden, but it is still a powerful building that makes a statement for its time. The facade's rounded corners act as foils for its flat walls, its delicate iron railings set off the brick

113

and terra cotta, and its overall lightness of design contrasts
with the massiveness of the place.

To make sure that this seventeen-story building was absolutely fireproof, Stokes made the interior masonry partitions about 3 feet thick, creating what is reputedly the best
soundproofing in any New York apartment house. It has been
a haven for an impressive list of musicians, among them Stra-
vinsky, Toscanini, Caruso, Pinza, and Pons.

St. Regis–Sheraton Hotel 1904

2 East Fifty-fifth Street, southeast corner of Fifth
Avenue
Trowbridge & Livingston, Architects

*All conservative decoration aside, New York's tallest hotel in
1904 was equipped with some futuristic gadgets that put it
light years ahead of its competition.*

It made sense to John Jacob Astor IV that if skyscrapers could
make money as office buildings, then skyscrapers could make
money as hotels. The hotel that Trowbridge & Livingston
designed to his specifications was, at eighteen stories, the
tallest in New York. It was also one of the most elegant hotels
of the day, bettering even the original Waldorf-Astoria on
Fifth Avenue and Thirty-fourth street.

Astor realized that the wealthy liked to surround themselves with a feeling of elegance and permanence, although
they might in fact only be inelegant transients. He built his
hotel at the southern end of what was then New York's most
exclusive district. He named it for a monk who had been
canonized for his hospitality to travelers. He had each room
equipped with an automatic thermostat, and air that was
heated, cooled, moistened, or dried was pumped into the
rooms through wall ducts. He had a vacuum-cleaning system
installed that allowed a maid to attach a flexible tube to an
outlet in the room and apply the nozzle to a dusty surface or

a piece of trash. Presto!—the dirt was sucked into a system of pipes and down to a giant garbage bag in the basement. There were forty-seven Steinway pianos for the guests to play, a library with three thousand volumes to be read, and in the dining room a complete solid-gold flatware service.

Neither the architects nor the interior decorators adhered to any specific style, but "International Looie" might describe it. Money was no object. A simple straight-backed chair supplied by Arnold Constable for the Palm Room cost $55. Up to $6,000 was spent to decorate some suites. (The building took about $4 million to build, and another $1.5 million to furnish.)

The facade is a rich potpourri, with graceful French windows and iron balconies, garlands of stone flowers and fruit, balustrades, an escutcheon perched precariously at the fourteenth floor, all topped by a slate mansard roof with bull's-eye windows and copper cresting. Ten windows down Fifty-fifth Street the rich decoration of Trowbridge & Livingston gives way to a more restrained facade, which is an extension designed by Charles Platt in 1928. (This is where, in the ground-floor restaurant, you will find Maxfield Parrish's famous Old King Cole mural.)

Restaurants originally occupied most of the lobby floor on Fifth Avenue. There were the dining room, a cafe, and a palm room, considered a must at the turn of the century because smoking was permitted there during all hours and in all company.

Across Fifth Avenue is the perfect companion, the Hotel Gotham, built one year after the St. Regis from designs by Hiss & Weekes.

Cartier, Inc. (L) 1905

(Originally home of Morton F. Plant)
651 Fifth Avenue, southeast corner of Fifty-second Street
Robert W. Gibson, Architect

This neo–Italian Renaissance mansion was built on land that had been bought with the understanding that the site would remain residential for twenty-five years.

This was Vanderbilt country in 1902, and America's wealthiest family wanted to keep it that way. Already Fifth Avenue was commercial in the upper teens and twenties, Benjamin Altman was quietly assembling a plot for his department store on Thirty-fourth Street, and the Windsor Arcade, filled with art galleries and showrooms, was as near as Forty-seventh Street. William K. Vanderbilt, who lived on the northeast corner of Fifth Avenue and Fifty-second Street, felt the inexorable northward movement of commerce. Whether commerce was pushing residences before it or commerce was being pulled after residences did not concern Vanderbilt—he just wanted commerce to stay away. He owned the 50-by-100-foot plot diagonally across the avenue from his house, and when Morton F. Plant wanted to buy it, Vanderbilt placed one restriction on the sale—the site would remain residential for twenty-five years. Plant agreed.

The florid, five-story marble and granite neo-Italian Renaissance mansion Plant built for himself, with its address on the avenue but its entrance on the side street, was a private palace, befitting a businessman whose worth was put at $32 million in 1919 and who was called the Commodore because of his function at the New York Yacht Club. By 1916, however, Plant had grown weary of the neighborhood. Fifth Avenue homes between Forty-second and Fifty-ninth streets taken over by commerce had become so common that the transactions were hardly worthy of comment. Already the northeast corner of Fifty-second Street had an eight-story "loft" on it, with six floors rented by a dressmaker.

Although his block was holding out, Plant could not stand the pressure of more commercial encroachment, and he began to build a new mansion at 1051 Fifth, on the northeast corner of Eighty-sixth Street, far from the madding crowd. It was only then that the announcement was made that William K. Vanderbilt was buying the Plant mansion for a reputed $1 million (the assessed valuation of the land and the house was $925,000). Since it was Vanderbilt who had struck the "no commerce" bargain with Plant, Vanderbilt was not bound by the deal and had the power to nullify it. He casually inquired what 5 percent on $1 million was, and agreed to rent the house to Cartier for the $50,000 a year, one of the highest rentals on the avenue for a business. It all smacked of a deal worked out in advance by the three parties, but, in any case, there went the old neighborhood. The rustication and domestic fenestration on the first floor gave way to display windows, a clock was added, and the jeweler's name appeared in a few places on the facade. The first two floors still contain the original paneling. At the very least, it should make Cartier feel right at home.

B. Altman & Company   1906

Fifth Avenue to Madison Avenue, between
Thirty-fourth and Thirty-fifth streets
Extensions, 1911, 1914
Trowbridge & Livingston, Architects

The first major department store to leave the bosom of
Ladies' Mile and venture east to Fifth Avenue.

In 1902, Macy's left Ladies' Mile and moved up Sixth Avenue
as far as Herald Square, landing on Broadway between
Thirty-fourth and Thirty-fifth streets. Four years later Benjamin Altman left his blockfront store on Sixth Avenue at Nineteenth Street and moved not only as far north as Macy's, but
east to Fifth Avenue. (Like Macy's, Altman's could not immediately acquire the corner lot on Thirty-fourth Street and
would not until 1911; Macy's still has not acquired its.)
Across the street was A. T. Stewart's marble palace, then the
Metropolitan Club. Diagonally across Thirty-fourth Street
was the Waldorf-Astoria. Two new McKim, Mead & White
buildings were also neighbors, Gorham on Thirty-sixth Street
and Tiffany on Thirty-seventh. And uptown on Fifth lived
the greatest accumulation of wealth in the nation.

Not to be cowed by all this, Altman had his architects
design his store in the style of an Italian Renaissance palace,
with cornices setting the stage for the three-part theme.
Fluted Doric columns with major and minor bands of egg-
and-dart motifs as capitals flank the Fifth Avenue entrance;
otherwise the columns are plain. If the building somehow
reminds you of France rather than Italy, it might be because
it was built of limestone imported from France, the same
limestone used for so many Parisian facades. The bowed marquees seem especially French, and they add a touch of elegance to the building, an elegance that is continued in the
mahogany-paneled entrances. Fortunately, no iconoclastic
interior designer has come along and torn out the molding
in the name of progress.

The Thirty-fourth Street facade clearly reveals the extension that was added so artfully it eludes most people's eyes. The facade shows the roofline cornice ending abruptly, and the eight-story Fifth Avenue building becoming thirteen stories on Madison. The differences are subtle—for instance, on the Madison Avenue entrance the elaborate marquees are missing and the Doric columns are plain.

When Altman's moved here in 1906, Fifth Avenue was already in transition. Since about 1885, when families started moving out of their homes, the brownstone fronts were being knocked out and store fronts installed in their place. And new buildings were going up, as were the prices. A midblock lot on Fifth Avenue that measured 25 by 100 feet was worth about $125,000 in 1901. By 1907 the same lot was worth as much as $400,000, and assembling a blockfront was becoming a virtual impossibility. Altman himself had done it under an assumed name before the rush, and even then it took him from 1895 until 1905 to do it.

But he knew what he was doing. By 1907, Fifth Avenue between Twenty-sixth and Fiftieth streets was the longest street in America exclusively devoted to a high-class retail trade. And the store that anchored Fifth Avenue never hung out its sign.

Morgan Library (L) 1906

33 East Thirty-sixth Street, between Madison and Park avenues
McKim, Mead & White, Architects

It only cost an additional $50,000 to erect the first building in America to approximate the ideal of classical Greek building principles. The marble blocks were cut to fit together perfectly, abrogating the need for mortar.

J. Pierpont Morgan, the bankers' banker at the turn of the century, was doing innovative things with money on a huge scale, and he set out to acquire works of art, especially rare books and manuscripts, on the same scale. He lived in an unpretentious brownstone on the corner of Thirty-sixth Street and Madison Avenue (the last of the family compound, now owned by the Lutheran Church in America, is still standing on the southeast corner of Madison Avenue and Thirty-seventh Street—see page 35), but the library in his home was neither big enough nor grand enough. What he wanted was a jewel box.

118

Morgan hired McKim, Mead & White to design one for him, and Charles Follen McKim was given the choice assignment. McKim wanted to do in Murray Hill what had been done at the Erechtheum on the Acropolis in Athens—use no mortar, just marble blocks that were cut with tongues and grooves to fit together perfectly. Morgan thought it was not a bad idea, and told McKim to go ahead with his scheme. The investment of an additional $50,000 was small potatoes to pay for perfection in a building that would finally cost $1,154,669 to build.

The building's facade is basically little more than a Palladian porch flanked by a pair of niches. Its strength, its purity of design, come from this simplicity.

The sculptured panels, by Adolph A. Weinman, represent on the left *Truth* with *Literature*, *Philosophy*, *History*, *Oratory*, and *Astronomy*; on the right, *Music* is inspiring the *Arts*. True to classical antiquity, where architects never signed their works, McKim would not have his name chiseled in this facade. Instead, his face was sculpted in bas-relief as the sphinx.

Guarding the library are a bronze fence with marble posts; a pair of crouched lionesses, sculpted by Alexander Phimister Proctor; and sixteenth-century bronze doors.

Morgan's will stipulated that after his death his home should be torn down and the library extended. Benjamin Wistar Morris intentionally designed the extension subordinate to the library. The 1928 extension is the entrance now used.

Between McKim's facade and Morgan's den, the Morgan Library shows how a few gentlemen of taste and fortune lived in the early twentieth century.

East Twenty-third Street Bath House (L)   1906

Asser Levy Place, between First Avenue and the FDR Drive
William Martin Aiken and Arnold W. Brunner, Architects

An extravaganza of a neo-classical facade masked the serious municipal undertaking of providing free bathing facilities for the unwashed masses.

At the turn of the century well over a million New Yorkers lived in old-law tenements, and 96 percent of them had no bathing facilities except a common sink in the hallway. It's not that there were no opportunities whatsoever for bathing, it's just that they had to be assiduously sought out. As early as 1852 there were some bathing facilities on Rivington Street, and there were the "floating baths," little more than barges filled with salt water along both rivers' edges. But reformers were slowly scoring their point, and the idea that cleanliness was indeed next to Godliness, and a good way to create good citizens to boot, began to overcome municipal indifference. In 1889 the first public bathing house appeared, with hot or cold water, "depending on the season." By the 1890s the New York State Legislature consented to give the bath movement legislative support. And in 1903 the City took steps to provide twelve new public baths, which according to the great tenement-house reformers Robert DeForest and Lawrence Veiller were "all situated in the more crowded tenement house districts."

By 1905 there were the Free Public Baths, "Dedicated to the People by the City of New York," in John Jay Park at Seventy-eighth Street. There were thirty-eight showers for men, and twenty-five showers and ten tubs for women, as well as a "plunge bath," or swimming pool. A year later the West Sixtieth Street Bath House was built, with all interior surfaces having rounded corners, providing easy "washdown" surfaces. Its capacity was estimated at 2.5 million baths a year (actually, there were no baths at all, since by then showers were preferred because tubs were considered unsanitary and too difficult to keep clean).

The biggest and most impressive public bathing facility was the East Twenty-third Street Public Baths, with 155 shower compartments and a "natatorium." Its facade is basically a pair of Roman arches flanked by pairs of Doric columns, not unlike Hunt's facade for the Metropolitan Museum of Art. One major difference is that in this case the carvings on the attic story have been completed, with the urns every bit as symbolic to a bath house as Hunt's idea for the four ages of civilization is to a museum. This extravaganza of a facade reflects the City government's approach to municipal buildings at the turn of the century, an approach that led to competitions and architecture of a high quality. The mere fact that the building exists attests to an awakening on behalf of the City to the needs of its populace, an awakening that had already been manifested in the developing professionalism of municipal services.

Trinity and U. S. Realty Buildings   1906

111 and 115 Broadway, between Trinity Churchyard and Cedar Street, with Thames Street intersecting them
Francis H. Kimball, Architect

The Twin Towers, with Gothic variations, 1906.

The Trinity Corporation, one of New York's foremost landowners, took the site of today's Trinity Building in the 1840s and built what is reputedly the first building erected in New

York exclusively for offices. It was designed by Richard Upjohn, and stood five stories high. Take the same site about
sixty years later and consider one fact—there will not be another skyscraper thrown up immediately south of the Trinity
Building until after the sound of the last trumpet, since that
plot is Trinity Churchyard. With a guarantee of light and air
you could put up a building and take it as high as you dared
in 1906, say 290 feet, or twenty-one stories.

But consider the narrowness of the original building site,
which was only 35 feet, and figure out how to get more space.
With Trinity Church as the landlord, the answer was easy—
arrange with the city to shift Thames Street and widen it by
9 feet in the bargain. Then all you'd have to do is build twin
towers (with slight variations), each over twenty stories high,
and each using the 30-foot-wide Thames Street as little more
than an air shaft. Put both the buildings' services on the
Thames Street side—elevators, staircases, toilets, and a few
offices on the upper floors, with the majority looking south
over the churchyard or north over Cedar Street, and hope that
some other monster would not be built on the north side of
Cedar Street and hog all the light.

Tell the architect to design the office buildings in the
pseudo-Gothic style to blend in with the distinguished neighbor to the south (it is the same conceit that Upjohn practiced
in the original Trinity Building and which James Renwick,
Jr., practiced in the office building just north of Grace Church,
at 808 Broadway). The preponderance of Gothic-style trim is
in the lower and upper floors. Between, you find an occasional Gothic-style finial atop a false buttress (it's all for effect—these buildings are built on steel frames with facades
of blue Bedford Indiana limestone). You will find trefoil windows, lancet windows, and flamboyant Gothic-style windows; you will find windows in pairs and threes to appear
as rose windows; and you'll find windows in Francis I arches
and crenellated towers. Along with all the marble, bronze,
and gold leaf in the lobbies are the elevator banks, likewise
in the Gothic style. The elevators were the hydraulic plunger

type, which meant that for every foot the elevator went up, the plunger had to go down one, 300 feet in all, straight into bedrock.

U. S. Custom House (L)   1907

At Bowling Green, bounded by State, Bridge, and Whitehall streets
Cass Gilbert, Architect

New York's second great public Beaux Arts building, this one with all its sculptural faculties intact.

If the ideal Beaux Arts building is a marriage of sculpture and architecture in a French neo-classical motif, then this building was made in heaven. Gallic neo-classicism is rampant, as is the statuary. The four sculpture groups in front of the building are the most dramatic. They are from designs by Daniel Chester French and represent four continents, each symbolized by a woman surrounded by icons (from left to right): *Asia,* imperiously sitting on a throne of skulls; *North America*, clear-eyed and forward-looking; *Europe*, regal and sanguine; and *Africa*, the sleeping giant, complete with a weathered sphinx. All stereotypical clichés, but powerful nevertheless.

Atop the cornice stand six paired statues in period costume, each representing the great seafaring nations. The third statue from the right had represented Germany, until, in a fit of "victory cabbagism" during World War I, the name Germany was effaced and replaced by Belgium. The cartouche in high relief, crowning the facade and breaking the attic balustrade, is by Karl Bitter. The seal of the United States is flanked by loosely draped, winged women, one representing a nation at peace (she holds a sheathed sword), the other representing a strong nation (she holds a fasces), the whole topped by a federal eagle.

Like the classical ideal, the Custom House has a beginning, middle, and end, clearly delineated in its horizontal-vertical-horizontal theme, which begins in the rustication of the first floor, continues in the engaged, colossal Corinthian columns, and culminates in the two top stories.

122

This building was constructed as the headquarters for the U. S. Custom Service in New York City, and housed the collection of custom duties on revenues realized from commerce across the seas. Architect Cass Gilbert included marine symbols as a motif, including dolphins and scallop shells (he even went so far as to substitute tridents, symbol of Poseidon, for the usual anthemion as the antefixes), and because the business of the Custom House was business, he incorporated the head of Mercury, god of commerce, within all the Corinthian capitals. Ironically, the building turns its side to its source of wealth, fronting on Bowling Green instead of State Street and the harbor beyond.

If there is one building in New York that approaches the Paris Opera House in scale, site, and philosophy, this bit of imperial grandeur is it. Incredibly, the Custom Service itself has abandoned this granite beauty in favor of the sterility of the World Trade Center.

The Plaza (L) 1907

Fifth Avenue, between Fifty-eighth and Fifty-ninth streets
Extension, 1921
Henry J. Hardenbergh, Architect

Blessed by its charming site, graced by its harmonious facade, the grandest dame of New York's Edwardian Age is still as grand as ever.

Built for the staggering sum of $12½ million in 1907, the Plaza opened to the huzzahs of millionaires, many of whom instantly rented whole suites of apartments for themselves.

Built on one of the few sites in New York City where you

can view a building in its entirety from two sides, this hotel replaced one that had been erected only seventeen years before on the same site and with the same name. Edwardian tastes, however, found the old eight-story, brownstone hotel neither grand nor elegant enough. Everyone agreed that its replacement, with its marbled elegance, could placate even the most sophisticated.

The Plaza is loosely modeled after buildings from the French Renaissance. Its Fifth Avenue facade, for instance, is divided into thirds, like all good things classical: a loggia and granite rustication for the base; ten stories of matte-glazed brick with terra cotta trim as the shaft; and a major cornice, another loggia, and a monumental green-tiled mansard roof with copper cornices and finials as the capital. Architect Hardenbergh linked the building laterally by projecting the wings. To soften it, he rounded off the corners, incorporating oriel windows that rise from the fourth floor to be capped by individual dome roofs (you'll find similar treatment, although at midbuilding, in the Dakota.)

Several hotels had already suffered from growing pains when the Plaza was being designed, so, planning ahead, additional land was bought on Fifty-eighth Street and Hardenbergh allowed for an extension in his plans. In 1921 the three-hundred-room extension was added.

After more than seventy years there have been changes at the Plaza. Gone are the water-powered hydraulic elevators, the summer dining room in the Fifth Avenue lobby, and the leaded-glass domelight in the ceiling of the Palm Court. In 1971, in an effort to be "now" and "with it," the hotel had its elegant Edwardian Room done over as the Green Tulip Room, which supposedly extended the freshness of live greenery from Central Park. Fortunately—greenery be damned—in 1974 the Edwardian Room was restored to its Edwardian splendor.

It is just the things about the Plaza that don't change that have attracted guests like Cary Grant, Zelda and F. Scott Fitzgerald, Frank Lloyd Wright (he liked the Plaza almost as much as if he had designed it himself), probably every politician since Teddy Roosevelt, undoubtedly the entire New York Social Register at one time or another, and, for Lord's sake, Eloise.

Singer Building   1907

561 Broadway and 88 Prince Street
Ernest Flagg, Architect

Fifty years after the Haughwout Building, and the next logical step—bands of floor-to-ceiling windows and terra cotta panels hanging from a steel skeleton.

Architects of turn-of-the-century skyscrapers like 15 Park Row and the Flatiron Building stingily inserted windows in their walls of limestone or granite, as if the walls were supporting the building. They could have opened up the walls with windows, a possibility fully explored in the 1850s by

architects of cast-iron buildings, but they chose instead to design buildings that appeared substantial but belied their potential.

In the twelve-story Singer Building, architect Flagg realized the possibilities inherent in skyscraper technology. From the frame of steel, encased in brick as a fire retardant, he hung bands of floor-to-ceiling windows (actually they are French doors under glass transoms) alternating with bands of terra cotta across the wide central bay. Flanking the bay are windows set in terra cotta panels. Glass almost completely fills the frame. The result is the lightest facade of its time in New York, the first true skyscraper with an obvious curtain wall. And before the advent of air-conditioning, it must have been one of the coolest. To admit the cool breezes of summer, the French doors could be opened wide. And to protect the offices and loft spaces from unnecessary sun streaming through the windows, the balconies act as awnings, shading the offices.

The delicate wrought-iron railings, as well as the arch spanning the second floor and the other spanning the tenth and eleventh floors, add a Gallic air to the building, probably emanating from a primordial memory of Flagg's from his days at l'Ecole des Beaux Arts. (Flagg must have adored arches—he designed so many of them: his second Singer Tower, which was at Broadway and Liberty Street before its untimely demise, was basically a Beaux Arts tower with arches; his Engine Company No. 33 on Great Jones Street is essentially a building built around an arch; and his Scribner Building on Fifth Avenue at Forty-eighth Street has an arch spanning the lower floors.)

This delicate little L-shaped building is really twice as lovely as most people bargain for, because it has one facade on Broadway and another on Prince Street. Unfortunately, the entrance on Broadway was modernized, so admiration should begin at the second story.

Metropolitan Life Tower   1909

Southeast corner of Madison Avenue and
Twenty-fourth Street
Napoleon LeBrun & Sons, Architects

At 700 feet this astigmatic vision of the Campanile of St. Mark's, Venice, was the world's tallest building.

By the turn of the century, corporations were beginning to use their headquarters as corporate symbols, as advertisements for their products. Every time a tour guide or a proud citizen pointed out the next great breakthrough in skyscraper technology and attached a company name to the building, the company's products would be given that much more free publicity. It was a theory as valid for selling insurance policies as it was for boosting five-and-ten-cent stores.

The original plans for this tower called for a building 560 feet high, which would have made it the world's tallest, making it one of the buildings most written about, most talked about, most gaped at, and most snapped at in the world. The final plans called for a building 700 feet high, or "fifty-two stories, inclusive of the basement." This height ensured its claim to the world's tallest title and all of the concomitant free publicity, while setting itself up as the building that Frank W. Woolworth wanted to top.

The tower, only 75 feet wide on Madison Avenue and 85

126

feet wide on Twenty-fourth Street, was admittedly inspired by the Campanile in Venice, but at best it is an astigmatic vision. (The architects did win a Medal of Honor from the Architectural League of New York for their design, nevertheless.) Originally built as an annex to a former Metropolitan Life Building next door (the company has expanded at least thirteen times on this site), the tower had a balustrade above the tenth floor which united it with the cornice of its past neighbor (when the old building was torn down, the balustrade went with it). Now the tower rises unencumbered to the face of the clock, 350 feet up (the building's boosters relished describing the clock as the largest four-dial clock in the world, bigger even than Big Ben). Then the Renaissance, which so far has been quietly represented in the quoins, begins to roar, encircling the building first with a balustrade, then a three-story loggia, then another balustrade (this one topped by urns), the tower in turn topped by another element, including still another balustrade, a choragic monument, and a gilded lantern. The lantern flashes one, two, three, or four times in red to indicate the quarter-hours; after the fourth red light has flashed, a white light flashes to indicate the hour. The bells sound a measure by Handel on the quarter-hour as well.

The observation gallery, which cost fifty cents to visit as early as 1911, was reached first by elevator to the forty-fourth floor, then by steps. The booklet given to visitors claimed that from the highest lookout, the balcony of the fiftieth floor and 660 feet up, were visible "the homes of over one-sixteenth of the entire population of the United States." With the population of the consolidated Metropolitan New York at about 16 million, it's a claim that would be equally valid today, with one exception—the seventeen taller buildings in Manhattan would severely block the view.

Belnord Apartments (L) 1909

225 West Eighty-sixth Street, between
Amsterdam Avenue and Broadway
Hiss & Weekes, Architects

With the coming of the subway in 1904, several large apartment houses were built on the West Side. Here was the world's largest.

From the 1860s on, property owners along the upper stretches of Broadway held on to their property in the belief that its value would rise. With the coming of the subway in 1904, the promise finally came true.

The thirteen-story Belnord, built around a central courtyard that measures 94 by 232 feet, is over 50 feet deep from the street to the courtyard. Overall, it is 350 feet long, 200 feet wide, and 150 feet high, making it in 1909 not just the largest apartment house in New York, but the largest apartment house in the world.

Originally there were 175 apartments in the Belnord, ranging in size from seven to fourteen rooms. They rented

from $2,100 a year, or $175 a month, "and upward." To many New Yorkers who did not consider themselves poor but who nevertheless craved some sunlight, comfort, tasteful surroundings, and some sort of luxury, $175 a month seemed a staggeringly high price to pay. The *New York Times* predicted that with the coming of huge, luxurious, and expensive apartment houses like the Belnord, there would soon be few private dwellings on Manhattan Island, except the palaces of the very rich.

Granted, Belnord residents did receive some pleasant amenities, like the cost of electricity and "artificial refrigeration" included in their rent. Their doors were made of mahogany, their walls had wainscoting in the style of Louis XIV, storerooms were provided free of charge in the basement, and on the roof was a laundry room with tubs, ironing boards, and drying lines.

Beneath the planted courtyard was a great breakthrough in city planning—an off-street truck delivery system. Just off Broadway on Eighty-seventh Street is a ramp that leads down to the basement. If you follow it you will come to an underground driveway that leads to the building's eight service elevators. Tradesmen could deliver directly to the building, and the tenants would be completely unsullied by their presence.

The Belnord, costing $3 million and built in the style of the neo–Italian Renaissance, is hardly as elegant as its cousin, the Apthorp Apartments on Broadway at Seventy-ninth Street, but some touches are beguiling, like the pair of arched portes cocheres on Eighty-sixth Street with the sgraffito in their ceilings.

Old New York City Police Headquarters (L) 1909

240 Centre Street, between Grand and Broome streets
Hoppin & Koen, Architects

A great neo-classical palace for New York's old police headquarters, tucked away and hardly ever seen.

One of the fascinations of New York City and eclectic architecture is that you can turn a corner and unexpectedly be confronted by a building that turns back the clock to another time and takes you on a trip to another place. With the old police headquarters, the time could be the seventeenth century, and the place Paris or Rome.

If this were a Baroque city, or even a provincial French capital, the police headquarters would probably have a grand boulevard leading up to it, or at least a square laid out before it. As it is, about the only hint from afar that this beauty exists is when you look north from the Municipal Building along Park Row. The hint is its dome, looming just above the low-lying buildings.

One of the forces that created this secret phenomenon, and the one that hems it in, is lower Manhattan's narrow streets, many of which follow original land grants. In this case, the strange confluence of streets marks what used to be the western border of the East Bayard Farm. As a result, the old police headquarters is built to fill an irregular plot—the building is 46 feet wide at the Broome Street end, and 88 feet at Grand Street.

This neo-Renaissance building, with its granite base and Indiana limestone facade, took about eight years to complete. Now deserted (the police department moved out in 1973), its future might hold a community center for the neighborhood. One thing that is not uncertain is the building's statement of quality. In the true Beaux Arts tradition, everything is balanced and carefully framed, from the rustication on the first floor to the quoining on the second and third to the five heroic statues bearing plaques inscribed with the names of the boroughs. The seated statue with the scepter serves a double function: it identifies both Manhattan and New York City, which until 1898 and the creation of Greater New York was the same place anyway.

Main Branch, New York Public Library (L) {1911}

Fifth Avenue, between Fortieth and Forty-second streets
Carrère & Hastings, Architects

The nation's third-largest library is housed in one of the brightest gems in New York's crown of neo-classical municipal buildings, a restrained Beaux Arts facade with dignity.

If Chicago and Boston had great public libraries by the 1890s, then New York was not to be outdone. The Astor and Lenox libraries were already ensconced in their own buildings, but they were hardly capacious or splendid enough to top the rival cities. And the $2.5 million bequeathed by Samuel J. Tilden was hardly enough for the Tilden Trust to assume the building costs for the kind of library that would be adequate to the job. Since the building had to be the best, there would hardly be any money left over for books. "Click" went the light bulb over the heads of the trustees of the Tilden Trust and the Astor and Lenox libraries. After much negotiation, they merged, creating the New York Public Library. Despite its name, it is still a private library that is open free to the public. All that the City agreed to do, as requested by the trustees, was to "furnish a proper site, and provide thereon a suitable building."

The design for the "suitable building" was chosen from a field of eighty-eight entries, and then refined. The original winning design was more florid, more Beaux Artsy, more French. The roof over the main reading room was elevated and bowed, victory columns flanked the building, and eight rostral columns, just like the ones at the Paris Opera House, were set into the balustrade. The building that transpired is a restrained Beaux Arts design with dignity, a design with roots in Claude Perrault's east front of the Louvre (1665). Everything is in harmony. The central Roman arch in the portico is flanked by paired Corinthian columns, the portico itself is flanked by matching wings terminating in mini-porches of their own, and the vertical thrust of the columns is tempered by the horizontal base and the rooftop balustrade.

Statuary abounds. In the attic story it stands in pairs or singly, continuing the line of the columns below: Paul Wayland Bartlett's *History* and *Philosophy* stand alone, flanking *Romance* and *Religion* (left) and *Poetry* and *Drama* (right).

130

Frederick MacMonnies sculpted the allegorical figures in the niches: *Beauty* is represented by a woman, *Wisdom*, by a man, reflecting the stereotypes of contemporaneous society. The library's most famous statues—they have almost come to symbolize it—are the pink Tennessee marble lions by Edward Clark Potter. They have been criticized (not regal enough), joked about (when you go to the library, be sure to read between the lions), nicknamed (Patience and Fortitude, Lord and Lady Astor), and finally, reproduced (appropriately enough, as bookends).

With more than 2.5 million books, the NYPL is the third-largest reference library in the nation—only the Library of Congress and Harvard's Widener are larger. Most of the books are in the west end of the building, taking up 63 miles of shelves on seven floors of stacks, with the floors constructed of steel beams fitted with floor slabs of 1½-inch-thick marble. Viewed from Bryant Park, their windows show a purely functional facade, unlike the other facades of this neo-classical building.

The estimated cost of the building was $2.5 million, which would have exhausted all of the Tilden Fund. The contract went to the lowest bidder, but the building still cost about $9 million, or about $3 a book to house. A bargain.

998 Fifth Avenue 1911

Northeast corner of Eighty-first Street
McKim, Mead & White, Architects

If there is a watershed in New York Society's living habits, it is this apartment house. When 998 was erected, 90 percent of Society lived in private homes; within twenty-five years, 90 percent of Society would be living in apartments, with much of the change due to the kind of quality this house inspired.

Bottocino marble lined the entrance, and French walnut paneled the elevator walls. Apartment walls were given nine coats of paint, bedroom closets secreted wall safes with combination locks, and in the days when most steam heat was either on or off, valves regulated the intake. Reception rooms measured 14 by 36 feet and were usually copied from the Long Gallery, Haddon Hall, England. Their walls were paneled in English oak, and their ceilings were plastered in the geometrical patterns of the Tudors. A refrigerating plant cooled a private wine room in each apartment, and butler's pantries were supplied with plate-warmers. Salons that averaged over 300 square feet could be either oval or octagonal, and one apartment dweller devoted his room in the southwest corner of the building to the gentlemanly game of billiards. Six to nine servants' rooms per apartment were common (there was no more upstairs-downstairs, of course, but there was front, for the family, and back, for the servants), and the service elevator opened directly onto the servants' wing. Some apartments were duplexes that took up two halves of the building, others were simplexes, and two apartments took almost two entire floors. The second largest was about twenty rooms, and went as a loss leader to Senator Elihu Root for $15,000 a year. The largest had about twenty-five rooms, and was rented for about $25,000 a year by Murry Guggenheim.

Guggenheim had a stained-glass ceiling suspended from the structural ceiling of his 15-by-34-foot conservatory and had it backlit (his former home on West Seventy-sixth Street had one, too). He also had all the hardware removed and sent to Tiffany & Co. to be gold plated. It made sense—since gold never tarnishes, it never needs polishing, so metal polish never slops over from the window fixtures and light brackets and door hinges and handles to mar the woodwork in the paneling or the paint on the walls.

If Fifth Avenue was Millionaires' Row, then No. 998 was justifiably called the Millionaires' Apartments. The land value alone was worth $100 a square foot, or $1,280,000 for the lot, and the building fetched $3.5 million when it was sold in 1913. When it was built, 90 percent of New York Society was living in private homes. Twenty-five years later and the reverse would be the case, with 90 percent of Society living in apartments that were usually lesser, but nevertheless grand, versions of 998 Fifth. This Renaissance-style apartment house, complete with battered walls, set a standard of excellence that was often aspired to but seldom achieved.

903 Park Avenue   1912

Northwest corner of Seventy-ninth Street
Warren & Wetmore, Architects

New York's most expensive house in 1912 was also its tallest, overcoming the fire and height restrictions imposed by the City and setting the standard for the next fifteen years.

By 1912 the style for first-class apartment houses was well established. The biggest averaged twelve stories, and most bore a limestone facade for the first story, or even the first few. Above, the buildings were almost always brick. The facade could be Gothicized, like 44 West Seventy-seventh Street, or Francis the Firstified, like the Alwyn Court at 182 West Fifty-eighth Street, but the preferred trim was neo–Italian Renaissance. It lent itself gracefully to grand entranceways, cornices, and an occasional balcony. Most importantly, it created an image of money and prestige and solidity.

New York's most expensive apartment house for 1912, 903 Park Avenue, held true to form, with two exceptions—it was seventeen stories, and granite was used on the lower floor. The apartments were designed to be as spacious as private houses, and private-house dwellers were the market the builder hoped to tap. And it seemed to be working—former home dwellers were indeed shifting to apartments. And no wonder. At 903 Park, for instance, there was one apartment to a floor, and, depending on the layout, it could mean an apartment of fourteen to seventeen rooms, with five or six bathrooms (the ground-floor apartment was the only one that was any smaller). The rents were $9,000 to $10,000 a year, the top paid by Carl Tucker, treasurer of the Maxwell Motor Company, who rented the apartment on the seventeenth floor. At seventeen stories, 903 Park Avenue was New York's, and the world's, tallest apartment house (the Ansonia was considered an apartment hotel), and by paying the premium, Tucker got the world's highest apartment.

New York City law required that any apartment house taller than twelve stories had to be absolutely fireproof and the apartment houses could not be taller than one-and-a-half times the width of the thoroughfare they faced. The first restriction led to increased construction costs in relation to the house's added height, one reason that No. 903 was 1912's most expensive apartment house to build. It necessitated a huge leap in height to make the investment worthwhile, leading the builders to erect houses to their maximum allowable height. Park Avenue is 140 feet wide, and 903 Park is just under 210 feet high. Its seventeen stories set the standard for later apartment houses on both Park and West End avenues, two streets that today are apartment-house canyons.

With the increased possibilities came the concomitant rise in prices: a corner at Seventy-fifth and Park was sold in 1911 for $175,000; by 1930 its value was estimated at $800,000.

Grand Central Terminal (L)   1913

Forty-second Street and Park Avenue
Warren & Wetmore and Reed & Stem, Architects

After the Beaux Arts terminal was completed and the tracks up Park Avenue were covered, Park Avenue north from the terminal emerged with all its trappings of luxury.

It is remarkable that this railroad terminal, built in the heart of one of the most densely developed sections of the city, operates so efficiently and with so little intrusion. Much of its success takes place under and around the building, absolutely hidden from view.

Until 1903, steam-powered trains operated as far south as Fiftieth Street on Park Avenue in a partially covered cut, fanning out into an open train yard as they approached the old terminal, which had stood in various stages on this site since 1871.

With electrification, Chief Engineer William J. Wilgus realized that the tracks could be completely enclosed in tunnels. Instead of fanning out, tracks could be stacked, one on top of the other. Instead of roundhouses to turn around locomotives, entire trains could loop around the terminal on special sets of tracks. Instead of the prime real-estate property above the tracks going to waste, the New York Central Railroad could sell its air rights for buildings, multiplying the value of its holdings.

Using Wilgus's guidelines, Reed & Stem won the architectural competition for the new terminal. They designed an elaborate system of pedestrian ramps within the terminal, and around its periphery, an elevated "circumferential plaza"

that allowed traffic to continue downtown without being dumped on Forty-second Street.

After the contract had been signed, Reed & Stem were persuaded to team up with Warren & Wetmore. It was Reed who had conceived of the concourse, which is topped by a celestial barrel-vaulted ceiling, but it was Beaux Arts–trained Whitney Warren who brought the refined detailing to the terminal. Together they created New York's finest extant interior space, and the glory of the place still shines through.

Warren's Forty-second Street facade is simple—three triumphal archways, each flanked by a pair of doubled columns. Jules Coutan's sculpture—*Mercury* (transportation), flanked by *Hercules* (strength) and *Athena* (civilization)—is an integral part of the facade. The columns, but not the statuary, are repeated on the eastern and western facades. Stories have it that the size of the arches was determined by the width of Forty-third Street—if the City should ever decide to reopen that street, a ramp could theoretically be built through the concourse linking Vanderbilt and Lexington avenues.

Within about fifteen years from the coming of this terminal, a swath of prestigious buildings had been erected up both sides of Park Avenue. Buildings built on railroad-owned land, most erected over the tracks with no basements, included eleven office buildings, ten apartment houses, eight hotels, and one club. The economic theory of air rights had become an economic fact. In 1903 the railroad's property was valued at $77,631,787. By 1923 the value had risen to $327,951,701.

Scribner Building
1913

597–599 Fifth Avenue, between Forty-eighth and Forty-ninth streets
Ernest Flagg, Architect

The smartly modish Parisian design for Scribner's new store cum offices made an elegant commercial foray into residential Fifth Avenue.

More and more commercial ventures were moving uptown onto residential Fifth Avenue, and the worst fears of the Vanderbilts were being realized. In 1911 art dealer M. Knoedler joined the northward trek, moving from Thirty-fourth Street to 556 Fifth Avenue, at Forty-sixth Street. Two years later, publisher and bookseller Charles Scribner's Sons would be leaving their elegant little building at 153 Fifth Avenue, between Twenty-first and Twenty-second streets, and would likewise be moving north. The architect for their buildings on lower Fifth Avenue had been Ernest Flagg, and he was asked to design the company's new building as well, incorporating the same features—a large store with double-height ceiling ringed by a mezzanine, and with offices above.

Flagg's design for the Forty-eighth Street building incorporated a bold horizontal-vertical-horizontal theme, with all the elements neatly assembled for the ten-story building. Its facade of Indiana limestone and iron and glass is filled with beguiling details. A pair of Boucher-like cupids playfully suspend an escutcheon under the first floor cornice, within which is inscribed "Charles Scribner's Sons" (today's awnings simply say "Scribners"), while up on the mansard roof a pair of caryatids act forthright and mature. The architectural ornamentation is carefully executed, like the unobtrusive frets at the base of the square pilasters with a variation on the pattern above in a cornice. Amidst elegant Renaissance detailing on the fourth floor are four medallions of great printers (from left to right: Benjamin Franklin, William Caxton, Johann Gutenberg, and Aldus Manutius). The only wood in the steel-framed building was in its furnishings and fittings, indicative of Flagg's obsession with fireproofing materials.

The storefront, one of the few in the city that has remained pristine so long, is an elegantly detailed metal frame faced with brass. A pair of slender, bowed French Renaissance–style columns flank a semi-elliptical arch, one of Flagg's favorite shapes. The Scribner logo is worked within the pedimented doorway; and everywhere, even surrounding the roundels, is delicately wrought iron.

When the publishing company moved into its new building it only occupied four of the office floors, renting out the remaining space (Scribner's occupies all but two floors today). Its printing and manufacturing was done at the Scribner Press, on West Forty-third Street. Great American writers who have been published by Scribner's include Edith Wharton, Henry James, Thomas Wolfe, Ernest Hemingway, and F. Scott Fitzgerald. Their books are often proudly displayed in the store's windows.

Municipal Building (L) 1913

Centre Street, straddling Chambers Street
McKim, Mead & White, Architects

This blockbuster of a neo-classical building was designed to house the burgeoning bureaucracy created by the formation of Greater New York.

Until 1873, when Westchester County shed some of its southern self and the west Bronx was absorbed into the city, Manhattan Island had been New York City. In 1898, with the incorporation of the counties of Queens, Richmond, and Kings, which was also a city in its own right (Brooklyn), came the creation of Greater New York. Within twenty-five years New York City had ballooned from a city of about 14,000 acres to a city of 325 square miles, and its population had swelled from less than a million to 3,393,252.

There was no question about the city's focal point—when the celebratory fireworks were to be fired from City Hall, nobody went to Brooklyn's City Hall (now Borough Hall); instead everyone flocked to Manhattan's. With the centralization of so much power came the concomitant problem of so much paper work.

To house the expanded bureaucracy in one building would require a blockbuster, and in 1908 an architectural competition was held. The building had to conform to an awkward site. It had to provide adequate floor space (this building has 648,000 square feet). And it had to accommodate

Chambers Street's traffic through its base as well as a new subway station in its basement.

The award-winning design by the firm of McKim, Mead & White is at worst a classical stew with a soupçon of Greek and a large dash of Roman, but taking a peculiar site, they did some interesting things. They shaped the building like a flattened V, using a Corinthian colonnade to link the two wings. (The original design called for statuary atop the colonnade, a la Bernini's St. Peter's.) The columns act as an arch screen, and as you walk through them the looming building is diminished, and you enter a Roman triumphal arch, complete with coffered ceilings and rosettes. With no true basement because of the subway, the fourth floor, neatly masked in the frieze, houses the mechanical equipment.

Above the twenty-fourth floor, the building is topped by a ten-story tower, comprised of colonnades, balustrades, urns, obelisks, pyramidal domes, one choragic monument, and a 25-foot-high statue, *Civic Fame*. In her left hand she holds a crown, shaped like a turret. The five parapets represent Greater New York's five boroughs.

Many believe that this building is City Hall, and understandably. It's big, and when people say they are getting married at City Hall, this is the place they mean.

Woolworth Building
1913

233 Broadway, between Barclay Street and Park
Place
Cass Gilbert, Architect

*This masterpiece of the eclectic vertical skyscraper design,
with everything outsized but with its components in perfect
scale to each other, was the world's tallest building from
1913 until 1930.*

The Woolworth Building opened to a public-relations blitz
that resulted in about two million words in print and cul-
minated in President Wilson's pushing a button in Washington that lit 80,000 light bulbs throughout the building's sixty
stories. And why not? At 792 feet it was the tallest building
in the world, a building that synthesized the American dream
and advertised one of its peculiar institutions, the five-and-
ten-cent store. (Even today, only three U.S. cities have buildings that are taller than the Woolworth Building.)

Frank W. Woolworth, who paid $13.5 million cash for
the building, had long admired London's Houses of Parliament, and what he wanted for his new headquarters was
something that looked Gothic, like Parliament, but was taller

than the Metropolitan Life Tower, then the world's tallest building. Architect Cass Gilbert obliged, creating one of the masterpieces of the eclectic vertical skyscraper design, basically a tower rising from a setback, everything outsized but in perfect scale. Nevertheless, a steel-framed, sixty-story building is a paradox when covered by a neo-Gothic skin.

Since skyscraper construction was still a relatively new science, Gilbert overengineered the building, incorporating a frame for the first twenty-eight floors that was comprised of portal arches, girders whose undersides arch to meet the vertical columns. From the twenty-ninth to the forty-second floor is a system of diagonal struts between the girders and columns, both top and bottom. It was all redundant, but reassuring to the tenants, who were told that the building would stand in winds as high as 200 miles an hour.

What everyone takes to be stone carving on the facade is in truth terra cotta; only the first three floors are covered in limestone. Neo-Gothic trim is everywhere, from the gargoyles that do not funnel rainwater to the buttresses that do not support the pyramidal belvedere.

The lobby is one of the most elaborate in the city. Greek marble lines the walls, marble staircases lead grandly to the mezzanine, Gothic-style mailboxes incorporate the letter W in their designs, and mosaics cover the three-story-high, barrel-vaulted ceiling. Tucked away beyond the mosaic ceiling is a stained-glass ceiling, with two dates in it: 1879, to celebrate the opening of Woolworth's first store, in Lancaster, Pennsylvania; and 1913, to celebrate the opening of the tallest building in the world.

Not to be outdone by the real Gothic McCoy, a corbel representing Woolworth counting nickels and dimes is at the southeast transept of the lobby, and at the southwest transept of the lobby is another showing the architect himself cradling a model of the building.

Frick Collection (L)   1914

(Originally the home of Mr. and Mrs. Henry Clay Frick)
1 East Seventieth Street, at Fifth Avenue
Carrère & Hastings, Architects

The last block-long mansion to be built in Manhattan, and the next to the last of the great mansions of any sort to be built on Fifth Avenue.

By 1900, Fifth Avenue had only two vacant corners between Fifty-ninth and Seventy-ninth streets, and ten years later the avenue would be practically a solid wall of mansions from Fifty-ninth Street to Ninety-sixth. With the avenue's popularity, lots had become expensive and large assemblages rare, so when the contents of the Lenox Library were transferred to the new public library and the old building was torn down, Henry Clay Frick saw his chance and plunked down about $2 million for the site. Frick, chairman of the Carnegie Steel Corporation and a director of U.S. Steel, had been collecting art for years, and the value of his collection at his death would be estimated at $50 million. Although he had made his money in Pennsylvania, he believed that Pittsburgh was not the place to build a jewel box to house his collection. For one thing the air was too dirty. For another, nobody would see it. He had long admired Fifth Avenue, and as a young man had mused about the cost of maintenance on William K. Vanderbilt's mansion. Fifth Avenue was where everybody who had it was flaunting it, and if Vanderbilt's expenditure of $3 million on his mansion had impressed Frick, Frick's own total expenditure of $5.4 million would certainly impress his neighbors. His investment would buy the next to the last great mansion on Fifth Avenue (the last was Otto Kahn's, built in 1918 and today the Convent of the Sacred Heart).

Frick's art dealer was the shrewd Lord Duveen, a perfectionist with exquisite taste. He did not want his client to house a collection of old masters in just any old mansion. It was Duveen who knew art, it was Duveen who knew architecture, and it was Duveen who was instrumental in the selection of Thomas Hastings as Frick's architect. Hastings designed an elegant Louis XVIII *palais*, a palace in the true sense of the word—there were apartments for the Fricks, and there were reception rooms in the north wing where the art was displayed for their friends. The elegance is cool, understated, even austere, but tucked away are such sweet touches as the heavily ornamented ceiling of the north wing's portico.

The underlying principle of design was for the Frick mansion to become the Frick Collection upon the deaths of Mr. and Mrs. Frick, as stipulated in their will. Upon Mrs. Frick's death in 1931, Duveen stepped in again. To remodel the interior became the responsibility of one of his protégés, John Russell Pope. His interiors are as carefully thought out as Hastings's facade, a standoffish and precise design, the whole greater than the sum of its parts.

Hotel des Artistes   1915

1 West Sixty-seventh Street, west of Central Park West
George M. Pollard, Architect

Statuary representing painters, writers, musicians, and architects adorns this studio/apartment building that was erected by a syndicate of artists.

New York's first building designed to house artists' apartments and studios was the Studio Building, 51–55 West Tenth Street, erected in 1857 to plans by Richard Morris Hunt (demolished, 1954). Despite the success of the Studio Building, banks and loan companies were reluctant to provide mortgages to syndicates of artists who sought sponsorship for cooperative apartment/studio buildings. Bankers dismissed the idea as visionary and the artists who advocated it as impractical. In 1905 ten artists, among them Childe Hassam, gathered enough capital to build 27 West Sixty-seventh Street, the block's first studio/apartment building. The artists occupied half the building, and rented out the other half. The impractical artists and their visionary scheme produced a 23 percent return on their investment, the kind of return that can turn a banker's red line into an okay on a loan application.

Within about ten years there were seven artists' apartment/studio buildings on this block alone, most of them designed by George M. Pollard, with others in the neighborhood, like the Gainsborough Studios on Central Park South. Of them all, the seventeen-story Hotel des Artistes is the largest and most famous—Howard Chandler Chrysty used to live there, and Mr. and Mrs. John Lindsay still do.

The rich, neo-Gothic facade, complete with its statuary above the second floor, is reflected in the interiors of the apartments. Many have wood-paneled dining and living rooms in the style of the English Renaissance, several have beamed ceilings, and almost all have wood-burning fireplaces. Most of the apartments are duplexes, with double-height ceilings in the living rooms and balconies from the bedroom floors overlooking the elegant scene below.

Because of its name, many people mistakenly believe that this cooperative apartment house is now or originally was a hotel. Granted, none of the apartments originally had kitchens, and all the cooking was done in communal kitchens (tenants were provided preparation areas in their apartments, where they could prepare their food to the point of cooking, and then send it down to the kitchens by electric dumbwaiter); telephone switchboard service was provided; and maids could be hired for twenty-five cents an hour. "Hotel" in this case is the second or third meaning in French, a town house or mansion, words that define the quality of the building which is far removed from the usual garret image of *la vie bohème*.

Yale Club   1915

50 Vanderbilt Avenue, at Forty-fourth Street
James Gamble Rogers, Architect

A classic example of the "modernized Italian Renaissance" style that characterized the Terminal group of buildings.

A remarkable thing happened in this area between 1915 and 1930—like Athena, it was born full-grown. A 1914 photograph shows nothing but empty building lots on Park Avenue from about Forty-ninth Street south to Forty-fifth. In the southwest, the most visible building was the Hotel Biltmore. Rising before it was the steel framework of the Yale Club. Fifteen years later and the twenty-one-story Yale Club would be completely obliterated by its neighbors to the north and east, buildings that, like it, were erected on the air rights of the New York Central Railroad.

Architecturally, the style of this remarkable development was fairly homogeneous, something described at the time as the "modernized Italian Renaissance." The few buildings still standing from the period that are in the style include the Biltmore, Barclay, and Roosevelt hotels, and the Postum and Vanderbilt Concourse buildings. The Yale Club is the best-preserved of them all, a classic example of the style that characterized the Terminal group of buildings.

If it were only five stories high, or as high as its rustication, the Yale Club could pass itself off as a Florentine *palazzo*, especially with the easily defensible position it assumes. But it is twenty-one stories, and rising from its base is the brick shaft, with good Renaissance-style balconies added to the facade. The capital comes complete with escutcheon and colonnade, and all is topped by one of New York's greatest cornices. Its twenty-one stories made it the largest building in the world devoted exclusively to clubdom. The lower floors consist of public rooms, and the fifth and sixth floors include a gymnasium, swimming pool, and squash courts. Eleven floors are devoted to 165 bedrooms, all with private baths. (The seventh floor housed a special service for gentlemen members who did not have time between the workday and evening to go home to change into formal attire, with dressing rooms installed especially for the purpose.) The top floors consist entirely of dining rooms and kitchens, while in pre–air-conditioning days, a roof garden topped off the building.

Although entirely fireproof, the fire laws and building codes compelled architect James Gamble Rogers (Yale, '89) to include three interior fire stairs, evidently to his disliking—in his eyes they were redundant and took up so much space that he was forced to abandon his plans for ceremonial stairs.

When the club opened in the fall of 1915, its week-long celebrations started on a propitiously festive note—Yale beat Princeton in football.

Equitable Building   1915

120 Broadway, between Pine and Cedar streets
Graham, Anderson, Probst & White, Architects

The last of the buildings to rise straight up from the building line—this one for forty stories—blocking the sun from the streets below. In its shadow, the City wrote the Zoning Law of 1916, requiring setbacks for future skyscrapers.

One of the clichés that describe the Financial District is the "canyons of Wall Street." Cliché or not, the canyons are there, canyons where sunlight seldom reaches the sidewalks below, canyons that rise straight up for 500 feet or more, canyons created not by erosion but by greed.

It was buildings like the Equitable—an H-shaped edifice that rises 537½ feet, or forty stories, straight up from the building line without a setback—that created those canyons. At its completion it had room for 15,000 workers on 1,200,000 square feet, or 45 acres, of floor space, all built on a plot only slightly larger than an acre.

It's not that other buildings were any better—the Liberty Tower (at Liberty and Nassau streets) is 401 feet high on a plot of land that measures only 58 by 82 feet, and 108–112 West Fortieth Street was proud to be the world's tallest office building ever erected on its size plot—it's just that no other building flaunted its bulk so cavalierly. The City realized that this madness could not continue.

As early as 1885 New York City had passed a law restricting the height of apartment houses to 70 feet on streets and avenues not wider then 60 feet, and to 80 feet on avenues wider than 60 feet. By 1913 the law had changed, stipulating that apartment houses could be no higher than one-and-a-half times the width of the street. In 1916 the city was divided into commercial and residential zones, and allowable building heights were regulated within each zone. It was the first zoning law written in the country, and it said that some areas were "zoned" for taller buildings, especially in commercial areas, and some were zoned for not such tall buildings, as on residential side streets. For builders of all types of buildings, commercial or residential, the Zoning Law of 1916 said one thing that would affect the city's skyline more than anything, except technology, for the next fifty years: buildings could start at the building line, but above a certain height they had to be set back from that line. To find the height of the setback, an imaginary hypotenuse was drawn from the center of the street to the perpendicular of the building. Where the line hit the building, a setback was required. To keep every building from looking like a pyramid, the law said that a building could go as high as the builder wanted to take it, so long as the tower was built on no more than 25 percent of the site.

With this in mind, it is understandable why the Equitable Building will probably remain standing until an act of God knocks it down: no builder today could get as much bulk from the site as this building claimed in 1915.

St. Bartholomew's Church (L)   1918

Park Avenue between Fiftieth and Fifty-first streets
Porch, 1903; dome, 1930
Bertram Grosvenor Goodhue, Architect; porch, McKim, Mead & White

One of the earliest of Park Avenue's second-generation buildings, this church is distinguished by its three-portal porch from a former edifice.

This was the edge of the city when the F. & M. Schaefer Brewing Company built its brewery here in the 1860s, with railroad tracks at grade and only other brewers and manufacturers, like Steinway Pianos, as neighbors. By the 1900s work was progressing on the tunneling and electrification of the approaches to Grand Central Terminal, and by the 1910s there was a paper city along Park Avenue just waiting to be turned into brick and mortar. In 1914 the brewery sold its site for $1.5 million to the congregation of St. Bartholomew's Church, and the second generation of Park Avenue's buildings was begun. It was clearly the avenue to invest in, the one site to have when you were having only one.

Park Avenue would soon be vying with Fifth Avenue in elegance, and its buildings would be grand and ostentatious.

This church, even in its small details, is no exception. Its salmon-colored brick, for instance, was handmade, so there are permutations of color, even of size, providing a rich facade. Its style was, according to its architect, "Romanesque of the Italian type," although Byzantine decoration predominates. Clearly, the Stanford White–designed porch, which is set free of the facade, bears little resemblance to the building. It was not designed for this edifice, but as an addition to its Lombardy-style predecessor, which was designed by James Renwick, Jr. In both roles the porch has acted like a stage flat, added on to the previous church in 1903 and with the new church created around it in 1918, a prop that plays its role of grandeur admirably. Its inspiration was an early Romanesque triple marble porch on the church at St. Gilles in the south of France, a design with which White was smitten in 1878. This porch is one of his few ecclesiastical designs, but it shows his capacity for invention on a borrowed theme and his sagacity at hiring the best to do his sculpting, artists like Daniel Chester French, Philip Martiny, and Herbert Adams, among others. The porch was paid for by Vanderbilt money, and on the bottom of the door (stage left) of the central portal is an inscription in uncial lettering: "To the glory of God and in loving memory of Cornelius Vanderbilt, born 1843, died 1900. These doors are erected by his wife and children."

"Saint Bart's" has always managed to keep up with New York Society, moving from the fashionable Lafayette and Great Jones Street when it became commercial to Madison Avenue and Forty-fourth Street, until that site, too, became commercial. Now the residential neighborhood which St. Bartholomew's moved into has itself been encroached upon. *Plus ça change* . . .

Halloran House   1924

(Originally Shelton Hotel)
Lexington Avenue, southeast corner of Forty-ninth Street
Arthur Loomis Harmon, Architect; remodeled, 1978, Stephen B. Jacobs & Associates

Its thirty-four stories made the Shelton the world's tallest hotel in its time, and its massing and good use of the envelope of space accorded by the zoning law made the design a twofold gold-medal winner.

The Zoning Law of 1916 said that if you wanted to build a building straight up from the building line, you had to set it back above a certain point. If you wanted to build on 25 percent of the site, however, you could take the building straight up as high as you could technologically go. The effect on the skyline would be dramatic, creating slim towers rising from solid bases. If great tall towers were not the builder's goal, however, the law's effect could also be stultifying, leading to buildings with one box monotonously piled atop another, with each cubic mass diminishing in girth.

The first tower erected under the new law was the Heckscher Building at Fifth Avenue and Fifty-seventh Street (1923), considered a clumsy artistic failure. Then came the thirty-four-story Shelton Hotel, the world's tallest hotel in its day, and considered such an aesthetic success that its architect was awarded a gold medal by both the Architectural League of New York and the American Institute of Architects. Because it is a hotel, which necessitated a facade with windows that basically reflect the same-sized room ad nauseam, architect Harmon created a series of vertical recesses, one or two windows wide. These recesses break up the monotony of one room after another horizontally, while creating a third dimension vertically through the shadows created by the recesses. He used entasis in the tower, a slight bulge to overcome the optical illusion of sagging. And on the lower floors he incorporated batter, a slight incline from the vertical to create an illusion of height. But it is the Shelton's basic form and the grouping of its massing that make this building work so well within the envelope of space, making it a building with scale.

It is still eclectic, depending on borrowed interest from the Venetian Gothic and pseudo-Romanesque detailings in its trim. A two-story loggia is its entrance, and variations on its arches are found at the rooflines of each setback. Trefoils, chevrons, vaulting shafts, even the winged lion of St. Mark, were incorporated, but subtly, never overwhelming the building with miscellaneous tripe that could have made it overbearing.

Although women were soon admitted as guests, the Shelton was originally intended as a club-hotel for men only. A swimming pool was in the basement, and the top floors housed a gymnasium and squash courts, activities reflected in the statuary above the capitals in the loggia. Rooftop dining and lounging amidst gazebos were provided on the sixteenth floor setback. The hotel was refurbished and renamed in 1978.

26 Broadway   1924

(Originally the Standard Oil Building)
At Beaver Street, facing Bowling Green
Carrère & Hastings and Shreve, Lamb & Blake, Architects

The clash with reality: the architects wanted a veneer of neoclassicism, the setback law required a tower, but the engineers provided the breakthroughs, including the first push-button elevators.

If you want to catalog classical elements without concerning yourself with classical form, 26 Broadway would be a jolly good place to do it. The building sports the three Greek orders in its columns. It has four floors' worth of serious rustication, and some interesting quoins for the rest of the building. It has balusters and the concomitant balustrades; it has keystones and pediments, obelisks and urns, triglyphs and bisons, rosettes and frets, eggs and darts, dentils, friezes, and antefixes. And topping it off is a twelve-tiered extravaganza of a pyramid surmounted by an urn that seemingly burns incense in the winter, but which is only a cleverly masked vent issuing steam. The architects just couldn't figure out how to make the transition into the 1920s.

The Zoning Law of 1916 stipulated that buildings had to be set back above a specified height. Since 26 Broadway faces Bowling Green, the building's initial setback could be higher than if it faced the usual narrow street in Lower Manhattan, but a setback it has. Its right-angled tower rises from a convex base on Broadway, a base that follows the course of Broadway and, as a result, presents one of New York's more interesting cityscapes.

This pile of Indiana limestone is not really a pile at all, of course, since the limestone is only a skin over a remarkable frame of steel. Work on the building was begun before all the former buildings on the site had been torn down, so the building was erected in sections, around and even over other buildings. A Childs restaurant, for instance, was housed in a five-story building at 3 Beaver Street, with a lease that was not to expire for several years. Undeterred by its presence, the engineers cantilevered the framework over the low-lying building in a virtuoso performance for steel, and the new building was built atop the old. And digging the foundation, the engineers hit water and shale instead of bedrock, requiring a "pan" of steel and concrete to be lowered onto pilings to enclose the cellar in watertight walls.

The marvel in 1924 was not so much the complexity of the building's construction, but the simplicity of its Otis elevators. Gone were the old-fashioned handles that elevator operators pushed one way or another to go up or down, replaced by a tablet with two rows of buttons. For the first time, the operator had only to touch a button for the desired floor, and the elevator would do the rest.

American Radiator Building (L)   1924

40 West Fortieth Street, between Fifth Avenue and the Avenue of the Americas
Raymond Hood, Architect

A free-standing tower with chamfered corners that hinted at things to come, a dramatic shift in the design of office buildings.

Skyscrapers like the Equitable Building had risen straight up as high as they could reach, and others like the Standard Oil Building had risen in towers from setbacks with neo-classical *chotchkes*, but no New York building had ever risen as a pure, unembellished tower from a low base on a midblock site. The American Radiator Building was not as tall as some

150

skyscrapers, nor as dramatically situated as others, but its free-standing tower made a statement about the aesthetics a skyscraper could attain. Gone are the obelisks and urns and Italian Renaissance trim and Francis I windows twenty-five stories up, replaced by a cubist's dream of massing in setback forms that hinted at things to come. The style is beyond the Woolworth Building but has not yet reached the old McGraw-Hill Building.

Furnaces and heaters were the products of the American Radiator Company, so what could be more appropriate for its corporate headquarters than a building that looked like a piece of coal with glowing embers at its terminals. Its black bricks and mortar were selected because architect Hood believed that windows during the day looked like black holes punched into the facade, with their regular spacing making the building look like a waffle. Black makes them less apparent. To accentuate the crown of gold and amber, the top of the building was floodlit to advertise itself in the night sky.

There are no right angles; instead, the corners are chamfered, lending a soft, almost huggable quality to the building. The beveled corners were the result of some elementary deductive reasoning: in a steel-framed building where columns extend to the corners, the corner columns support a quarter as much weight as the interior ones. Hood eliminated the corner columns and cantilevered the three windows and their piers from the columns on either side. It was a building principle whose influence would be felt through the 1930s.

Since the core of the building is taken by elevators, the building's working space is like a square doughnut. And since the building is small, over 90 percent of its floor space is within 25 feet of the windows. Just as the building was created with windows to look out from on all sides, so it was created to be seen from all sides. There are no blank walls anticipating the arrival of buildings next door, nor is there inferior brick in the rear, where supposedly nobody will ever see it. It is an integral part of the block, yet a tower in the city.

New York County Courthouse (L)　　　　1927

60 Centre Street, at Foley Square, between Pearl and Worth streets
Guy Lowell, Architect

It took fourteen years to get this courthouse built, and some funny things happened on the way from the drawing board to its completion.

This is no OTB office. A no-nonsense Corinthian portico indicates that this building serves a governmental purpose of great seriousness and should be approached with reverence. The portico is three columns deep and ten wide, and its richly carved pediment is balanced by three heroic statues, *Law* flanked by *Truth* and *Equity*. The courthouse behind

the portico is hexagonal, built to fill an awkward site, but the building is upstaged by its portico, which to many is the building. This is the so-called Temple of Justice.

What was originally planned was a Palace of Justice, and it was the design for a palace that won the architectural competition for Guy Lowell in 1913. The award-winning design called for an extravaganza of a building. It was round, 500 feet in diameter, and 200 feet high, with Rome's Colosseum as its model. There were four entrances, one every 90 degrees. Each was a four-story-high portico with eight colossal Corinthian columns. Atop each pediment stood eight heroic statues. Between the seventh and tenth floors was a band of Doric pilasters—eighty of them. At least five major cornices girdled the building. There were three setbacks, and sitting on one were eight statuary groups. If true wedding cake architecture had ever had its moment, this would have been its finest hour.

But a funny thing happened on the way from the drawing board. Debates raged over the suitability of the foundation— the site had originally been the Collect, a freshwater pond that had been improperly drained. On the site stood the Five Points Mission House (in the mid-nineteenth century this area was New York's worst slum). During World War I, barracks were built on the site. And by 1919 Lowell's design was considered so outrageously expensive—$21 million— that he submitted the $7 million hexagonal design.

It would still be criticized. It included a private bar for judges, designed during the wet Teens but illegal during the dry Twenties. It was on too grand a scale, but not large enough—an extra $302,000 had to be spent remodeling it even before it opened. It finally cost, according to some estimates, about $30 million. And it seemed to make some people a lot of money—one construction company alone was accused of skimming $500,000 off the top by substituting inferior stone. With figures like that, this courthouse almost belongs in the same league as the one it was built to replace, the notorious Tweed Ring Courthouse.

Sherry-Netherland
Hotel   1927

Fifth Avenue and Fifty-ninth Street, northeast corner
Schultze & Weaver, Architects

With a distinctive Francis I flèche for its roofline, this was the world's tallest apartment hotel when it was built.

The 1920s and 1930s witnessed a great change in the New York skyline. Thirty-, forty-, even fifty-story towers became commonplace, with each of their rooflines making a statement of individualism. Some towers, like the Hotel Pierre or Hampshire House, would end in massive mansard roofs. Others would end in Art Deco detailing, with bolts of electricity emanating from the roof, as in the G. E. Building, or with geometric "Gothic" massing, as in 60 Wall Street. The Ritz Tower would terminate in an obelisk reflecting its neo-classicism, and the Sherry-Netherland Hotel, likewise reflecting its eclecticism, would end in a flèche that would feel at home atop the chapel of a hunting château in the Loire Valley.

The Sherry-Netherland Hotel was built on the site of the former Hotel Netherland, a fourteen-story pile of brownstone built in 1892 during the Romanesque Revival. The Sherry-Netherland's fifteen-story tower alone was to be the height of the old hotel, but it stood atop the twenty-three-story body of the hotel-apartments, making the thirty-eight-story building 570 feet high and the tallest apartment hotel in the world at the time. The building occupies the entire lot up to the

twenty-fourth floor, and tiled terraces were built on the setback for the private use of a few residents.

Elegance in the form of the Loire Valley of Francis I was
used for the motif. The roofline is complete with gargoyles,
neo–Loire Valley window frames, and the flèche (one wag
quipped that the "flèche was willing but the spirit was not").
The walls of the entrance to the lobby are lined with sculptured panels that were salvaged from the mansion of William
K. Vanderbilt, designed by Richard Morris Hunt and demolished in 1925. Most of the tower floors had only one apartment each, with living rooms averaging an ample 17 by 31
feet. A duplex was installed on the thirty-sixth and thirty-
seventh floors.

After the building had been topped out, one of New
York's most spectacular fires occurred. The fire started after
quitting time on the wooden scaffolding that surrounded the
building, and soon the scaffolding was enveloped in flames.
No water could be brought to the upper floors because the
standpipes were not operating, and the fire department's
pumpers were useless. Burning embers landed on roofs for
blocks around, threatening a huge conflagration. By mideve-
ning the fire had attracted so great a crowd that to get a good
view some swells rented rooms at the Plaza with Fifth Avenue exposures.

The usual calls for reform ensued, as did one modest
proposal, this from architect Schultze—that the tower be
equipped with large tanks of water and a 200-horsepower
pump that would throw a stream of water one block, the
device to be used as auxiliary fire-fighting equipment for the
fire department. If it was ever installed, nobody seems to
know about it.

Fred F. French Building   1927

551 Fifth Avenue, northeast corner of Forty-fifth
Street
Fred F. French Company, Architects

*A classic example of a 1920s setback office building with
faience at the setbacks and covering the water tower.*

The tops of skyscrapers are a whole study unto themselves.
Some tops are pyramids, others are mini-Parthenons, while
still others are choragic monuments or belvederes. The Fred
F. French Building was one of the first to end with a flat
roof—no Renaissance-style cornice, no statuary, nothing but
a flat plane. Below the roofline, and cleverly masking the
water tower, is New York's most colorful faience, and some
of New York's most arcane symbolism to boot. The architect
who designed the thirty-eight-story office building was H. D.
Ives, who believed that a building's intended use should be
expressed by decorative symbols. Since this edifice was to be
the flagship building of the Fred F. French Company, one of
New York's most prestigious real-estate companies (Tudor
City, finished in the same year, was one of French's developments), the symbolism had to speak of the company. And

since the building was a commercial one, the symbolism likewise had to speak of commerce.

The panels on the southern and northern ends of the building show the rising sun as their central motif. This represents progress. Winged griffins, representing integrity and watchfulness, flank the sun, with golden beehives and bees symbolizing thrift and industry. Panels on the east and west sides contain stylized heads of Mercury, the god of commerce.

The building is elegantly detailed, with bands of faience at the setbacks, and with massive bronze doors and a frieze of Assyrian griffins above the first floor. To define the building as a skyscraper with neo-Assyrian trim, however, is ludicrous, and even architect Ives admitted that he was at a loss to describe the building in historical terms. Suffice it to say that here is a building designed to fill the maximum envelope of space allowed under the law—and in 1927 that meant setbacks—a building that did it artfully, with ziggurat setbacks climbing up the east end of it, and with a seemingly free-standing tower in its west end on Fifth Avenue. It is such a classic example of setback architecture that the *American Heritage Dictionary* used a picture of this building to illustrate the word "setback." As a newspaper advertisement proudly proclaimed in 1926, "these tower office floors are as perfect as human ingenuity can produce."

The building's 78½-by-200-foot corner lot was described as being "at the peak of commercial Fifth Avenue," and was brought for $275 a square foot. Fifteen years earlier, the peak of residential Fifth Avenue (998) had cost about a third as much. The boom was on.

Hearst Magazine Building   1928

(Originally International Magazine Building)
959 Eighth Avenue, between Fifty-sixth and
Fifty-seventh streets
Joseph Urban and George B. Post & Sons,
Architects

*A peculiarly stunted building that makes the transition to a
modernist's use of classical elements.*

"A beautiful building is the sandwich board of its owner,"
said the quotable architect Joseph Urban, and for William
Randolph Hearst this was a sandwich board that was a hero.
It is one of the earliest New York buildings to make the transition to sculptural modernism, in both its architectural elements and its statuary by Henry Kreis (from left to right, *Sport
and Industry, Comedy and Tragedy, Music and Art, Printing
and the Sciences*). The building's facade incorporated classical ornamentation, but its classical elements differed from
the ones used by the traditional neo-classicists—Joseph Urban's were stylized studies in geometry that hinted at the Art
Deco to come. Some elements were outsized, like the keystone over the arched entrance and the urns that act as finials,
and some elements were, by contrast, diminutive, like the
balusters. It was all for effect, "wedding beauty to ballyhoo,"
as Urban described his style.

Urban was first and foremost a set designer whose cath-
olicity embraced the Metropolitan Opera and Ziegfeld's Follies with equal fervor. While at the Follies he met Marion
Davies, and through Davies, William Randolph Hearst. Hearst
hired Urban to design sets for some of Marion Davies's movies, including *Little Old New York*, which premiered at the
Cosmopolitan Theater on Columbus Circle, renovated for the
occasion after Urban's designs in 1923. By 1928 Urban had
designed the Ziegfeld Theatre for Florenz Ziegfeld, the International Magazine Building for Hearst, as well as a pro-

posal for his third employer, the Metropolitan Opera (the Ziegfeld Theatre was demolished by 1967 to make way for Burlington House, and his Met design was never built).

This building seems stunted, as if it were striving to be more than it is, as if its colossal columns should be doing something more. The building occupies a 200-by-200-foot site, yet only the first two of its floors are built to the property line, and although it has only six stories, it has six elevator shafts, a ratio of elevators to floors that is double or triple the norm. All of these peculiarities make sense with the realization that the building was designed to be constructed in two parts, its six-story base first, and a further seven stories added at some undetermined later date. The building's foundations and steel columns were calculated to support the additional weight, as, clearly, was its scale.

This site was zoned for residential use in the 1920s, and the original building application was turned down. A variance was granted, resulting in a westward extension of commerce, making the west side of Eighth Avenue a buffer zone.

Paul Laurence Dunbar Apartments (L) 1928

Bounded by Seventh Avenue, 149th Street,
Eighth Avenue, and 150th Street
Andrew J. Thomas, Architect

An experiment in cooperative housing for middle-class blacks in Harlem that failed.

In the 1880s the coming of the elevated railroad awakened the sleepy village of Harlem. By the 1890s, row after row of one-family brownstone homes had been built, and by 1910 large and luxurious apartment houses lined the wide north-south thoroughfares. The traditional pattern that plagues so many speculative real-estate ventures plagued Harlem—it developed too much too fast, and supply soon exceeded demand. European immigration was shut off during World War I, and Southern rural blacks started flooding the city for jobs. Since the apartment houses in Harlem provided a ready housing stock, blacks started moving into the vacancies.

Like most immigrant groups, the majority of the Southern blacks were either single or members of small family groups. They could not use the large apartments nor could they afford the high rents, so boarders were taken in or the apartments were broken up into small ones. When blacks moved into apartments, white home-owners started moving out. With more people living here and paying more for less—the average working-class white paid approximately 20 percent of his wages for rent, while the average black Harlemite paid 33 percent or more—Harlem had become the worst slum in the city by the time these model houses were built.

It was John D. Rockefeller, Jr., who decided to do something about the egregious housing conditions for blacks in Harlem. In the tradition of the City & Suburban Homes, he built this group of six five-story buildings with 513 apartments on only 49.7 percent of the site, devoting more than half the area to light and air, with gardens, courts, and playgrounds. But these apartments were cooperative, with a down payment of $50 a room required, and monthly charges averaged about $14.50 a room. Every room was designed to have cross ventilation, lodgers were banned, and a nursery was provided. Tenants were carefully screened, and only middle-class blacks were accepted. The serious plight of the underemployed and the underhoused was, therefore, ignored.

Came the Depression and the newly affluent middle-class blacks, as well as other minorities and women, dropped a financial notch. Rents that had been affordable in the 1920s suddenly became oppressive. What had happened to Harlem twenty years earlier happened in microcosm to the model apartments—lodgers were allowed in, large apartments were broken up, and the halcyon days were over. Although the cooperative venture failed and the apartments became rental in 1936, the deterioration that has plagued Harlem since World War II has not happened here.

Helmsley Building   1929

(Originally New York Central Building)
230 Park Avenue, straddling Park Avenue
between Forty-fifth and Forty-sixth streets
Warren & Wetmore, Architects

With a variation on the Baroque outside and George F. Babbitt Modern decor inside, this building set the scale and tone for the Park Avenue of the 1920s.

Here's a piece of urban design that worked. For fifty blocks
north of Forty-sixth Street you could see the New York Central Building straddling Park Avenue, its embracing arms
continuing the cornice line and enclosing the vista, its thirty-
five stories acting as the avenue's capstone and setting its
tone. It was built to command, built to consume conspicu-
ously, built to convey the power and the glory that was the
New York Central Railroad.

Now the railroad is bankrupt, the building's name is not
the same, and the scale of Park Avenue has changed. Where
there had been buildings fifteen to twenty stories high in the
1920s, fifty-story-plus towers had appeared by the 1960s.
With the coming of the Pan Am Building in 1963, the New
York Central Building was dwarfed almost to the point of
obliteration.

It is unfortunate, because this building, from its monumental entrance to its frieze of bisons and its splendid crowning lantern, is absolutely glorious. The tower is essentially
a Baroque drum, complete with a band of Corinthian columns
supported by volutes, only it is square, and the roof is a pyramid instead of a dome. This rectilinear tower is flanked by
curvilinear wings. The facade was refurbished in 1978, when
some architectural ornamentation was gilded as well.

The lobby is unadulterated George F. Babbitt Modern,
one of the most ornate in the city, a drummer's paradise. Its
walls are of travertine and Jaspé Oriental marble. Great rococo
grilles support elevator indicators; and the elevators, although now automatic, still retain ceilings with clouds drift-
ing lazily in the painted sky.

This is one of Grand Central Terminal's "air rights"
building. It had to be built on stilts over two levels of tracks,
a problem further complicated by the tracks and platforms of

one level not aligning with the tracks and platforms of the other. Compound the problem by the vibrations caused by the seven hundred trains that daily rumbled in and out of the terminal, and the solution is an engineering marvel. The steel columns are insulated with lead and asbestos. When columns and tracks are adjacent, a 4-inch layer of compressed cork has been placed between them. It adds up to a floating building. (You can stand with one foot on Park Avenue and the other in the building and feel the vibrations outside but not inside.)

The great arches through the building funnel automobile traffic onto Grand Central's elevated "circumferential plaza." Just as the engineers separated the building from track vibrations, so they separated it from automobile vibrations. The building has two holes punched through it, with the viaducts separate from it within their own tunnels.

55 Central Park West 1929

Southwest corner, Sixty-sixth Street
Schwartz & Gross, Architects

Under the spell cast by Art Deco, Schwartz & Gross designed this apartment house around the theme of the ziggurat in form, trim, even brickwork.

The 1920s did indeed revolutionize the nation. Even if most Americans had never seen Paree, there was a new kind of elegance in the air, and by the end of the decade it was finding its way into brick and mortar.

Schwartz & Gross, who had been designing Renaissance-style apartment houses on the Upper West Side for twenty years, fell under the spell of the decorative arts show held in 1925 in Paris (*l'Exposition des Arts Decoratifs*: hence, Art Deco). Just as the Armory Show had synthesized modern art a dozen years earlier, the Paris show on decorative arts synthesized modernity and influenced all commercial and dec-

orative art, from magazine covers to automobiles and architecture. The theoreticians did not believe that less was more:
theirs was a philosophy somewhat to the left of the glitzier
the better. The accent was on geometry, with stylized Aztec
and Egyptian art frequently incorporated into the design.

At 55 Central Park West, a ziggurat building itself, the
architects took the ziggurat as their theme, incorporating
three-dimensional ziggurats as buttresses and finials, always
in the style of building blocks, always lower on the flanks
and rising to the apogee. The theme is even incorporated in
the awning, a whole ziggurat skyline in microcosm. Adding
to the overall look of the ziggurat is the brickwork, an expensive undertaking with reddish-brown bricks at the base
that decrease in intensity until they are pale beige at the top
of the building.

The apartments on the setback floors are generally large
(up to nine rooms), and have terraces. However, most of the
apartments range in size from three rooms to six. The building boasted sunken living rooms, which became a hallmark
for apartments during the next decade. The building also
boasted that the "ideal six-room suite . . . is actually a seven-
room apartment, for the gallery is 17 feet long and 9 feet
wide." Looking at the building from across Central Park West
you can find this "six-room suite" or "seven-room apartment" by counting windows. The third window from the left
is the 15-by-25-foot living room, the fourth is a 12-by-20-foot
bedroom, the fifth is a bathroom, and the sixth is a 13-by-20-
foot bedroom. The dining room (16 by 17 feet), kitchen (9 by
12 feet), pantry (5 by 13 feet), and maid's room (10 by 8 feet)
all overlook the rear court of this U-shaped building.

Chrysler Building (L)   1930

405 Lexington Avenue, between Forty-second
and Forty-third streets
William Van Alen, Architect

*Its Art Deco spire, the ultimate architectural statement of the
Jazz Age, made the Chrysler Building the first structure to top
the Eiffel Tower.*

The race was on during the 1920s for the world's tallest
building, and it was neck and neck between 40 Wall Street
and the Chrysler Building. Architect Van Alen released his
plans, claiming that the Chrysler Building would rise 925
feet. Construction on 40 Wall halted two feet higher.

The surprise came when the unannounced Art Deco
spire was bolted into place above the radiant arches. It created the Chrysler Building's most distinguishing feature and
brought its height to 1,048 feet. That made it 64 feet higher
than the Eiffel Tower, and the world's tallest building until
the Empire State Building opened in 1931.

Van Alen had originally designed it as a speculative office building, but Walter P. Chrysler bought the lease on the
property. Van Alen and his plans went with the deal. It was

Chrysler himself who asked Van Alen to design a distinctive tower (the original plan called for a stunted, mosquelike dome). Presumably Chrysler also asked for the automobile icons, like the winged Mercury radiator caps and the frieze of hubcaps and mudguards on the setback at the base of the tower. Van Alen used geometric patterns throughout the entire facade, including triangles in the spire and bands of chevrons and stripings in the tower.

The sleek, mirrorlike quality of stainless steel made it a favorite Art Deco building material, even though it was exorbitantly expensive. There is probably more of it on the Chrysler Building than on any other New York building. Its finials, its radiator caps, its gargoyles, and its spire are all made of stainless steel.

The walls of the Lexington Avenue lobby are lined with expensive African marble, the lighting is indirect, and the shape of the lobby is reflected in a perfect ziggurat in the ceiling. An artist's rendering of the building itself is painted on the ceiling, with its spire pointing, like a compass, to the west. The elevator doors are like a field of blooming flowers on a cubist's canvas. And everywhere, it is sleek, it is chic, it is "modern."

Daily News Building   1930

220 East Forty-second Street, between Second and Third avenues
Howells & Hood, Architects

Reduce a building to its simplest cubistic forms, peel off all ornamental trim, rely on bands of windows and dark spandrels to achieve an illusion of height, and you have the Daily News Building.

Until the Daily News Building was built in 1930, skyscrapers usually ended with elaborate temples, mansard roofs, flèches, choragic monuments, anything but an extension of the tower itself. Raymond Hood, however, decided to top off this thirty-seven-story building and hide the water towers not by building a baroque extravaganza, as his peers were doing, but by extending the tower and creating an unbroken look. For his extended tower Hood used entasis, an idea perfected by the Greeks in their columns. Entasis fights the optical illusion of concavity, or sagging, by incorporating a slight convex curving of the vertical.

To achieve an illusion of height, Hood set dark, vertical stripes into the white brick walls at regularly spaced intervals. Within the bands, windows alternate with red and black brick spandrels. In one of the greatest manifestations of "form follows function," Hood ascertained the width of the windows—hence the width of the distinctive vertical stripes running up the facade of the building—not by what looked good but by the ease with which a woman could open a window. The widest window that could be opened comfortably, he discovered, was 4½ feet wide, so that's how wide the windows were made.

Since the steel columns only had to flank every other window, Hood figured that he would wind up with a horizontal cross-section that would include a steel column, window, false pier, window, steel column, etc. What to do with the false nonstructural piers was neatly resolved by using them for pipes, conduits, and ducts, necessities that until then had hugged columns.

This radically new tower houses the newspaper's printing presses on its first nine floors—you can see the loading docks on Forty-first Street—with offices above. The lobby was designed to be an area of special interest, the kind of place that acts as a destination for school outings, and it was then and still is filled with meteorological paraphernalia. A huge revolving globe is set into the floor. When it was unveiled, it was spinning the wrong way.

The New School for Social Research   1930

66 West Twelfth Street, between Fifth Avenue
and the Avenue of the Americas
Joseph Urban, Architect

A glass and masonry bay is cantilevered from a frame of black granite, an elemental design with a high degree of refinement and sophistication.

Joseph Urban's design for the New School is so elemental that is seems implausible that no New York building had ever looked like it before. It is basically a square front, or cube, cantilevered from a square frame. The bay facade consists of horizontal bands of glass in rolled-steel window frames that are painted black. The continuous bands of windows, which wrap themselves around the corners, alternate with continuous horizontal bands of black and pale-buff brick spandrels. This glass and masonry bay is projected from a frame of Coopersberg black granite, the bay finding the perfect foil in the slick, polished frame, with everything reduced to basic forms.

This seems such a perfect piece of straight-edged geometry because Urban accounted for the ancient realization that perfectly perpendicular buildings sometimes create the illusion of leaning outward, so he battered the cantilevered

164

section, setting back the sills a few inches every foot. As a result, the top floor is cantilevered over the street one foot less than the second floor.

The design, especially the building's coloration, went through several permutations. Urban believed that architecture should be colorful and vibrant. For the New School he tried various color schemes, including window frames that were yellow or blue or green, colors that would play off the horizontal bandings of mortar. He also tried white masonry against silver window frames, with the name of the New School running along the bottom spandrel from edge to edge in a sans-serif, block typeface. His final design called for muted tones for the facade, but with color behind the windows provided by the walls of the classrooms, which were to be painted in vibrant hues.

The idea for the design stems directly from the notion that form follows function. Fire stairs and elevators are ordinarily windowless, so they are housed within the windowless frame that flanks the building. Classrooms need natural light as well as peace and quiet, so the windows are double-paned, insulating the classrooms from street noises (the insulation factor is twofold since the double-paned windows also reduce heating bills by 25 percent). And since classroom routine creates an ebb and flow of students and the concomitant bunching, the 3-foot overhang acts as an awning, so when crowds try to enter the building in the rain, they are protected by the building itself.

River House   1931

433–437 East Fifty-second Street, between First
Avenue and a dead end at the FDR Drive
Bottomley, Wagner & White, Architects

*An ambivalent design for what is indubitably a "posh"
cooperative apartment building, one that used to sport its
own private dock on the East River.*

There are apartment houses and apartment houses. At the Sovereign, 425 East Fifty-eighth Street, where the rents are reputedly the highest of any new apartment building in the city ($765 to $2,130 a month), the tenants talk about the residents of River House as being "posh." Its sixty-four "suites" originally consisted of simplex and duplex apartments ranging from eight to thirteen rooms in the fourteen-story body of the building. In the tower were only duplexes, all with seventeen rooms and seven bathrooms, with a triplex on the twenty-fourth, twenty-fifth, and twenty-sixth floors. The triplex also had seventeen rooms, but with nine bathrooms, terraces on every level, and a purchase price in the depths of the Depression of $275,000. River House was not then, nor is it now, an ordinary cooperative apartment house.

The building was erected on the easternmost plot of a 200-by-200 foot site, with a landscaped driveway in the west. Before the FDR Drive was built, the East River lapped at the side of the building, a la Venice. Tied up to River House and

accessible by private entrance was a floating dock to harbor the yachts of the tenants and any passing Astors. (Another building with a private dock was built at about the same time. Designed by Cross & Cross, it is at Gracie Square, and originally bore the unfortunate name of Watergate.) What was once a riverside terrace is still used by tenants for private parties. Another deluxe feature, this one incorporated within the building, is the River Club, complete with squash and tennis courts.

Clearly the architects could not make up their minds about the best style for River House, an ambivalence that is manifested in microcosm in the gates. Ziggurated, molded, Art Deco stanchions topped by stylized eagles flank rococo iron gates, disparate styles that would ordinarily clash yet seem to work fine together, with a willing suspension of disbelief. Ambivalencies and all, the architects were awarded an honorable mention for their design of a tower-type apartment house by *Architectural Record,* the tower, of course, mandated by the zoning laws. (A bonus from setbacks is that they provide the terraces that had come into vogue among luxury-apartment dwellers by the end of the 1920s.)

Before the building was even completed, Marshall Field and William Rhinelander Stewart had already bought apartments in it. Further proof that this building was indeed first class: twenty of the mechanics who worked on it were awarded certificates for their skilled and superior craftsmanship by the New York Building Congress.

326 West Forty-second
Street 1931

(Originally the McGraw-Hill Building)
Between Eighth and Ninth avenues
Hood & Fouilhoux, Architects

*Volume that is geometrically bounded with absolute
regularity and minimal decoration: in short, the International
Style.*

The thirty-four stories that comprise the McGraw-Hill Building's distinctive setback silhouette still stand out in the New
York skyline. In 1931 the building was like a beacon. To
begin with, its facade is green (it might have been Prince-
tonian black and orange, or even Chinese red). Alternating
with the bands of sea-green terra cotta are bands of windows that stretch horizontally across the facade, windows
that open corners and daringly reveal the building's steel
frame. And there is hardly any decoration, no pseudo-Greek
temples or friezes of locomotives or ears of corn.

Instead of mass there is volume; and instead of schmaltz,
there is minimal decoration. In short, here are the tenets of
the International Style as laid down by Henry-Russell Hitchcock and Philip Johnson in their book, *The International
Style*. This was the only New York building included in their
book, but they believed it still lacked the essence, the purity
of the movement begun at the Bauhaus and synthesized in
Mies van der Rohe's "less is more." They felt, for instance,
that McGraw-Hill's crowning pyramidal feature was "unnecessary" and "inexcusably heavy," a feature that nevertheless captures for others all those fantastic, futuristic designs
in Raymond Massey movies of the 1930s.

Within a year of each other, and on the same street, the

167

New York Daily News Building had opened east of Third Avenue and the McGraw-Hill Building had opened west of Eighth. Why were two of the most daringly avant-garde skyscrapers of their time, both housing socially acceptable businesses, so remote from the prestigious avenues between Fifth and Lexington? Just as the Zoning Law of 1916 explains setbacks and towers on broad bases, so the new law explains the placement of both buildings. Light industry had been zoned out of the heart of midtown, and since both buildings housed printing presses as well as offices, both were forced beyond the pale.

When McGraw-Hill took occupancy, the Depression was not yet a word to be capitalized, and the publishing company needed 75 percent of the space. By 1939 the publishing company occupied only 34 percent, and its printing presses had long been sold. But the building had been a bargain, only $6.47 a square foot, or little more than the average loft building of its day. Not a bad price to pay, considering it included the initiation fees into the prestigious International Style Club. What a pity for McGraw-Hill that it is now headquartered in the antiseptic corporate row on the Avenue of the Americas.

Century Apartments   **1931**

25 Central Park West, between Sixty-second and Sixty-third streets
Irwin Chanin, Architect

This twin-towered apartment house wears a brave, new, and worldly style.

Four twin-towered apartment houses were built on Central Park West within about a year of each other. One of them, the San Remo (Seventy-fourth to Seventy-fifth streets), fell prey to neo-classical trim, including choragic monuments to hide its water towers. Another, the El Dorado (Ninety-first to Ninety-second streets), was trimmed in Art Deco. The Majestic (Seventy-first to Seventy-second streets) and the Century, both designed and built by Irwin Chanin, are cool, cut down to their essentials, with bold massing and clear statements of strength.

The Century maintains a delicate balance between vertical and horizontal elements. Six sets of bay windows run up the building's base. Tempering the vertical thrust is the fenestration of the corner apartments, where sets of casement windows wrap themselves around the cantilevered frame. The horizontality is accentuated by cantilevered concrete terraces at the breaking point between the body of the building and its towers, a motif that is reflected again in the building's soaring capstones, its water towers.

The office of Irwin Chanin had its own engineering, construction, and interior decoration departments, all of which contributed to time- and labor-saving amenities that were built into these apartments. And there were novel permutations, such as one-bedroom duplexes, and old standards of luxury, including eleven-room apartments with mini-level changes. The rear court, which in a lesser building would have been barren concrete, is instead a landscaped garden.

The Century's building site teaches a good lesson in real-estate economics. Even then, the only economical development was large scale, and the sale that was easily closed was the best one. To assemble a vast plot was becoming increasingly more difficult, especially if the management had to go to many separate owners. Word spreads that a big deal is about to be made, owners hold out, and the price of the land becomes inflated. This makes buildings on large sites particularly vulnerable, especially if they are only marginally profitable. The sale of this site was consummated in one deal—with the owners of the Century Theatre, a huge, neo-classical building that had stood on the site for only twenty-one years. Many of the city's landmarks, like the original Waldorf-Astoria, the old Metropolitan Opera, the Hotel Savoy Plaza, and the Astor Hotel have vanished as a result of such easily made deals.

Starrett-Lehigh Building   1931

Twenty-sixth to Twenty-seventh streets, Eleventh to Twelfth avenues
Russell G. Cory and Walter M. Cory, Architects; Yasuo Matsui, Associate Architect; Purdy & Henderson, Designing Engineers

One of the greatest examples of concrete column-and-slab framing behind one of the most dramatic skins a building ever wore.

Great horizontal bands of concrete, brown brick, and glass alternate with each other for nineteen stories of undulating rhythm in this building that combines manufacturing, freight handling, and warehousing. Built over the tracks of the Lehigh Valley Railroad, the Starrett-Lehigh Building was originally designed so that fully-loaded boxcars could be transported from the tracks below to the warehouse above, but the tracks within the building were never installed. Nevertheless, three elevators acted as a "vertical street," linking the railroad spurs to all floors.

Today, the railroad tracks have been torn up and freight is delivered by trucks. Those as long as twenty-nine feet and weighing as much as fifteen tons can be taken upstairs directly to the desired floor by one of the three elevators.

This huge building, with some ceilings as high as 20 feet and the lower floors with 124,000 square feet of floor space, has been the scene of some interesting goings-on. San Benito wines were made on the third floor, or the "cellar in the clouds," from the end of Prohibition until the 1950s. A "cottage"—complete with garden—was built on the roof in 1937 and lived in for three years by Mr. and Mrs. Ludwig while they tested new materials and products. And when the Ludwigs weren't living on the roof, a flock of homing pigeons was.

The frame for the building is fascinating. The first two stories are traditional steel columns and girders supporting concrete slabs. The mezzanine supports the floor above by trusses and is a transitional floor. Above it, the concrete slabs—none thicker than 8¼ inches—are supported by concrete columns with mushroom capitals that spread the concentrated load over a large area. Since the slabs are cantilevered at least 8 feet from the center of the peripheral columns, the curtain wall can contain the unobstructed bands of concrete, brick, and glass.

The windows, too, are fascinating. You will notice a subtle change in the windows within the bandings, those opening from the lower second- and third-fifth of the band alternating with windows opening from the upper third- and fourth-fifth of the bands.

The center of the building, on Twenty-sixth Street, is a classic example of the setback law of 1916.

The Starrett-Lehigh Building spawned many ideas for later office buildings, including Frank Lloyd Wright's Johnson Wax Building in Racine, Wisconsin (1939), the Look Building in New York (1950), and Philip Johnson's Post Oak Central Building in Houston (1977). This is indeed an influential though often overlooked building.

Waldorf-Astoria Hotel   1931

301 Park Avenue, between Forty-ninth and Fiftieth streets
Schultze & Weaver, Architects

The Park Avenue of the 1920s suddenly encountered the sleek elegance of 1930s Art Deco, and a whole new scale was born.

The buildings that were erected over the New York Central's air rights during the 1920s were considered majestic, but just a few years later their majesty was eclipsed by the new elegance and scale of the Waldorf-Astoria's 625-foot towers rising forty-seven stories above Park Avenue. It was a scale that changed Park Avenue and New York's hotels as well (you could very neatly have tucked the original Waldorf-Astoria into the body of this one).

The glory of this Waldorf is that it was no pale imitation of the original's Victorian elegance. It was up to date, chic, what some described as "modernistic" and others called Art Deco. Its strong massing reveals two buildings—the 1,800-room hotel topped by apartments in a pair of towers reaching for an Art Deco sky. (The Waldorf Towers have a private entrance, complete with concierge, on Fiftieth Street.) The Waldorf's building plans were filed on July 25, 1929, and its construction was underwritten by bankers a month later, two months before Black Tuesday. Construction forged ahead regardless. From the White House on opening day came a nationwide broadcast by President Hoover (there was a radio in every room at the Waldorf) describing the Waldorf's completion as an "exhibition of . . . confidence to the whole nation."

Little had been spared to deserve the accolade. To decorate one ballroom, paneled walls from the estate at Basildon Park, England, had been shipped over. Mantels of English design had been certified by a curator of the Victoria & Albert Museum, London; likewise, mantels of French design had been certified by a curator of the Carnavalet Museum, Paris. So that guests arriving by private railroad car could circumvent ordinary railroad stations, a private siding was constructed from the New York Central's tracks. (The Waldorf is built over the New York Central's air rights; the lobby is up one flight, the kitchens up two.) The grand ballroom and adjoining salons could be joined by sleight of hand to constitute the largest entertainment suite in the nation, accommodating six thousand guests. On the Park Avenue setback was the Starlight Room, with a ceiling that could be rolled back, revealing real starlight for the revelers on pleasant evenings. By the end of the 1930s all public rooms would be air-conditioned.

It seems fitting that what was dubbed "The Unofficial Palace of New York" is still one of New York's grandest hotels, and a direct descendant of New York's first, the Astor House.

Empire State Building   1931

350 Fifth Avenue, between Thirty-third and
Thirty-fourth streets
Shreve, Lamb & Harmon, Architects

Although no longer the world's tallest building, the Empire State Building and its distinctive Art Deco styling still symbolize the skyscraper to millions.

It took architects Shreve, Lamb & Harmon sixteen attempts to come up with a design for the Empire State Building that pleased them and the corporation. The building as they conceived it was to reach the dizzying height of eighty-six stories, or 1,100 feet.

To observe the zoning laws, the architects figured out

the volume of air with which they could work. Then they cut away at the building's girth, taking the cubic area that they cut away and adding it to the top, as if they were modeling in clay. What they designed was a five-story base for the building, with the tower rising from a 60-foot-wide terrace, the building's major setback. To create an even greater illusion of height than the slim, eighty-six-story building had on its own merits, the architects added gleaming stainless-steel mullions running up its sides, and set windows flush with the limestone curtain wall, creating a smooth facade.

But then one of the building's backers took another look at the design and decided it appeared unfinished. He said it needed a hat. So late in 1929 Alfred E. Smith, former governor and presidential candidate, and then president of the Empire State Building, announced that the building would be equipped for an age of transportation that was then only a dream of aviation pioneers—a zeppelin mooring mast, lifting the building's height from 86 stories to 102, or 1,250 feet. The zeppelin mooring mast never worked, of course, but the building was given a hat as distinctive as Al Smith's derby.

The building rose at the astonishing rate of four-and-a-half stories a week and was finished in less than the anticipated time. At $40,948,900, it cost less than the original estimate.

The dream building, envisioned in the boom of the Twenties but finished in the bust of the Thirties, opened in 1931 to great fanfare but few rentals, and it was soon nicknamed The Empty State Building. It has survived the Depression, as well as the B-25 that crashed into its seventy-ninth floor one foggy Saturday morning in 1945, and although it is no longer the world's tallest (Chicago's Sears Tower holds the record today, and the World Trade Towers are tied for second), it is, nevertheless, enduring.

Irving Trust Company Building   1931

1 Wall Street, between Broadway and New Street
Voorhees, Gmelin & Walker, Architects

A stylized flame is the motif for this elegantly restrained Art Deco building, a tower that would be one of the last to rise in the Financial District for the next thirty years.

There are subtleties to the plasticity of this fifty-story building that reveal themselves only gradually. The whole building is created to appear as a grooved shaft, with concave spandrels that accentuate shadows and with some piers that are brought forward to add even greater shading. At first glance the building appears to be one sheer tower, but setbacks begin at about the twentieth floor, and the tower is indeed only a tower. The body of the building is about eighteen windows wide on Broadway, the tower only six. Nevertheless, a sensation of great verticality is provided, an effect the architect was clearly seeking. Just as Shreve, Lamb & Harmon had cut away at the flanks of the Empire State Building and added the volume to increase the tower's height, so architect Ralph Walker cut away at the girth of the Irving Trust Company Building. However, he cut away right down to the first floor by making the corners beveled, a fact clearly evidenced by the brass property-line indicator in the pavement at the corner of Wall and New streets.

The spandrels carry a stylized flame motif the entire height of the building, a motif that burns itself into visitors' memories in the three-story-high banking room on Wall Street. Walls, columns, and even the ceiling are all covered in Venetian glass mosaic, with the flame as the motif.

The bank moved into its new headquarters with the same kind of military precision National City Bank had pulled off twenty-three years before (see page 28). Armored trucks that could beat off a gas attack bristled with machine-gun-toting guards as $3 billion in gold bullion, securities, and currency was transferred into the bank's vaults. Once its assets were in the vaults, management breathed easier, because these were no ordinary vaults. Only those of the Bank of England and the New York Federal Reserve Bank were larger than Irving Trust's. They were 72 feet down in bedrock and protected not only by a 6-foot-thick outer wall of concrete, iron, and steel, but by an interior wall of sheets of chrome steel and solidified chemicals. The chemicals would give off paralyzing fumes under the heat of a "cracksman's" torch, or so said the newspapers.

The bank was named for Washington Irving, and its headquarters are at a propitious site—Irving reportedly began work on Diedrich Knickerbocker's *A History of New York from the Beginning of the World to the End of the Dutch Dynasty* while living at 3 Wall Street, the very spot where the mosaic-lined banking room now stands.

George Washington Bridge   1931

From 178th and 179th streets across the Hudson River to Fort Lee, New Jersey
Second deck, 1962
Othmar H. Ammann, Engineer; Cass Gilbert, Architect

Its record as the world's largest suspension bridge was short lived, but its grace is timeless.

John Roebling said in 1868 that the Hudson could be bridged, and there was serious consideration given to the idea in the early 1900s. First Twenty-third Street and then Fifty-ninth Street were chosen as natural locations for the sake of business. In the 1920s Othmar Ammann recognized the 179th Street site as a natural location because of its topography—the Palisades on the New Jersey side and Washington Heights on the Manhattan side provided approaches at a height that allowed adequate clearance.

In 1927 work was begun, and when the bridge opened in 1931 it was the world's longest suspension bridge. Its main span is 3,500 feet, the height of its towers is 600 feet, and they add up to one of the most spectacular works of pure structural art, what Le Corbusier described as "the most beautiful bridge in the world."

But it was not planned that way. Tons of cement were waiting to be poured over the towers' steel frames, and the whole pile was to be covered with a facing of granite. The bridge's buoyancy, its grace, would have been drowned in the ponderousness of it all, and the vast geometry of its towers would have been lost. Thank God, as John A. Kouwenhoven says in *The Arts in Modern American Civilization*, "the 'unexpected' functional beauty of the steelwork fascinated people, and there was widespread popular protest against applying the masonry covering. . . ." The outcry, coupled with the realization on behalf of the Port Authority of New York and New Jersey that the amount of money budgeted for the casing could never be spent painting the girders to protect them, led the Port Authority to overlook Cass Gilbert's design.

Originally, too, the bridge was intended to have a second deck. The lower deck was not planned for the use of private cars, but for rapid transit. (The Brooklyn and Queensboro bridges both carried streetcars, and the Williamsburg and Manhattan bridges still carry subways.) The Port Authority, however, decided to kill the lower deck. Ammann acquiesced, figuring that the immense weight of the bridge would prevent sway, even without the strengthening trusses. He was right, but looking at the quality of our air today, the Authority was wrong. It only compounded its mistakes in 1962 when the second deck was added for cars.

Cars or no cars, at night its lights make the George Washington Bridge look like a diamond necklace strung across the

Hudson. By day it is a paradox of steel and air, reflecting Ammann's ideal of never making a small thing bigger than it should be, instead making large things light and graceful.

New York Hospital–Cornell Medical Center   1932

Sixty-eighth to Seventy-first streets, east of York Avenue
Coolidge, Shepley, Bulfinch & Abbott, Architects

A butte of glazed-white brick, with only the updated Gothic and bold setback massing for decoration, houses this great medical center.

The concept of bringing together in- and out-patient care, teaching, research, and social services in one medical center was new when New York Hospital opened. It took planning, but it worked, integrating the disparate but interlocking functions so that they flowed together.

This great complex is on 6¼ acres of land and has 45 acres of floor space, linked by a network of color-coded corridors that are 5 miles long within the buildings and by tunnels underneath. The artful arrangement of its eleven buildings makes this massive medical center appear as one. Its motif is the updated, slimmed-down Gothic. Otherwise, all is plain and unadorned. The central building rises twenty-seven stories, almost 400 feet, with three major setbacks and two southern wings. The wings terminate in apses, with great eight-story-high lancet windows. Continuing the feel for the Gothic above the second setback are more apsidal wings, these smaller, in scale with the flank of the building. Running up this flank are vertical recesses that add shadows, ending in pointed arches. And breaking the vertical thrust is a set of one-story lancets just below the third setback, acting almost like the arches in the triforium of a nave arcade.

As in Kansas City, everything here was up to date. The operating rooms had shadowless lights. The X-ray machine took pictures at 1/120 of a second. A huge ventilation system completely replaced the air every seven minutes, providing "conditioned air." The heating and plumbing pipes ran up the buildings within the outside walls. And where corridors crossed, the steel columns were recessed a foot on either side, so that the 8-foot-wide corridors became 10-foot-square crossings.

When the hospital opened, it instituted a free bus service with twenty-minute headways between 7 A.M. and 7 P.M. for its nearly one thousand daily visitors and patients. The buses ran east from Fifth Avenue on Sixty-eighth Street, picking up passengers but discharging nobody until the hospital had been reached. Its westbound trip on Sixty-seventh Street deposited passengers at the Second and Third Avenue els, the Lexington Avenue Subway, and all the bus and trolley lines along the way. Everything was up to date.

Rockefeller Center   1932–1940

The thirteen prewar buildings, between Forty-eighth and Fifty-first streets, and between Fifth Avenue and Avenue of the Americas
Hood & Fouilhoux and Reinhard & Hofmeister and Corbett, Harrison & MacMurray, Architects

The city's most important piece of urban design, a grouping of buildings that beautifully defines open spaces and creates a human scale where there could have been gigantism instead.

There is no missing the thirteen buildings that comprise the original Rockefeller Center. Built between 1932 and 1940, they are sheathed in gray Indiana limestone, and all have similar vertical wall treatments, with channeled spandrels to add to the verticality of the buildings and softened edges when the rooflines are reached. They include the RCA Building, La Maison Française, the British Empire Building, the International Building, and the Associated Press Building.

This is the city's most important piece of urban design, a grouping of buildings that beautifully defines open spaces and creates a human scale where there could have been more of the same kind of gigantism that was attacking lower Manhattan and midtown at the same time. The view down Channel Gardens, so called because its fountains and pools separate the British Empire Building from La Maison Française, just as the water of the English Channel separates the two nations, is now almost a cliché, but it dramatically shows the thought that went into the grouping. The slab tower of the RCA Building soars seventy stories, its height emphasized by the horizontal plane created by the Channel Gardens and the low-lying buildings. Often overlooked are the setbacks on the RCA Building. It had to be built within the allowable envelope of space, and despite the air rights given up by the low-lying buildings, setbacks were still required.

Several factors contribute to the joy of the place. This was the first large office building project in America in which extensive landscaping played an inherent part, even on rooftops and setbacks, providing a vernal oasis in midtown. Seasonal plantings are regularly made, including lilies at Easter and the famous tree at Christmas. Pedestrian circulation is

enhanced by Rockefeller Plaza, a north-south street that offers a multiplicity of choice in traveling the 900 feet from Fifth to Sixth avenues, or from one side street to another. The streets are free of trucks, because an elaborate truck-delivery system was built underground to serve all the buildings between Fifth and Sixth avenues. And linking all of the buildings is an underground pedestrian arcade, permitting the pedestrian to walk undercover from Forty-eighth Street and Fifth all the way to Fifty-third Street, west of the Avenue of the Americas. Along the way are newsstands, jewelry stores, restaurants, shoe repair shops, banks, a pet shop, and one rare-book store.

The sunken plaza in front of the RCA Building was installed as a lure to get people downstairs into the pedestrian arcade, but since people were not buying during the Depression, the idea was abandoned. Instead, the area is converted into an outdoor restaurant in the summer and an ice-skating rink in the winter.

The name of the original project was Metropolitan Square, and a new home for the Metropolitan Opera was its focal point. The project's number-one backer was John D. Rockefeller, Jr., and the year was 1929. With the Crash came such dire forecasts for donations to the opera's building fund that the company pulled out of the real-estate deal in December 1929, leaving Rockefeller holding the leases on several blocks of deteriorating brownstones. John D., Jr., businessman, sorely needed a revenue-producing scheme to cut the losses on his leases. At the same time, John D., Jr., philanthropist, realized that a massive construction program would ease the high unemployment in the construction and building industries. A new commercial center would do it.

For the now defunct Metropolitan Square project, architect Benjamin Wistar Morris had already figured out that the zoning law would allow the heights of buildings to reach an average of 250 feet if the buildings faced a large enough plaza. Compare that with the 90-foot-high buildings that were allowed on the average 60-foot-wide side streets, and you will arrive at the same conclusion as Rockefeller—a large open area would pay for itself in the increased heights of the buildings around it. Several permutations later and the stage was set for Rockefeller Center.

The one man whose stamp is firmly seen on the Center is Raymond Hood. It was Hood's idea, for instance, to install a fountain in the sunken plaza, giving something to the man in the street. He computed that to recirculate the required 30,000 gallons of water would cost only $8.30 a day, a small price to pay for such an amenity, one that has come to symbolize Rockefeller Center. He also advocated art in architecture, giving us Paul Manship's *Prometheus*, regilded and shining in the sunshine; Lee Lawrie's *Wisdom, Light, and Sound* over the main entrance to the RCA Building and *Atlas* in the reveal in the International Building; and Hildreth Meiere's plaques, *Theater, Dance,* and *Song,* on the Fiftieth Street wall of Radio City Music Hall.

Rockefeller Center's elegantly restrained Art Deco styling and crispness of design made it "modern" in the 1930s, and modern it still is. And for a walker in the city who is seeking scale and a sense of time and place, this is the spot to find them.

211 East Forty-eighth Street   1934

(Originally home of Mr. and Mrs. William Lescaze)
Between Second and Third avenues
William Lescaze, Architect

This is more than a remodeled brownstone with a daringly modern face—in the eyes of the architect it was modern because it met the needs and purposes of his business and family.

Before Lescaze, this building was another "respectable" brownstone. After Lescaze, with his rectilinear planes contrasting with curvilinear surfaces, industrial tubular railings

instead of wrought-iron balustrades, glass block panels instead of neo-Renaissance window frames, with all his tenets of modernism instead of Victorian propriety, Lescaze's building was a small revolution. And it was more than its superficial modernity, more than its stucco on brick and great expanses of glass that made it modern to William Lescaze—it was that this building was a purely functional object.

Lescaze did not believe that modernity had much to do with the merits of one form versus another, although he clearly preferred some forms over others, but that it represented a "process of thinking versus a total lack of thinking." If a building met the needs and purposes of the people who lived or worked in it, then it was modern. To ascertain their needs, Lescaze and his partner, George Howe, began asking potential clients how tall they were so that shelves could be placed at comfortable heights; they also questioned clients about the degree of privacy they enjoyed and how it might be guaranteed.

The design for Lescaze's own home/office incorporated his answers for both living and working spaces. His basement studios ran the length of the plot, and had a skylight in the extension. Above the rear of the studios, separated from the building itself by about 20 feet of open space, was his library, also skylit.

His home was about 60 feet long, and occupied the upper three floors. A skylight in the roof admitted light, and central air-conditioning kept everything cool. Extending the entire length of the top floor was the living room, with a wall of glass blocks in the south to admit light but keep out noise (remember, the Third Avenue El still rattled by). One floor down were the bedrooms, with front and back rooms separated by bathrooms and dressing rooms. Since the master bedroom in the rear faced north, Lescaze cantilevered a curvilinear window that snaked its way northwest, thereby admitting the morning sun from the east. The parlor floor housed a maid's room and kitchen in front, with the dining room overlooking the terrace. Everything was compact, everything was precise, right down to the crank-operating windows that swung open. The building caused a sensation, a result no doubt hoped for by the businessman in the architect, a sensation that led the owners to allow visitors in to see the house one hour every Monday. Mrs. Lescaze, the architect's widow, still happily lives here.

First Houses   1935

29–41 Avenue A and 112–138 East Third Street
Frederick L. Ackerman, Architect

The nation's first municipally built, owned, and managed housing project.

It had been about a hundred years since slums were recognized as a social problem in New York. The basic tenets for reform had been advocated for at least forty years, predicated on the belief that sunshine, space, and air are minimum housing requirements, yet never had the City taken any direct action. Aside from a few philanthropic efforts at model tenements, there had been little effort to improve the lot of the "underhoused." It finally took the Depression, with the New Deal's make-work programs, before the city and federal governments built anything. The start was First Houses, so called because these eight, five-story walk-ups were the first municipally built, owned, and managed housing project in the nation. Originally, this project was not designed to construct new buildings from scratch, but to renovate old tenements. Ultimately, however, almost entirely new houses were constructed, and only a few of the old walls and foundation supports were preserved. Essentially, every third house was torn down, creating light where there had been only air shafts. Whereas the old tenements had covered about 90 percent of the land, these houses occupied only about 42 percent.

When the New York City Housing Authority announced that it was taking applications on the 120 apartments in these eight, five-story walkups, four thousand families registered. A committee consulted neighborhood groups and screened the applicants, looking for families with steady incomes, thrifty habits, and a reputation for paying their bills on time. The 120 families that moved into the apartments had weekly incomes that averaged $23.20, yet eighty-one of the families had been living in tenement houses with inadequate plumbing, ninety-one had had no bathrooms, and twenty had had one or more windowless rooms. The fact was New York's housing stock for the middle and lower-middle classes had been ignored too long.

These apartments had at least one window in every room, 11-by-18-foot living rooms, 11-by-12-foot bedrooms, combination aerial and ground connections for radios, central heating and hot water, kitchens equipped with gas stoves and electric refrigerators, electric washing machines and dryers in the basements, and a playground and back yard landscaped by Robert Moses's Department of Parks. The rent was $6.05 per room a month—a sum that brought joy to many applicants when they learned that bathrooms, foyers, and closets were not counted as rooms. Many were already paying that much or more for less, with additional costs that averaged $5 a month during the winter for coal to heat their apartments and the year-long cost of ice for their iceboxes.

With Eleanor Roosevelt on the podium with him on opening day, Mayor Fiorello La Guardia said, with evident pride in the City's accomplishment and distaste for his critics, "This is boondoggling exhibit A, and we're proud of it."

United States Courthouse   1936

Centre Street between Duane and Pearl streets on Foley Square
Cass Gilbert and Cass Gilbert, Jr., Architects

The last gasp of neo-classicism in New York, a twenty-story tower bursting through the roof of a neo-classical temple.

A decision had been reached in Washington by the end of the 1920s that unofficially there was to be an official style for Washington's new federal buildings, and the decision favored the traditional time-honored classical forms against the modern. It meant more of the eclectic same. Cass Gilbert, whose taste ran the spectrum of eclecticism from Beaux Arts to neo-Gothic, chose the neo-classical for this federal building. It was not only to placate his client but it was also an effort to achieve a continuity with the New York County Courthouse to the north and the Municipal Building to the south, both designed in the prevalent style of the 1910s. This was Foley Square, named for Tom Foley, a local ward politician who ran taverns and Tammany with equal ease, and

it was designed to become New York's civic center. The hope was that the style of New York's Foley Square would evolve into that of Washington's Federal Triangle.

Gilbert said in 1929 that the "greatest element of monumental architecture is good proportion," a criterion he applied to this courthouse in a peculiar way. Broad granite steps lead up to the Corinthian portico of the courthouse, the 100-foot-wide entrance providing an impression of permanence and dignity in the approved "official" style of Washington and federal neo-classicism. However, this is New York, a vertical city, not Washington, a horizontal one; land values are higher here and exploitation of land greater. Everything that had to be housed in this building on its relatively small site could not be housed in a Washington-height building. There simply was not room for the offices of the U.S. District Attorney for the Southern District, the U.S. District Court and Circuit Court of Appeals, as well as a target range for G-men to practice their marksmanship in the basement.

Gilbert's resolution was to have a twenty-five-story neo-classical tower, complete with loggias and urns and pilasters bursting through the roof of a neo-classical temple. To make an interesting addition to the skyline, he topped the building with a gilt pyramidal cap and then added the requisite lantern. As much as Washington liked neo-classical buildings, neo-classicism was moribund, and this granite-faced courthouse was its last gasp in New York City.

Rockefeller Apartments
1936

17 West Fifty-fourth Street, between Fifth Avenue and the Avenue of the Americas
Harrison & Fouilhoux, Architects

The bold massing of the cylindrical bays is only one result of the architects' belief that the building's form had to follow its apartments' functions.

Bay windows were incorporated in many row houses because their interiors need all the light they can get. The same principle holds true for the average apartment, but the average apartment seldom gets a bay window. Straightaway, this building tells you that it is no ordinary apartment house. Cylindrical bays run up its facade, filling dining rooms with light. And since the bays are adjacent, their windows face away from each other, assuring some degree of privacy.

Architects Harrison & Fouilhoux made studies of living patterns, of the scale of furniture in relation to the scale of the interiors, even studies to ascertain the height at which a casement window can be opened comfortably. Their designs were presented to the man financing the research and paying for the building, John D. Rockefeller, Jr. He bought the plans because they made sense to him.

The apartments were distillations of ideas on urban living and interior design. The radiators, for instance, are concealed, with heat coming from registers in the walls. The proximity of the site to the burgeoning business district would probably mean that small families would be living in

185

the building, and some apartments might even be *pieds à terre*. Kitchens had to be complete, with adequate cabinets and work space, but they would probably not be the family's focal point. Dining rooms had to be provided, but they needn't be baronial—a room accommodating a round table for four or six would probably be large enough. And bathrooms had to be as convenient for tenants as for their guests.

The midblock site stretches from Fifty-fourth to Fifty-fifth streets, so the architects rejected the usual setback/tower building as being too ungainly. Likewise, they rejected the usual closed court. Instead, they designed what are essentially two separate buildings linked by an open-ended courtyard, assuring sun to the rear apartments, a steady flow of air, and, since noise would not bounce back and forth, quiet. (The bedrooms fronting the streets are equipped with air filters and noise silencers to blot out traffic noises.)

The facade is clear and straightforward—there is no subterfuge here—with the bold massing of the cylindrical bay windows acting as the perfect geometric foil for the flat planes.

With only the plans to go by, a third of the Rockefeller Apartments were rented before the steelwork was even started, 86 percent were rented by the time the steelwork was finished, and 100 percent by the time the building was finished.

25 East Eighty-third Street   1938

Northwest corner of Madison Avenue
Frederick L. Ackerman, Architect; Ramsey &
Sleeper, Associates

A crisply designed facade for New York's first apartment house built with central air-conditioning.

By the 1930s the popularity of air-conditioning for comfort's sake was spreading. Some industries were already air-conditioned, as were select hospitals, stores, and theaters (banners showing penguins would be hung from marquees to advertise the coolness inside). The spread of air-conditioning for domestic use, however, was slow because it was expensive. In 1936 the apartment house at 400 Park Avenue was completely gutted, its huge apartments (vintage 1916) broken up into smaller units. With the complete remodeling came the first centrally air-conditioned apartment house in New York (the building has since been demolished).

The first apartment house in New York that was constructed with built-in central air-conditioning was this one, a house so artfully designed that there is no air-conditioning equipment in any of the apartments themselves. All the equipment was built into public areas with access for the building's workers, so that if something should go wrong, the repairmen could get at the problem. The air was filtered and dehumidified, and, depending on the season, heated or

cooled and sent through the same system. All air was recirculated, except the air from kitchens and bathrooms, which was vented through rooftop ducts. The air-conditioning plant consisted of two freon compressors, and each apartment had its own built-in thermostat and humidistat.

The apartments ranged in size from studios to two bedrooms, and despite all their modernity, conservative trim, such as neo-classical fireplaces, was still built in. Because the apartments were compact, with no space in them for a maid's room, some maid's rooms were provided on the main floor in the rear. That way a resident could essentially have a live-in maid who nevertheless lived out, an arrangement that assured some privacy for all involved.

The facade expresses the modernity of the building's innovation, a carefully scaled design with bands of glass blocks to admit sunlight, with casement windows either flanking or being flanked by glass blocks. (What the sole air-conditioning unit is doing in the window on the top floor is a mystery.) By recessing the facade, Ackerman created extra light where ordinarily there would have been little, and by beveling the corners he created even more. By today's standards the building is still crisply, some might even say coolly, designed.

Criminal Courts Building and Prison   1939

("The Tombs")
Centre Street, between Leonard and White streets
Harvey Wiley Corbett and Charles B. Meyers,
Associate Architects

*A ziggurat design of elegant simplicity that makes a
fundamentalist statement—none of that neo-classicism here.*

One look at these *moderne* office buildings, with their cubist
massing and their facades stripped down to plain facings of
Indiana limestone and glazed terra cotta, and visions of Rockefeller Center dance in the head. The window-spandrel configuration is similar, the vertical stripings are similar, even
the cresting is similar (Corbett was one of Rockefeller Center's
architects). The difference is scale. These buildings make no
bones about the setback law and project themselves as ziggurat buildings. They are not slim towers, but fully occupy
three-quarters of their site, early manifestations of Corbett's
belief that buildings in New York should be lower than the
great skyscrapers of the 1930s, and with simpler designs. The
wings project from the building itself, and pairs of free-standing monoliths, like the watchful eye of the law, flank the
courtyards. The whole effect creates entrances that are impressive, yet just a bit Orwellian. The sleek, cool modernity
is carried into the lobby, which could just as easily be the
Promenade deck of the *Queen Mary* as a courthouse.

The northern wing, connected to the criminal courts
building by two bridges and a utility tunnel, was designed
to look like any other office building in the neighborhood,
but it was a jail and it was in use until 1974. Since this jail
was for prisoners who were awaiting trial, hence presumed
innocent, its design was not modeled after Leavenworth.
Glass blocks that are 2¼ inches thick were set into steel and
mortar. The glass area is small enough so that even if the
panes were smashed, no jailbreaker could squeeze through
the space, yet light floods the cells without the psychologi-
cally depressing effect of bars. The 835 prison cells were
intended to house one prisoner each, and they were consid-

ered model penal facilities when erected. By the 1970s, however, the overcrowding was so horrendous that the jail was closed because the conditions were considered cruel and unusual punishment.

These were "The Tombs," so called because a jail built in 1838 in the style of the Egyptian Revival reminded New Yorkers of Egyptian tombs. The nickname stuck through three generations of New York jails (the original Tombs was demolished in 1902, and its successor was vacated in favor of this one; prisoners are now incarcerated at Rikers Island).

Another New York tradition religiously observed in these buildings is for impecunious collegians to bring their dates to night court on Saturday night. Their explanation is sociology.

Museum of Modern Art 1939

11 West Fifty-third Street, between Fifth Avenue and the Avenue of the Americas
Edward Durell Stone and Philip L. Goodwin, Architects; extensions, 1951 and 1964, Philip Johnson

Plunked down on a residential street of brownstones and Beaux Arts town houses in 1939, the starkly modern Modern was even more dramatic then than it is now.

If modern American architecture has its intellectual roots anywhere, it is within the museum that this building houses. Founded in 1929, the museum's goals were to develop and encourage the study of modern arts and furnish popular instruction. In its first year of existence, Philip Johnson mounted a show on architecture's twentieth-century greats, including Le Corbusier, Mies van der Rohe, Walter Gropius, and Frank Lloyd Wright. Three years later, he and Henry-Russell Hitchcock mounted another show on modern architecture, a show that had an impact on the American consciousness as great as the Armory Show had on art in 1913, resulting in their epoch-making book, *The International Style*.

Until the MOMA, museum curators and directors considered themselves conservators, whereas MOMA's considered themselves innovators. The innovations, of course, spilled over into the kind of home that would be built to house the collection, a building that the museum could safely include in its own show on modern American architecture held in 1944.

The strongly horizontal facade manifested a crispness of design that had not yet surfaced in the United States (there was a definite time lag between the U.S. and Europe, where the Bauhaus School had been both preaching and practicing its style since the 1920s). What the design did to Fifty-third Street was to drag it away from nineteenth-century brownstones and Beaux Arts town houses into the twentieth century. Its steel and concrete frame construction is faced with white marble, with a horizontal swath of Thermolux glass to light the exhibition galleries on the second and third floors. Set out to the building line, hence nearer to the curb than the brownstones to its east, the original wing had THE MUSEUM OF MODERN ART running down its eastern flank in a modern, sans-serif typeface. The original canopy (since removed) was curvilinear, a soft, free-flowing design that contrasted with the building's angularity.

The museum is built on a side street with no perspective, hence no attraction from afar. To attract passersby, Stone and Goodwin created the inviting, glass-enclosed lobby. The land for the museum was donated by Mr. and Mrs. John D. Rockefeller, Jr., land that had been the site of the home of John D. himself (4 West Fifty-fourth Street). The Rockefeller interests explain why there was once a plan to cut a midblock plaza from Rockefeller Center to Fifty-third Street. The bold lines of the museum would have acted as northern anchor, while the plaza would have provided the perspective so sorely lacking. Since its opening, this building has been modified and flanked by exquisite extensions by Philip Johnson, extensions that point up how good the original building really is.

Stuyvesant Town   1947

Fourteenth to Twentieth streets, First Avenue to the FDR Drive
Gilmore D. Clarke, Chairman of the Board of Design; Irwin Clavan, Chief Architect

Manhattan's first massive housing project encouraged middle-class families to live in the city when decent housing was scarce and the suburbs beckoned.

The eighteen blocks where Stuyvesant Town now stands were in a decline by the 1940s. In 1920 the neighborhood's population stood at about 27,000. By 1942 it had slid to about 11,000. And no wonder: 75 percent of the housing dated from pre-1900; 75 percent of the buildings lacked central heating; and 66 percent of the apartments were without bathrooms, while 20 percent had no private toilets. By the 1940s New York State had passed a law allowing the condemnation of blighted districts by nonprofit corporations. If ever there was a blighted neighborhood, this was it, and the Metropolitan Life Insurance Company decided to take advantage of the urban redevelopment legislation and build a massive housing project for the middle class.

Metropolitan Life's return was to be limited to 6 percent, which required a deal on taxes. The City agreed to tax the Stuyvesant Town Corporation on the assessed valuation of the area for 1943, or before improvements, for twenty-five years. Then taxes would be paid on the true assessed valuation. It seemed a fair *quid* for the *quo*—the area's density would be doubled, some of the middle class would be better housed and not lost to the beckoning suburbs, tax collection would be simplified, and tax delinquency would be abrogated. With ex-neighborhood residents installed in new quarters found through the Metropolitan Life Tenant Relocation Bureau, the wrecking ball started swinging in 1945 and down came over six hundred buildings. Urban renewal on a massive scale had begun.

Thirty-five fireproof buildings were built, each twelve or thirteen stories high, with ten-story wings. The estimated occupancy in the 8,755 apartments was 24,000, or just a little less than the population on the same site twenty-five years before. There were differences, of course. There were no schools in Stuyvesant Town, no places of worship, and not a single candy store for a good chocolate egg cream. And with funny addresses like "6 Stuyvesant Oval" and nary a distinguishing architectural feature or landmark to guide the visitor, this standardized chaos could have led to the question asked by a lady of her mailman in Robert Day's cartoon version of a Levittown: "I'm Mrs. Edward M. Barnes. Where do I live?"

Its anonymity aside, the arrival of Stuyvesant Town was propitious. It came at the same time that the federal government was giving GI loans for private homes and sponsoring huge highway projects for private cars, encouraging suburban and urban sprawl. Here was a project that encouraged middle-class families to stay in a concentrated area in the heart of the city. With GI's given preference, the response was overwhelming—200,000 applications were received for 8,755 apartments of one to three bedrooms, renting from $50 to $91 a month. Today the waiting list is shorter, but if you want a one-bedroom apartment a year from now, you'd better sign up today.

Look Building   1950

488 Madison Avenue, between Fifty-first and
Fifty-second streets
Emery Roth & Sons, Architects

Continuous bands of strip windows around a curvilinear frame makes the Look Building the Starrett-Lehigh (see p. 169) of office buildings almost twenty years after.

What new office construction the Depression did not halt, World War II did. The first awakening took place in 1947 when a twenty-one-story tiered office building rose at 445 Park Avenue. Ten years later and there would be sixty-four postwar office buildings already built, with another twenty under construction. It would mean about 40 million square feet of new office space, with most of it between Thirty-fourth and Fifty-ninth streets, and most of it mediocre. Like Bordeaux wine, there would be few first growths. Designs like Lever House and the Seagram Building would set a standard for the world. The Look Building is perhaps the first of the second growths for the vintages of the 1950s.

Its daddy is clearly the Starrett-Lehigh Building. Continuous bands of strip windows wrap around a curvilinear frame, and its setback shape is almost a carbon copy. (Adulterated variations on its setback theme would abound throughout the 1950s.) This is the wedding-cake look.

Quick to use it in the postwar construction race were Percy and Harold Uris, whose names would become synonymous in the vocabulary of critics with the kind of architecturally uninspired office buildings that characterize most of the Fifties. Uris Brothers plunged right into the race in 1950, constructing two major blockfront office buildings on Madison Avenue, one on the site of the Ritz Carlton Hotel (400 Madison Avenue), and the Look Building on the site of Cathedral College. They entered the construction race to win, with no secret weapon except determination. At 488 Madison, the builder employed three crews of seven men and seven riveting gangs to erect the steel framework. Although the job was complicated by the curved channels at the corners of the building, its steelwork was "topped out" merely twelve weeks after the first delivery of steel, setting a postwar record. The pace of the bricklaying was even faster, progressing at a rate of four floors a week.

By November 1949, at least two months before the building would be ready for occupancy, 488 Madison was fully rented. Clearly the comfort of air-conditioning was an attraction, and the continuous ribbons of windows provided an air of modernity while promising light for the offices and a concomitant feeling of spaciousness. By the spring of 1950, 488 Madison would be named the Look Building for one of its major tenants. Another tenant, Esquire, unsuccessfully sued, asking the court to enjoin 488 Madison from becoming the Look Building, since it might imply that Esquire and its publications were under the aegis of Look. It was a Pyrrhic victory for the original Look. Esquire is still there.

Manhattan House   1950

200 East Sixty-sixth Street, between Second and Third avenues
Mayer & Whittlesey and Skidmore, Owings & Merrill, Architects

New York's first "modern-looking" apartment house is more than just modern looking—its structure is of reinforced concrete, a building material that combines both tensile and compressive qualities in one plastic material.

Le Corbusier's 1925 vision for Paris was his "Voisin Plan," free-standing, X-shaped apartment houses with H-shaped wings. Manhattan House is a straight-edged version, several H-shaped buildings linked together on a plane, as if the apartment house could be repeated ad infinitum at either end. The lobby is a great, glass-enclosed space running through the center of the building. It has all the lightness of a small private home instead of a lobby for a nineteen-story building with 581 apartments, a lobby like Le Corbusier's Savoie House in Poissy, France. And Manhattan House was con-

structed of reinforced concrete, Le Corbusier's favorite building material, a material that provides tensile strength from rods of steel, compressive strength from concrete, and great plasticity, since it can be molded into practically any shape without sacrificing its inherent qualities.

Reinforced concrete would revolutionize apartment-house construction, replacing steel as the dominant material for the framework of tall apartment buildings in New York by 1960. Carpenters first build wooden forms in place for the columns and beams. Then ironworkers install thin, flexible lengths of steel. Concrete is poured into the mold, and usually within twenty-four hours the concrete has hardened enough to bear the weight of the next tier in wood. Within twenty-eight days, the reinforced concrete will have ninety percent of its strength and the building will be ready for its facade.

With the Third Avenue El still rumbling past in the 1940s and tenements in greater propinquity than the luxury of Park Avenue, this area was hardly the "posh" East Side when the building was planned. And it was not supposed to be a luxury building, since its builder, the New York Life Insurance Company, was forbidden by New York State law from building high-rent buildings ("luxury" rents in 1950 averaged $80 a room; Manhattan House rents averaged $65 a room). Nevertheless, there were still deluxe features. Granted, there was no central air-conditioning, but there was adequate wiring, balconies for most apartments above the sixth floor, fireplaces in many apartments above the twelfth floor, two floors of penthouses, direct telephone service not only with the lobby and the doormen but with every apartment in the building, and five separate elevator banks, providing intimate landings.

Despite Manhattan House's true modernity, its model apartment was furnished by B. Altman's in eighteenth-century traditional. Ironically, Sachs Quality Stores had furnished a model apartment for the Sedgwick Housing Development in the Bronx at the same time, using all modern pieces, including some prize-winning designs from the low-cost furniture design competition sponsored by the Museum of Modern Art.

Philip Johnson's House   1950

(Originally the Museum of Modern Art Guest House)
242 East Fifty-second Street, between Second and Third avenues
Philip Johnson, Architect

If you saw only the upper section of this town house, you would swear that it was the Seagram Building.

Architect Lescaze and others broke through the gingerbread barrier in the 1930s, refining lines and using industrial products. Philip Johnson, under the hypnotic spell of Mies van der Rohe, went one step further, reducing elements to their most basic. Johnson took geometric forms and a concern for classicism and put them to work in this house, which is hardly a house at all but more an efficiency apartment on its own lot with its own walls.

The base of the house is brick, in the same hues employed by Frank Lloyd Wright for Robie House in Chicago. In the center is a door that is as high as the wall of brick, so it splits the wall cleanly. Above are six windows, three short ones which act as a base, three tall ones which act as the vertical element, and all set into exposed steel. Like Urban's New School, an elemental design.

Within are two rooms, the living/kitchen/dining room separated from the bedroom by a garden pool in the core of the house. The compact kitchen is behind the brick wall. When closed off by folding doors, the kitchen ceases to exist. When in use, the open folding doors act as a wall to direct visitors into the living room. The ambience is half Japanese, half Roman, as if the serenity of Japan had settled on an atrium house. Like a *palazzo*, the house is convoluted, absolutely turning its back on the street, shutting it off, and contemplating itself.

It is not a family house, and was not intended to be. Its intent was to be a guest house, a *pied à terre*, and it was commissioned by Mr. and Mrs. John D. Rockefeller III and used by the Museum of Modern Art as an apartment for visiting dignitaries. Since 1972 Johnson has rented the house from its owners as his own town house, a short walk from his offices in the Seagram Building.

Johnson started his professional career not as an architect but as a critic and polemicist. With Henry-Russell Hitchcock he defined the International Style, and he mounted shows for the Museum of Modern Art. At thirty-four he returned to Harvard, this time for his degree in architecture. While there, teachers like Hugh Stubbins told him not to imitate Mies van der Rohe, but to build on his style. Clearly he was a good student.

United Nations 1952

First Avenue, between Forty-second and Forty-fifth streets
United Nations Planning Staff, Architects; Wallace K. Harrison, Director, and Max Abramovitz, Deputy Director, USA; N. D. Bassov, USSR; Gaston Brunfaut, Belgium; Le Corbusier, France; Ernest Cormier, Canada; Ssu-Ch'eng Liang, China; Sven Markelius, Sweden; Oscar Niemeyer, Brazil; Howard Robertson, United Kingdom; G. A. Souileux, Australia; Julio Vilamajo, Uruguay.

The International Style reaches the next plateau in New York: wide walls of glass alternate with narrow walls of marble in the Secretariat, its angular slab meeting the perfect foil in the sway-backed roof of the General Assembly.

The International Style said no to Victorian excess and no to eclecticism, offering instead an anoretic's heaven, where slimmer is better, less is more. It was a new morality that took the 1920s' love affair with the machine age and toned it down. The United Nations combines the International Style with Le Corbusier's ideal of the Radiant City, tall towers and low, functionally shaped buildings set apart from each other in large landscaped areas. To many, Le Corbusier's idea is a sanitized version of what a city is all about, an idea that is anti-pedestrian and pro-automobile, anti-urban and pro-suburban sprawl. But despite all the anti-urban notions—the purity of the buildings set off by themselves in a park—this complex is vitally important.

New York's first building with all glass walls—both windows and spandrels are set in an aluminum grid—was the Secretariat, a thirty-nine-story slab whose glass walls on the east and west sides are 544 feet high and 287 feet wide, and whose marble walls on the north and south sides are only

seventy-two feet wide. When the Secretariat was being built in 1950, its slab shape reminded some New Yorkers of an upended shoe box, but its prestige rose during the Fifties and well into the Sixties, when its influence on contemporary architecture was finally challenged, and then only timorously. This graceful, slim tower is in perfect contrast to the General Assembly Building, an elegant, free-form building with a dome-topped sloping roof. One without the other, like a yin without its yang, would be weak and pointless.

This is the greatest international colony in the world, with 150 member nations represented, making New York the greatest international city. Other cities were vying for the UN's presence in the late 1940s, and it did not come easily to New York. But Mayor O'Dwyer realized its importance and was willing to give concessions. The UN's demands were high, including tax exemptions and the promise of housing for its workers. Lures that were proffered included the tunneling of First Avenue for through traffic and the widening of Forty-seventh Street. And then there was the site. In the 1940s, this was hardly a prepossessing neighborhood, since it was filled with slaughterhouses and coal yards (which explains why Tudor City, built between 1925 and 1928, turned its back on the east, concentrating its windows inwardly on its own system of parks). William Zeckendorf, real-estate wizard, had acquired an option on the land east of First Avenue between Forty-second and Forty-seventh streets for $6.5 million, or $17 per square foot, a low price to pay for midtown property. John D. Rockefeller, Jr., offered him $8.5 million for the site. After the sale was consummated, Rockefeller simply contributed the parcel to the cause. The spirit of goodwill still pervades the United Nations.

Lever House   1952

390 Park Avenue, between Fifty-third and Fifty-fourth streets
Skidmore, Owings & Merrill, Architects

A horizontal and vertical slab of blue-green glass and stainless steel hovers above Park Avenue. It's the Americanization of the International Style.

Until 1952, Park Avenue was a solid canyon of brick and limestone. Then came Lever House, the first chink in the great wall of Park Avenue, a delicate curtain of blue-green glass and stainless steel. It was Park Avenue's first all-glass building, but it was something more, too. The more, of course, is less. The building is barely a building at all on the street level. The space includes a glass-walled lobby with elevator banks, an auditorium, an open interior courtyard with a garden, and a pedestrian arcade defined by square, steel-clad columns (they are set back 10 feet from the Park Avenue building line to avoid the tracks below). A low horizontal slab seemingly floats above the building site. From it, and separated by a one-story-high notch in the facade, is the tower, eleven windows wide on the avenue, a slab tower that is set off center and hovers above the horizontal slab.

One shade of glass is translucent, to allow light to enter the offices. The glass for the spandrels is dark, opaque, reflecting the steel beams. Adding the necessary foil to the blue-green glass and cementing the rectangular forms within a grid are vertical and horizontal bands of stainless steel. The extra horizontal strip within the spandrels creates a natural balance. Some of the mullions are functional, since in reality they are flanged stainless-steel tracks for the window washers' motor-driven gondola to ride up and down. (Since no windows open, the gondola was an ingenious solution to the cleaning problem.)

The glass-and-steel curtain wall created a revolution that would set the tone for contemporary commercial architecture. In less capable hands, however, it could be banal. One look at its neighbor to the north is all that is needed to prove the point. Four hundred Park Avenue was erected five years after Lever House, and it seems the architects told their client that the building would be just like Lever House—all glass and steel. What they ignored, and what Lever got, was a sense of scale. The law permitted a tower of any height without setbacks, providing the tower did not occupy more than 25 percent of the lot. Lever's lot measures 200 feet on Park Avenue, 155 feet on Fifty-third Street, and 192 feet on Fifty-fourth Street. Lever's tower measures only 53 by 180 feet, its frontage almost precisely one-quarter of the lot. Its 290,000 square feet of office space could have been housed in a traditional eight-story building, but Lever wanted a prestigious headquarters that was lean and squeaky clean, and the building created a sensation. New Yorkers and visitors alike would gape at it, especially at night, with the ceiling lights so visibly harmonious, and with the vertical columns so countable between every fifth mullion. Each component is the perfect foil for the other, the horizontal versus the vertical, the wide versus the thin, solids versus voids. After Lever House came the Americanization of the International Style in the eyes of the world, to the degree that Lever House *is* the American corporate style.

Manufacturers Hanover Trust Company   1954

510 Fifth Avenue, southwest corner of Forty-third Street
Skidmore, Owings & Merrill, Architects

This jewel box, New York's first glass bank, still lights up the Fifth Avenue night with its grace, its serenity, its precision.

New York had never experienced a building like this before, a five-story glass jewel box for a bank. Its design reveals the consummate skill of its architects, whose aesthetic had appeared only two years before in Park Avenue's Lever House.

The bank is symmetry itself. Its windows are perfectly clear, acting as an invisible building material, reflecting nothing, but splendidly showing off the geometry within. The polished aluminum mullions and the dark spandrels act as the perfect foils for the clear windows and together they create an ordered precision. The mullions especially act as a foil for the windows, bringing a third dimension into play by not being set flush with the wall but by projecting 10 inches from

199

the glass. The clarity of the facade and the openness of the interiors are made possible by the cantilevered floors, with only eight interior columns supporting the entire weight of the building.

Imagine 1954 and how stunning this building must have been compared with the bank style of the period. Hardly any banks had been built since the 1920s, so people in 1954 were accustomed to the kinds of banks that Bonnie and Clyde had made a business of holding up, seemingly impregnable Italian Renaissance *palazzi*, built with 3-foot-thick walls and barred window openings, their tellers ensconced behind cages and vaults safely encased in concrete in the sub-basements. But here was a bank with walls of glass, with tellers separated from the customer by only a counter, and with a stainless-steel and polished bronze vault door right there in the Fifth Avenue window. Banking had thrown off its shroud of stuffiness and gone into merchandising. If the building does not strike you as so extraordinary today, it is because of its lackluster imitations.

The decision to make the building compact in size was influenced by practicality. If the building had become the standard skyscraper, it would have been set back 25 feet from the fifth floor because of its neighbor's air rights, diminishing its rentable tower space. Also, the banking area on the main floor would have been nibbled away by the necessity for a lobby and elevator banks, and off-street loading platforms. On a 100-by-125-foot plot, the bank decided to eschew the skyscraper, with all its drawbacks, and instead create a building of elegance and substance. Today the bank occupies only the first two floors, with tenants above.

Socony-Mobil Building   1955

150 East Forty-second Street, between Lexington and Third avenues
Harrison & Abramovitz, Architects

The largest metal-clad office building in the world was an expensive advertisement for the steel industry.

In the early 1950s the steel industry was worried. With the coming of the UN Secretariat, Lever House, and Manufacturers Hanover Trust, glass was clearly the facade of the future. And in 1952 the Alcoa Company thumbed its nose at the steel industry and built a corporate headquarters in Pittsburgh, the heart of steel country. Alcoa's building, of course, had an aluminum curtain wall. The steel industry responded by meeting any bid on the Socony-Mobil Building by the aluminum industry and bettering it. The difference was written off as the cost of promoting steel, making the Socony-Mobil Building the loss-leader building of its day. And what the steel industry got was, if not a winner, at least a whopper.

It was the largest metal-clad office building in the world. It was the largest centrally air-conditioned commercial structure ever completed. Its second floor, with 75,000 square feet of rentable space, was the biggest office floor in the city. And as a first for a big New York office building, all elevators were self-service, continuing the push-button precedent set by the Standard Oil Building thirty years before.

Its stainless-steel skin is only .037 of an inch thick. It is backed by a masonry wall, not to help support anything, but to satisfy the requirements of New York's building and fire codes. The skin is a stamped, faceted design, sort of a "Doodle on a Triangular Theme," but a practical design since its facets offset the tendency of sheet metal to bend slightly. What's more, the wind scours the splayed patterns and prevents a buildup of dirt. The windows are not washed by the innovative gondola system but by a conservative method. They actually open. And so the window-washer never has to dangle precariously outside, the windows pivot vertically.

This is a speculative office building, built for the "bottom line." To be kind, its design is uninspired. In fact, it could be at home in any 1950s airport, especially the long, arching, stainless-steel canopy on Forty-second Street.

This building is the southeasternmost link with the undercover passageways of Grand Central Terminal. During inclement weather it is possible to walk from Third Avenue and Forty-first Street as far as Madison Avenue and Forty-sixth Street during normal business hours and stay warm in the cold and dry in the wet.

It is ironic that one year after this building opened, the world's largest aluminum-faced office building, the Tishman Building at 666 Fifth Avenue, opened. The race was over, both entrants tied for last.

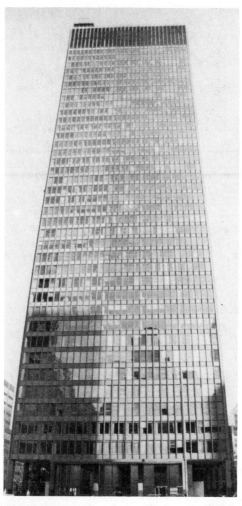

Seagram Building   1958

375 Park Avenue, between Fifty-second and
Fifty-third streets
Ludwig Mies van der Rohe and Philip Johnson,
Architects; Kahn & Jacobs, Associate Architects

*Cool, precise, classical, the ultimate statement of the
International Style. If, as Mies said, "less is more," the
Seagram Building is, at the very least, the most.*

202

Its colonnade stands like a multi-legged Parsons table. Rising off the six square columns is the shaft, 150 feet wide, 90 feet deep, and almost 500 feet high. Reflecting the post-and-lintel frame are five bays, with six windows to a bay, a formula repeated thirty-seven times in what could be monotonous banality but is sublime grace. It was Park Avenue's first building to rise straight up without a setback, and to conform to the zoning laws it was set back 90 feet from the building line, creating a 27,000-square-foot plaza before it. To project an image of sobriety, the Seagram Building is masked in a curtain wall of amber windows and bronze mullions and spandrels. And to keep itself trim, it was reduced to essentials, a sonata form that takes you linearly through its introduction, development, and recapitulation.

Sculptors say that their job is simply to cut away the stone to get at the sculpture that already exists within. It is this cutting away for which architect Mies van der Rohe is so famous, and he did it brilliantly in the Seagram Building, cutting away the extraneous to get at the essence. The Seagram Building is the quintessential Mies, the ultimate statement of the International style.

Seagram rejected the run of the mill for excellence. Doors were floor to ceiling, even in the elevators. Hardware of brushed aluminum and stainless steel was custom designed and proved so popular that it became a standard. The monolithic elevator banks, so visible through the glass of the lobby, are sheathed in travertine. It did not come cheap, but it is grand. Philip Johnson has his own offices on the thirty-seventh floor, for instance. And since the building could charge higher rents, and get them, Seagram's magnanimous investment in excellence paid off. Almost.

In one of the City's less enlightened decisions, and one upheld by the State's Court of Appeals in 1964, Seagram was forced to pay higher realty taxes per square foot than any other office building. The tax, said the Court, was not to penalize a corporation for contributing a monumental and magnificent structure, but by the traditional method of assessing a commercial structure, the Seagram Building, which cost over $40 million, should only have cost $17 million. The discrepancy was explained by the building's intangible (e.g. advertising) value to its owners. It was "specially built to suit the tenant," declared the Court, a category that would cost Seagram an extra $383,000 a year in taxes. Less would have been more like it.

Solomon R. Guggenheim Museum   1959

1071 Fifth Avenue, between Eighty-eighth and Eighty-ninth streets
Frank Lloyd Wright, Architect

Manhattan's only Frank Lloyd Wright building and one of the world's most distinctive architectural shapes—a logarithmic spiral that seems to float atop a horizontal slab.

The *Times'* headline introducing Frank Lloyd Wright's Guggenheim Museum to a startled world could have run in 1958. ULTRA-MODERN MUSEUM TO RISE ON FIFTH AVE. TO HOUSE NON-OBJECTIVE ART COLLECTION. It wasn't 1958, however, it was 1944, and master architect Frank Lloyd Wright had already been working for two years on his plan which was considered as daring and revolutionary at its announcement as it was fifteen years later at its completion. It was essentially a simple idea. Take a logarithmic spiral and cantilever from its interior walls a continuous spiral ramp with a grade of 1¾ inches every 10 feet. Poured concrete would provide the plasticity required for the project, with its structural calculations figured in terms of cantilever and continuity instead of post and lintel. For illumination, put a skylight in the 95-foot-high dome and run continuous bands of windows parallel to the ramp. Visitors can take an elevator to the top of the ramp and gravity can bring them down.

The building that was originally proposed was not the one that ultimately evolved. The original site ran only 145 feet north from Eighty-eighth Street, so the great horizontal slab was truncated (it took from 1947 to 1951 to acquire the full-block plot). To create the greatest interior space the lot allowed, the top of the upended spiral shell was to project about 24 feet beyond the building line. And to use natural light, glass was to be incorporated heavily. The New York Bureau of Standards and Appeals, which reviews proposed structures vis à vis the City's building code, vetoed the overhang, even after it had been pulled back to 6 feet. It likewise vetoed so much glass, because glass had not been accorded a fire-resistance rating. Wright persevered, conceding some points but winning others.

Wright's original suggestion for a facing had been white marble, but the Guggenheim wound up with a facing of yellowish concrete (it reminded Robert Moses of jaundiced skin), rough to the point that faults are apparent from the formwork. The shape of the building was a startling sight on conservative Fifth Avenue, an avenue certainly accustomed to museums, but museums in the neo-classical mode. And the controversy did not stop with the overall shape of the building, but raged over whether it served art or art served it or any of the above. Few critics, it seems, from the proverbial New York cabby to the professional art historian, were willing to accept the symbiotic relationship between the two.

Time & Life Building 1960

1271 Avenue of the Americas, between Fiftieth
and Fifty-first streets
Harrison & Abramovitz, Architects

*The first of Rockefeller Center's westward expansion
buildings learned few of the lessons so plainly taught east of
Sixth Avenue almost thirty years before.*

In the mid-1950s there seemed an inexorable drift eastward
to Park Avenue for new office space. For Rockefeller Center,
however, eastward expansion was blocked by successful institutions on Fifth Avenue.

West of Rockefeller Center sat Sixth Avenue, a perfectly
serviceable though hardly glamorous avenue. Major devel-
opers, if given the chance, had turned their backs on the
avenue and chosen instead to invest in more prestigious addresses, like 30 Rockefeller Plaza. Neither the disappearance
of Sixth Avenue's elevated in 1939 nor its name change to
the Avenue of the Americas in 1945 had precipitated a building boom.

But if Rockefeller Center was not to stagnate, westward
expansion across Sixth Avenue was a must. With the Time
& Life Corporation willing to go into limited partnership with
Rockefeller Center, the leap was made. To give the building
added volume, hence greater profits, the famous Roxy Theatre would be torn down and its air rights transferred. Cou-

pling the Roxy's air rights with a plaza that would take up 25 percent of the plot and act as a major setback, it was possible to build a monolithic slab 308 feet long, 104½ feet wide, and 587 feet, or forty-eight stories, high.

To harmonize with Rockefeller Center's earlier buildings, the architects chose conservative building materials. The limestone-clad piers were brought forward to provide uninterrupted peripheral wall space, so office partitions could be shifted without encountering unmovable columns. The piers are tapered, like buttresses, giving a subtle battered look to the building and accentuating its height. Between the piers is an aluminum-and-glass grid, the mullions serving as air-conditioning ducts for the peripheral offices.

Within five years of the coming of the Time & Life Building, new buildings would stretch from Fiftieth to Fifty-fifth streets on both sides of the avenue, and their combined costs would amount to about $415 million. Finished by 1973 were the three Rockefeller Center buildings south of the Time & Life Building, the Exxon, McGraw-Hill, and Celanese buildings, so uniformly banal, so boring, and so brutalizing that few New Yorkers deign to distinguish one from another by name, cavalierly dismissing them as the XYZ buildings. Few of the lessons learned from the Rockefeller Center were applied to this stretch of New York, resulting in something called Sixth Avenooism—a canyon of corporate towers surrounded at street level by open spaces.

270 Park Avenue   1960

(Originally Union Carbide Building)
Between Forty-seventh and Forty-eighth streets
Skidmore, Owings & Merrill, Architects

A fifty-two-story tower that is elegantly crisp, with an unexpected softness at its corners.

At fifty-two stories, or 707 feet, 270 Park Avenue was, in 1960, the tallest building erected in New York since the RCA Building went up in 1933, and Park Avenue's tallest building, period. (Today Park Avenue's Pan Am and Citibank buildings are taller.) Its scale, clearly, is huge, but its aesthetic is elegant, the logical development of ten years of SOM's refinements on a theme. Instead of two tones of green, as in their Lever House, or two tones of brown, as in Mies's Seagram Building, 270 Park has stark black spandrels, clear windows, and stainless-steel mullions, crisp, like a pink button-down shirt with a black string tie.

The building was designed as two forms—the tower, tall and slim, and an annex, almost a cube. The computation for the building was based on the zoning law. The tower was set back 33 feet from the building line so that, with Park Avenue's width, it could rise straight up without setbacks. The annex on Madison Avenue was kept low, its twelve stories going straight up from the building line, its scale intended to harmonize with the then-existing buildings. Usable space

was pared from the Madison Avenue side and added to the Park Avenue tower.

During 270 Park's construction, a modification to the zoning law was being considered—to give a floor-area bonus to builders willing to set back their structures from the property line. It transpired, leading to a different kind of canyon and the disurbanization of some of New York's avenues. As it was, if 270 Park had been constructed as a typical ziggurat building, it could have added 200,000 square feet more to its existing 1.16 million. However, too much office space would have been too far from windows. Windowless offices mean low rents. Here, 65 percent of all office space is within 15 feet of a window.

The building's circulation is complicated. As in Lever House, a street-level arcade rings the periphery of the buildings on Park Avenue, but there is also a block-through arcade continuing Vanderbilt Avenue north for pedestrians. If you're looking for an entrance from Madison Avenue, odds are you won't find it. And if you're looking for the lobby, you'll find it one flight up. Since three-quarters of the building is erected over Grand Central's double set of tracks, the "basement" housing the elevator pits was put aboveground.

One of the subtleties of the building's design is found in its corners—where you would expect to find stainless steel mullions, you don't, giving the corners a certain softness, so that the building appears to fade away, the perfect foil for its otherwise crisp design.

Chase Manhattan Bank Building   1961

1 Chase Manhattan Plaza, bounded by Pine,
Nassau, Liberty and William streets
Skidmore, Owings & Merrill, Architects

*The first major building erected in the Financial District
since 1932 and the one that set off a building boom.*

The Financial District's greatest concentration of buildings
was found in its T-zone, with few major buildings further
than a block away from the corridors of Wall Street and
Broadway. There had been no major construction since 1932,
and there was desultory talk in the 1950s that Wall Street
was losing its attraction. Some banks were planning to move
to midtown, the stock exchange was grumbling, and a sense
of general malaise was in the air. David Rockefeller, president
of Chase Manhattan Bank and chairman of the Downtown–Lower Manhattan Association, resolved to save Wall
Street with one mighty building—and save it he did.

At 813 feet, his Chase Manhattan Bank Building was at
the time the world's sixth tallest building, the other five all
within a few miles—the Empire State, Chrysler, Cities Service, RCA buildings, and 40 Wall Street. It was lower Manhattan's first aluminum-and-glass-skinned building, with
8,800 panes of glass.

The building is two-faced. Piers divide its north and
south facades vertically, like Time & Life, but a grid of mul-

lions and spandrels distinguishes its east and west facades, like 270 Park. It boasted the world's largest air-conditioning unit, with its parts housed underground, on the roof, and on three mechanical floors. The building had a 500-kilowatt diesel generator that could power some of the building's forty-six elevators and provide light in the event of a power failure. And it had a 985-ton vault installed 90 feet below street level in bedrock, with the assurance that not even a tidal wave could wash it away.

The sixty-story building occupies less than 30 percent of its 2½-acre site, creating an 89,466-square-foot plaza around it. In 1961 that made it lower Manhattan's first plaza and the only open space in this built-up section except Trinity Churchyard. On the upper plaza is a 42-foot-high sculpture, Jean Dubuffet's *The Group of Four Trees*, installed in 1972. In the sunken plaza, seven basalt rocks from Japan's Uji River combine with marble and water to create Isamu Noguchi's image of islands in a sea of tranquillity. This is only a hint of the art housed within the bank's offices, a collection considered to be one of the largest ever assembled by a commercial organization. In David Rockefeller's washroom, for instance, was hung a color lithograph by Cézanne.

Within a decade of the coming of this building, a whole new city had sprung up along the East and Hudson rivers, taking the buildings of the 1920s, with their decorated towers that gently pricked the sky, and quite literally boxing them in.

Kips Bay Plaza   1961

Thirtieth to Thirty-third streets between First and Second avenues
North building, 1965
I. M. Pei, Associates, Architects

Instead of one bearing column every few windows, there is one bearing column at every window, making a load-bearing wall of reinforced concrete. "What you see is the structure," said the architect.

By 1960 the federal and local governments were engaged in urban renewal on a major scale. With Title I projects, they would share the cost of making a site available to a private developer at a marked-down price. The developer would build apartments, which could in turn be rented at affordable prices. To sweeten the pot, the Federal Housing Authority backed each room in an apartment with a maximum of $3,750 in mortgage insurance, enough for Webb & Knapp to take advantage of the scheme in Kips Bay Plaza, New York's first Title I project.

At the time, balconies were de rigueur in middle-class apartment houses, visibly separating middle-income housing from City housing, where balconies had been declared luxurious, hence forbidden. And the FHA defined balconies as rooms, so although a balcony cost nowhere near $3,750 to build, the builder could get that much in mortgage insurance. (A bathroom, according to the FHA, was not a room.) But, architect Pei considered balconies to be useless dirt collectors that could only be used a few months out of every year, and so he designed Kips Bay Plaza without them. If Webb & Knapp had to give up balconies, they needed something to make the project cheaper. Therefore, instead of one bearing column every few windows, Kips Bay features one bearing column at every window. Like anything stamped out of a mold, it saves money since the identical forms are easily repeated. This multitude of light, narrow columns—there are four every 17 feet—when joined to the usual horizontal members, creates a rigid structural form, and the walls almost become stress diagrams of the buildings themselves.

While creating New York's first exterior load-bearing apartment-house walls in reinforced concrete, Pei also created New York's first apartment houses with floor-to-ceiling windows, apartment houses in the full flowering of the International Style. The windows play an important role in the repetitive design—they are set in 14½ inches to provide shadows in the facade while shielding the apartments from sky glare.

Kips Bay Plaza has been criticized not for its inherent design, but for its sterile setting. Unrelated to anything but its own presence, Kips Bay is an example of twentieth-century towers set off by themselves in their own urban wilderness, solitary, isolated, and remote from street life.

Butterfield House   1962

37 West Twelfth Street, between Fifth Avenue
and the Avenue of the Americas
Mayer, Whittlesey & Glass, Architects

This thoroughly modern apartment house of glass and brown brick presents a thoroughly neighborly facade to a street whose scale is out of the mid-nineteenth century.

The human scale of Greenwich Village is one of the neighborhood's hallmarks, and Twelfth Street between Fifth Avenue and the Avenue of the Americas, with its predominantly mid-nineteenth century buildings, is one of the blocks that makes the Village justifiably famous. When news spread that a new apartment house with 102 apartments was being planned for the block, shudders rippled down its spine. What the block did not need was some towering box with balconies bristling from a hostile facade and plastic flowers in the

210

lobby. What the block got is a beauty, a thoroughly modern apartment house that bows to the mid-nineteenth-century scale of the street.

The site is an irregular one, 50 feet wide on Twelfth Street and extending north to Thirteenth Street, where the site is 215 feet. Sensitive to the scale and history of the place, architects Mayer, Whittlesey & Glass designed a seven-story building for Twelfth Street, where the seven-story building is taller than its immediate neighbors to the west but certainly no blockbuster. Since Thirteenth Street was already filled with tall loft buildings, the bulk of the apartments were placed there in a thirteen-story building.

Like the Rockefeller Apartments, Butterfield House is two buildings, here separated from each other by an open-ended courtyard and linked by a glass-enclosed arcade. The entrance is on Twelfth Street. Almost every apartment has either a balcony or a "garden room," balconies with jalousie windows that admit light and air but keep out rain. Every apartment has a bay window that affords a decent view, and where layouts permit, bedrooms overlook the landscaped courtyard. Kitchens have pantries, penthouses boast concrete gazebos, and a sense of neighborliness pervades.

Off Fifth Avenue in the Village is basically a family neighborhood, so no efficiency apartments were planned. In fact, only 12 percent of the apartments have just one bedroom; the balance are two- or three-bedroom units (the floor plans show the latter as two bedrooms with a library). The cooperative apartments did not come cheap. A two-bedroom apartment cost about $28,000 in 1962, with monthly maintenance charges of about $350. But elegance is expensive, and with the interplay of solids and voids, with the trapezoidal bays running up the building, and with the effect of the bays reinforced on Thirteenth Street by staggered walls, this is an elegant building.

Lincoln Center for the Performing Arts
1962–1966

Between Sixtieth and Sixty-sixth streets,
Broadway to Amsterdam Avenue
Chairman, architectural committee, Wallace K.
Harrison; Metropolitan Opera, Wallace K.
Harrison, Architect; Avery Fisher Hall, Max
Abramovitz, Architect; New York State Theater,
Philip Johnson and Richard Foster, Architects;
Library and Museum of Performing Arts,
Skidmore, Owings & Merrill, Architects; Vivian
Beaumont Theater, Eero Saarinen, Architect;
Juilliard School, Pietro Belluschi and Catalano &
Westerman, Architects; Fordham University,
South Building, Voorhees, Walker, Smith, Smith
& Haines, Architects; North Building, Slingerland
& Booss, Architects; Guggenheim Bandshell,
Eggers & Higgins, Architects.

A performing-arts center that sequesters itself from the fabric of urban life and can be as dead as the travertine that sheathes it or as lively as the performing artists and the audiences that fill it.

The idea came to "power broker" Robert Moses in the 1950s: many of the city's performing-arts groups were in desperate need of new homes. The Metropolitan Opera had been trying to get out of its 1883 house since the 1920s. The New York Philharmonic was having a tough time negotiating its lease at Carnegie Hall. Both the New York City Opera and Ballet were still performing in what had been the Shriners' Mecca Temple but had become City Center. And Moses knew that other institutions, such as Fordham University and the Juilliard School of Music, were interested in midtown buildings. To fill out the group, the library and Museum of the Performing Arts would be created. With the aid of Title I the Mosaic dream became a New York reality by the early 1960s, coming together as Lincoln Center.

An architectural committee headed by Wallace K. Harrison created an overall design that is latter-day Baroque in concept. An open-ended plaza is the focal point, with three colonnaded buildings, all sheathed in travertine, providing the walls of the plaza. Smack dab in the center of the plaza is a fountain, and around it are concentric circles with lines emanating from it like compass points, one of the few attempts in the city to create an interesting pattern in the pavement.

Dominating the plaza and providing its axial focus is the Metropolitan Opera with its five great Roman arches. Within the arches are set lights to illuminate the terrace, and through the arches shine the only vibrant colors in the facades of the complex, the colors of Marc Chagall's murals. The Met's side walls are usually ignored, but their closely spaced mullions act as a wonderful foil for the open spaces of the front. This is the most Baroque of Lincoln Center's buildings, reflecting the grandeur associated with the great opera houses of Europe. Spaciousness, red plush, gold leaf, crystal chandeliers, and a serpentine staircase provide a stage for all the actors. It is also the largest of Lincoln Center's buildings, with 3,800 seats, twenty rehearsal rooms (three of which are large enough to mount any stage action), and the world's most highly mechanized stage, with six 60-foot-long hydraulic lifts.

Avery Fisher Hall, with 2,836 seats, is the permanent home of the New York Philharmonic. It is a glass box with a peristyle before it and a hall within it, its shape clearly revealed through the glass. The placement of its balconies, which are cantilevered within the building's walls, is reflected in the promenades that encircle the loge and two "terraces." Breaking the severity of the geometry are Richard Lippold's brass sculptures, *Orpheus* and *Apollo.*

Completing the trio is Philip Johnson's New York State Theater, likewise a modernist's variation on the Baroque. The grand foyer on the first ring has tiers of balconies surrounding it, and off it is an outdoor balcony that is tucked into the peristyle, a favorite place for theatergoers to gather during intermission for a breath of fresh air, even on the chilliest evenings. Unlike the other halls, the orchestra is arranged in the continental seating pattern, with no central aisles.

Tucked away in the northwest corner and not visible from the plaza is Lincoln Center's most successful piece of design, Eero Saarinen's Vivian Beaumont Theater. It is simply a horizontal slab of concrete with boldly expressive columns for the porch, and a glass wall behind. Its scale is harmonious with the formal pool in front of it, and Henry Moore's sculpture acts as the perfect foil for the theater's horizontality.

If cities represent concentrations of industry then Lincoln Center is an urban place. But if urban places occur within the urban fabric, then it is anti-urban. There is little life on the sequestered plaza except when the crowds pour in and out, and that vitality lasts only as long as the doors are open. But the center can be a joyous place, a festival of the arts, gathering within its walls a striving for beauty and perfection that can be humbling.

Pan Am Building
1963

200 Park Avenue, between Forty-fourth and Forty-fifth streets
Emery Roth & Sons, Architects; Walter Gropius (The Architects' Collaborative) and Pietro Belluschi, Design Consultants

The scale of the Pan Am Building brought the building little but outrage at first and firm resolve now never to let another like it happen again. One trip to Pan Am is enough.

In a city whose resolve has always been to build 'em higher, wider, but not necessarily any more handsome, it is ironic that the Pan Am Building should have created such a storm of protest, a storm that has not yet subsided. If the reason for a city is concentration, if the function of a city is congregation, and if the attraction of a city is multiplicity of choice, then the Pan Am Building should be beyond reproach. Here, after all, is a vertical building in a vertical city, built at a public transportation hub with three commuter lines and five subway lines downstairs. The trains could bring the workers in and the elevators could take them up, all of the estimated 17,000 occupants and 250,000 daily visitors, a number greater than the 1970 population of Tucson, Arizona.

The Pan Am Building, erected over some of Grand Central's air rights, provides about 2.4 million square feet of rentable space—the only two buildings that were bigger at the time were the Pentagon and Chicago's Merchandise Mart—and it is all on a 3.5-acre site. Its forty-nine-story octagonal tower rises from a ten-story base. Its northern and southern facades are each sixty-two windows wide (a World Trade Center tower is only fifty-eight windows wide). Two mechanical floors, each with squared-off columns, attempt to unify the facade. And the facade is nothing more than one precast concrete panel after another, a marvel of expediency, no doubt, since the construction company only had to hoist up one panel, slap it into place, and go on to the next, taking the merest aesthetic to its grossest proportions.

What is lacking is any sense of scale, any sense of grace. This mass, this behemoth, rises straight up and looms over Park Avenue from both ends, dwarfing the New York Central Building to the north and Grand Central Terminal to the south, shouldering aside all sense of proportion and elegance in its gigantism.

The building's flat roof used to be a helicopter landing pad, linking the building directly with New York's airports. Imagine the chill that ran through the neighboring offices when a helicopter took off or landed—first a blast of sound reverberating amidst the canyons, then a shadow across the desk. Finally, the inevitable happened in 1977—a landing strut collapsed, killing people on the heliport and in the streets below. The helicopter battle is probably over, but not the desire of the bankrupt Penn Central to build an even bigger building directly over the terminal itself. Luckily for us, the Supreme Court has ruled in favor of Grand Central's landmark designation, sparing us another Pan Am behemoth.

The Premiere   1963

333 East Sixty-ninth Street, between Second and Third avenues
Mayer, Whittlesey & Glass, Architects

An apartment house that is sensitive to its surroundings and brings a visual diversity where it could have presented another white brick wall with windows stuck into it and balconies stuck out of it.

The first great wave of real-estate speculation on the Upper East Side took place in the 1880s. With the coming of the Third Avenue El, the avenues and side streets were lined with tenements and smatterings of brownstones. With the demolition of the Third Avenue El in 1955 came the second great wave of real-estate speculation, when block after block of new "luxury" apartment buildings was thrown up both on and off the avenues, most built within the maximum confines of the law but providing minimum amenities for the tenants and less grace for the cityscape. Ironically, they destroyed the very mystique of luxury they set out to exploit. Some, like this apartment house, were exceptions. This is a side-

street building which occupies a long lot, 200 feet wide and 100 feet deep. It could not legally go much higher, and it's unlikely that the building could have been built with more style.

To preserve the color qualities of the block, with its row of brownstones across the street, the Premiere was given a facade of buff brick. To preserve the tradition of private row houses, the Premiere was constructed with sixteen duplex apartments on the first and second floors. The front apartments have private entrances from the street, set behind little gardens, just like private homes would have, and the rear apartments have private back yards. To preserve the family image of the Upper East Side, not a single studio apartment was built, and two-thirds of the apartments have two bedrooms. To create visual interest, most of the balconies are recessed, with those on the top two setback floors cantilevered to the building line, all of which create light and shadow and varied planes. Small bits of detailing, which might at first escape the eye but add to the whole, include the notched piers whose line is continued even in the corners of the cantilevered balconies, and the upper floors of the front duplexes that have pairs of tall thin windows which create a base line for the building.

Every apartment in the front has a terrace, and every dining room has a double exposure, one facing south, the other facing east or west. So often terraces in New York apartments are desolate places, little more than soot-catchers, but here there are hanging plants and window boxes filled with geraniums and petunias. And the tenants have the use of the wind-protected roof-deck for sunning and a glass-enclosed recreation room.

216

Chatham Towers   1963

170 Park Row, on a triangular plot bounded by
Worth Street and Chatham Square
Kelly & Gruzen, Architects

*Solids and voids, light and shadow, as if the buildings were
carved out of gritty cliffs of concrete.*

This pair of remarkable towers was built by the Committee
for Middle Income Housing after some complicated public
financing deals, including Title I, as a cooperative housing
development for middle-income families. The equity invested for a three-bedroom apartment in 1963 was about
$9,000, with monthly carrying charges of about $270. For
their investment, the 240 coopers got several firsts in New
York housing, including the first use of entirely exposed
poured-in-place concrete, the first use of wallboard throughout, and the first use of Swedish-designed, double-paned
windows that pivot up and down for ventilation and easy
cleaning, complete with Venetian blinds incorporated within
the double panes of glass.

Such firsts, however, seem academic and trivial when
measured against the excitement in the form and texture of
these buildings. Nothing like them had ever been seen in
New York, a pair of towers that seem carved out of gritty
cliffs of concrete. To create the gritty effect, wood forms of
rough fir boards were used to imprint their texture in the
concrete walls, making vertical grooves that create light and
shadow, solids and voids. The same effect that is created
vertically in microcosm in the walls is created horizontally
in macrocosm in the massing by balconies and the lack of
them. This effect is further extended within the balconies
themselves by the solid walls and the voids that are the open
and shadowed places. These great jagged forms, topped by
Cyclopean heads, seemingly hover over Chinatown when
seen from the north.

When viewed close up, their entrances are hard to find, only because the buildings are set on an awkward site—it seems that the buildings turn their backs on everything and everyone (the entrances are from a driveway off Worth Street). Softening this seeming indifference are the various levels of horizontal landscaping that act as foils for the verticality of the buildings. This area is not the stereotype of the dead plaza, but is a creation that provides a real play area for children and a genuine contemplative area for adults (the buildings occupy only 15 percent of the site, with 85 percent of the land used for the plaza).

When visitors come upon Chatham Towers from neighboring Chinatown, they often believe that they see dragons in the form of the buildings, the kind of dragons that are dragged out and around every Chinese New Year. Is it a romantic conceit, or are the dragons really there?

CBS Building   1965

51 West Fifty-second Street, at the Avenue of the Americas
Eero Saarinen & Associates, Architects

When you gaze up at Eero Saarinen's only skyscraper, it stares you down, and you know that this is no ordinary skyscraper.

All the bad things about "Sixth Avenooism" have to be tempered when the subject is the CBS Building. Granted, it is a sheer skyscraper, set back from the building line on its own plaza, with another bank on its main floor. But this is no anonymous building; instead of being desensitized, its viewer is humbled, as if in the presence of some awesome, mysterious, almost sacred thing.

What distinguishes the thirty-eight-story building and creates an interplay of light and shadow is its 5-foot-wide, V-shaped concrete piers with a veneer of Canadian black granite that alternate with 5-foot-wide windows. Each column comes to a 90-degree angle and is set at a 45-degree angle from the building. At the corners, the columns merge, so what would ordinarily become another 45-degree angle becomes instead a flat 180-degree plane.

These closely and regularly spaced columns do triple duty: they set the somber tone of the building; they act as a bearing wall—not a bearing frame—in tandem with an interior core of reinforced concrete walls (there is a 35-foot span between the core and the perimeter); and the concrete is hollow, containing, with the spandrels, ducts for air-conditioning, electrical systems, etc.

The magical number for the facade is 5—5-foot-wide windows alternate with 5-foot-wide columns, making 10-foot modules. Five feet was determined because it is the minimum space required for revolving doors, and it is handy for interior decoration—a chair and a desk that measures 2½ by 5 feet will fit into a 5-by-5-foot space. Take this to its logical conclusion in the pecking order of corporate life and you can tell a worker's status by the size of his office, from a manager (10 by 10 feet) to a vice-president (15 by 15 feet) to the president (20 by 20 feet). If you looked for the president's office on the top floor, you would not find it, since then it would be directly under one of the utility floors (the other is the second). To shield the brass from any hums, rumbles, or buzzes, the top executives are housed on the thirty-seventh floor.

The building is approached not by ascending stairs but by descending them, five of them, of the same granite as the tower. Notice the bronze cbs/52 or cbs/53 by the handrails, and the same bronze motif over the entrances. No Pan Am neon here.

Eero Saarinen said in 1961 that he wanted his only skyscraper to be a building that would stand firmly on the ground and grow straight up. He got one, and more.

Whitney Museum   1966

Southeast corner of Madison Avenue and
Seventy-fifth Street
Marcel Breuer and Hamilton Smith, Architects

*An upside-down ziggurat, its west wall cantilevered toward
Madison Avenue, its personality a brooding fortress.*

The plot for the Whitney Museum measures only 104 feet on Madison Avenue and 125 feet on Seventy-fifth Street. On this

relatively small space was set an upside-down ziggurat, a dark, brooding fortress of a building with a facade of flame-treated gray granite and trapezoidal windows that pierce its skin and provide a sculptural contrast to the otherwise rectilinear facade. It is a startling building, but a most reasonable design for the museum, a design that fulfilled the Whitney's requirements brilliantly. The museum wanted a sculpture garden that did not sequester itself but which could be appreciated by passersby, so it was put in a moat where everyone could see it. This space was created by reversing the idea of setback building. Instead of setting back the building on its upper floors, the architects set back the building on the lower floors and cantilevered the rest of the building in "set-outs." The museum wanted a small cafeteria and lecture hall, so these were put in the basement, one of the floors with the least square footage. A bridge whose canopy reflects the angularity of the building leads across the moat to the main floor, which is likewise small, housing only a small gallery and the necessary accouterments of a museum—ticket sales, coat room, shop, etc. Each of the floors above, where the main galleries are assembled, project 14 feet further west than the floor immediately below. Since this is where the galleries are, it is where the greatest square footage is needed. It means that the top floor has a 42-foot overhang, yet it is the only floor that comes to the building line and extends the full depth of the 125-foot plot. The ceilings are high to accommodate paintings and sculpture.

The concept of the building was radical, but its architectonics, if anything, were conservative. The building is constructed of reinforced concrete, its north and south walls being load-bearing. The gallery floors are cantilevered, with the Madison Avenue walls a series of deep trusses spanning the cantilevered steps. When reduced to its elements, it seems absurdly simple.

Rugged and stark without, this building is very hospitable to the visitor within, quietly showing off the museum's great collection of contemporary American art to advantage. The galleries are large and airy, with comfortable flagstones underfoot. The trapezoidal bay windows that project 20 to 25 degrees from the walls keep out direct light, and their shapes provide exciting glimpses and new perspectives of East Side life.

University Village   1966

Between Bleecker and Houston streets, La
Guardia Place and Mercer Street
I. M. Pei & Partners, Architects

*Three crisply designed towers tugging for your attention
while Picasso's Sylvette gazes at you.*

One of the goals of the City Beautiful Movement in the 1890s and the organizations created in its wake, such as New York's Municipal Art Society, was to incorporate statuary in public spaces, a movement which generally sputtered along throughout the twentieth century. The Revised Zoning Law of 1961, which brought plazas and public spaces to the city, has resulted in a great upsurge in statuary placed on plazas, including *5 in 1* at the new Police Headquarters Plaza, *Cubed Curve* at the Time & Life Building, Dubuffet's *Group of Five Trees* at Chase Manhattan Plaza, and Noguchi's *Cube* at the Marine Midland Building. Sometimes the sculpture is just an afterthought, an appendage to the building with no relation-

221

ship between one and the other, but sometimes there is a collaborative effect that creates a tension, both the building and the statue tugging at the eye for attention yet both working harmoniously together. So it is at Marine Midland, and so it is at University Village.

The statue at University Village is Picasso's *Portrait of Sylvette,* enlarged from a small Cubist sculpture he created in 1934. The original stands 2 feet high; this 60-ton, sand-blasted concrete version stands 36 feet high. It was I. M. Pei who wanted a Picasso sculpture for the space, and it was Picasso who selected *Sylvette* to go there.

The other element in this visual tug-of-war is University Village, three thirty-story towers that manifest a functional clarity in their design that is filled with subtleties. The placement of the buildings, for instance, provides a view that shows one facade eight windows wide set against two facades four windows wide, or vice versa, depending on your vantage point. The placement of one building was simply rotated 90 degrees to create the diversity. The floor plan for each building is a squared-off pinwheel, with equally spaced windows neatly tucked within the crisp post-and-lintel system. A concrete facade that is about 25 feet wide acts as a foil for the light and shadow created by the windows. Each apartment has two windows per living room, and one window per bedroom. Inset in each facade is a row of windows that seems out of joint, a row that creates another kind of tension. It is a third window for living rooms in corner apartments which front on the facade around the corner. This window creates a naturally lit dining area, an unexpected fillip for middle-income housing (the tower nearest La Guardia Place is a Mitchell-Lama Project; the other two are New York University faculty and staff housing). These buildings show an attention to massing and detailing that many "luxury" houses ignore. The tenants get their money's worth, as do the passing pedestrians.

Ford Foundation   1967

320 East Forty-third Street, between Second and First avenues
Kevin Roche & John Dinkeloo Associates, Architects

The Ford Foundation headquarters presents elegant walls of granite, Cor-Ten steel, and glass to the street while embracing a garden within.

The trend of the 1960s was for office buildings to be plunked down behind windswept plazas. Safe and sequestered from the madding crowd, they marched up Park and Sixth avenues in drab, corporate uniformity, scattering a fountain here and a bush there. Then came the Ford Foundation, dispenser of largess to the world through its grants and to New York through its headquarters.

Instead of being set back and stuck up, the Ford Foundation achieves a continuity with its neighbors by coming out to the building line. At first glance from Forty-second Street, the pinkish-gray granite piers appear to be the entire building, a monolith of sheer, windowless piers (actually, the piers house stairs and utility shafts). Slowly the subtlety and grace of the building reveal themselves as you glimpse the facade of rusted Cor-Ten steel and glass coming into view, suspended between the piers. The building is on a 200-by-200-foot lot and presents itself as a cube, clearly delineated by the piers and openly transparent, light yet forceful, majestic, commanding.

Instead of a plaza open to the weather built around the periphery of the building, the Ford Foundation is built around a plaza that is closed to the weather, embracing a garden within. Rain or shine, hot or cold, the garden that is a third of an acre beckons and lures you inside like a siren song. Twelve stories above is a delicately patterned skylight, and at your feet are seventeen trees—trees, not bushes—as well as shrubs and perennials. A stream courses through it, and in a convoluted act of reciprocity, visitors toss pennies into the pools. Since Forty-third Street is topographically higher than Forty-second Street, the garden is on a hill, and rises one story.

The offices are built on the west and the north sides of the building, and most overlook the vernal scene below from a perch in the ell. The two top floors encircle the building, like a square doughnut. Inside, everything is brass and mahogany in an aesthetic that is elegantly uniform, whether you're the chairman or the chief assistant to the assistant chief. The entrance is on Forty-third Street, tucked into the side of the building with one of the city's most impressive portes cocheres leading up to it, complete with a brass-lined curb.

The garden took about one percent of the total building cost of $16 million, but here is a gift to the city that cannot be measured in dollars and cents. A hush, the feeling of being somewhere sacred, pervades, and to speak above a whisper would profane the power of the place.

Paley Park 1967

5 East Fifty-third Street, between Fifth and
Madison avenues
Zion & Breen, Landscape Architects; Albert
Preston Moore, Consulting Architect

*Urban materials and a touch of nature make this vest-pocket
park an island of tranquillity in a sea of activity.*

Olmsted and Vaux showed that 840 acres of landscaping
could create a major urban park. Andrew Haswell Green
showed that trees planted on sidewalks and median strips
could create parkways. Lillian Wald showed that a patch of
concrete with a swing or a slide stuck into it could make a
playground. Raymond Hood showed that landscaping just a
few open spaces and rooftops could create the vernal oasis
that is Rockefeller Center. And Zion & Breen have shown that
one waterfall, a dozen trees, a little ivy, and a few tables and
chairs can make a vest-pocket park that is an island of tranquillity in a sea of activity.

A "waterwall" acts as a magical, almost mystical attraction, providing the ceaseless fascination inherent in moving
water as well as a pleasant sound that drowns out traffic
noises. It is soothing both visually and acoustically. Ivy
climbs two walls, and underfoot is not the usual concrete, or
even terrazzo, but gray, granite pavers that rise about one
inch above the mortar, setting a rough-hewn tone for the park.
Even the honey locust trees, in rugged urban individualism,
thrive in them.

Instead of the concrete and wood benches the Parks Department deposits throughout the city's parks, it's a moveable
feast. Like Paris's Tuileries, individual chairs can be moved
around, providing privacy if one desires, or allowing a group
to gather around a table for a sense of camaraderie. (Unlike
the Tuileries, however, no woman will charge you a chair-
rental fee.) If you want something to eat, you may bring your
own, or buy a snack from the limited menu.

Any resemblance between the cool elegance of Paley
Park and the cool elegance of the CBS Building is not purely
coincidental, since the park was given to New York City by
William Paley, board chairman of CBS in memory of his
father (the Paley Foundation maintains it). Built on the site

of Sherman Billingsley's famous Stork Club, Paley Park proves that even a small plot measuring 42 by 100 feet can make a successful city park. (Vest-pocket parks that are sterile and hostile despite many of the components that work so well in Paley Park are the block-through areas behind the Exxon and McGraw-Hill buildings.)

Theoretically, Paley Park is extended by means of mid-block plazas that stretch south for two blocks, first through the Harper & Row Building, then through Olympic Tower. Unfortunately, these real-estate tradeoffs with the City act as little more than corridors, lacking all the grace and joy of Paley Park.

Marine Midland Building 1967

140 Broadway, between Cedar and Liberty streets
Skidmore, Owings & Merrill, Architects

Manhattan's most elegant tower finds the perfect foil in Isamu Noguchi's Cube.

In 1961, a major revision of the Zoning Law of 1916 granted builders permission to erect a building that, within limits, could rise straight up, providing the building was placed on only 40 percent of the lot. If the builder provided a plaza, he was allowed to erect a building that was 20 percent bigger. Of all the buildings erected under the revised zoning law, this is the most elegant, with its scale, textures, and uncluttered form contributing to its elegance.

225

Take the Broadway facade, for instance, which is really
the side of the building (the entrances are on Cedar Street).
The building presents horizontal bands of windows. Each
band is divided into three groupings of windows, and each
grouping is divided into six parts. This is a subtle variation
on the classic Chicago fenestration of Louis Sullivan and
company. Sullivan's windows at the Carson Pirie Scott store,
for instance, consist of one central, horizontal, unbroken pane
of glass, flanked by a pair of windows divided into two horizontal parts. The central pane is about twice as long as both
flanking windows combined.

In the Marine Midland Building, four central windows
act as this central pane and take up about three-quarters of
the module, and the two flanking narrower windows take up
about one-quarter. These flanking windows provide the necessary vertical contrast. The wide modular windows coupled
with the narrow bronze piers and spandrels express the supporting steel frame honestly and elegantly.

On the Broadway plaza is the perfect foil for the building,
Isamu Noguchi's *Cube*. (It's really not a cube at all, but a
rhomboid.) The cube is bright where the building's tone is
muted, and it is tantalizingly tilted where the building is tall,
lean, and erect.

The Marine Midland Building invites no one to clutter
up the cityscape—the only place to perch for a noontime
snack is on one of the three benches that surround the potted
plants on Cedar Street, and they provide no back supports.

Manufacturers Hanover Trust   1969
Operations Center

4 New York Plaza, northeast corner of Water and
Broad streets
Carson, Lundin & Shaw, Architects

*A building whose brick facade was intended to blend with
some of its nineteenth-century neighbors creates a new
medievalism instead.*

With the flowering of the computer in the 1960s came a new
twenty-four-hour-a-day industry, and the need for office
space to house it. For its back-office operations, Manufacturers Hanover Trust erected this twenty-two-story building.
The bank's computers occupy all but five of the building's
floors. The design could have been another glass-and-some-
thing facade, but architect Arvin Shaw looked around the old
neighborhood. Fraunces Tavern and James Watson's house
were both just down the block, and row after row of red-brick
Federal and Greek Revival commercial buildings lined South,
Front, and Water streets, many of them occupied by tanners
and coffee-roasters and fishmongers. To make this building
unobtrusive enough to blend with its neighbors, Shaw gave
it a facade of orange brick flecked with iron that would mel-
low to a brownish-reddish hue. He did not use ordinary 8-
inch bricks for the job, but Norman bricks which are about
12 inches long, giving a horizontal strength to the building.

And instead of bands of windows at regular spacings, he divided the bulk of the fenestration into strips, with the windows set in. Two sets of strips are three stories high, with a seven-story-high set between them. The whole is topped by individually framed windows. The narrow, vertical openings remind Robin Hood fans of the loop windows that were cut into the walls of medieval castles for archers, and the top seven stories are reminiscent of a battlement. Combine the strength of these beautifully detailed walls with the strength of the battered piers that reflect masonry-bearing walls and a new medievalism is created.

When work began on this building in 1967 there were already ten new buildings being erected in the Financial District, with five more planned. Ironically, these new buildings would toll the bell for the nineteenth-century buildings with which this one was to blend, and a whole new ambience would be created from the Battery to Fulton Street, little of it brick.

This building was also one of the harbingers of another change in New York, that of changing street names to reflect a real-estate promoter's dream of a prestigious address with "plaza" in it. Rockefeller Plaza and Chase Manhattan Plaza preceded this one, but then came the flood, carrying away perfectly understandable street names and numbers, leaving only confusion in its wake. Few people know, and, what's worse, can figure out, where New York Plaza is, or Astor Plaza, or Liberty Plaza, but to some, they sure sound nice.

49 East Eighty-ninth Street 1969

Madison Avenue, between Eighty-ninth and
Ninetieth streets
Birnbaum and Oppenheimer, Brady & Lehrecke,
Architects

*Its scale is so colossal that it creates its own wind pattern,
but its detailing in brick is elegant enough to make up for its
bulk.*

Brick as a facade for prestigious apartment houses had been
falling out of favor in the 1960s as quickly as it had for prestigious office buildings. Many luxury apartment houses were
being given facades of exposed concrete or even glass curtain
walls that looked as coolly slick as any Park Avenue corporate headquarters. Beginning with this building, brick began
a serious comeback for apartment houses. Like the Manufacturers Hanover Trust Operations Center, these are not the
common white bricks that had become so popular, but multi-
hued brown bricks with flecks of iron in them. They are about
8 inches long and 2½ inches high, and are set into mortar
that is about half an inch all around. This creates a strong
visual contrast, especially with the brick and mortar set off
by very thin but noticeable stringcourses at every floor. Even
the terraces, with floors of concrete, are walled with the same
brick and mortar. Continuing the theme to the street, all of

228

the plaza around the building is paved in brick, and the sliced-off pyramids for planters likewise have brick facades.

All of the apartments in this building have two or three bedrooms, all have terraces, and 9-foot ceilings, an amenity in new buildings that is almost unheard of. On the roof is another tenant perquisite—a year-round swimming pool and sauna.

This is not a warm and gentle building. Its terraces bristle, and its lower floors, with the slant-ins and moatlike entrance, give the feeling of a Romanesque fortress. Its scale is super-colossal, yet it is only five windows deep on the side streets. A two-story wing extends on Ninetieth Street beyond midblock (this open area is in essence the building's plaza, put behind the building instead of in front; it assures light for this building's rear apartments and for the apartments on Park Avenue). The tower does more than dominate the view from Central Park—its thirty-eight stories act as a solid wall to the prevailing winds. As they blow, the tower forces them down, creating a downdraft that might just blow your hat off.

77 Water Street   1970

Between Old Slip and Gouverneur Lane
Emery Roth & Sons, Architects; Rudolph de
Harak, Graphics.

A building with a sense of humor where there could have been a marble mausoleum.

From a distance, 77 Water Street's solar gray glass and aluminum skin looks like any other office tower, the likes of which you might find on the Avenue of the Americas or in L.A. It is svelte and slick, standing foursquare like a traditional corporate structure, its facade divided into two parts by louvers on the mechanical floors. However, traditional it's not. Its builder was Melvyn Kaufman, a man whose sayings should ensure him a place in Bartlett's. On the austere, corporate tower: "Marble and travertine are . . . terrific for the dead." On public areas: they should be "stimulating, exciting and valid rather than dull and stultifying." On his building a non-lobby for a lobby: "So what! It's dead space anyway."

He took his sayings and metamorphosed them into buildings that were designed by architects but whose direction came from him, buildings like this one and others—a famous neighbor is 127 John Street, with a playful clock and a neon-lit tunnel of corrugated metal for a lobby. He likes to play with lobbies: for instance, 77 Water Street has no lobby. Instead, it has a pebble-strewn stream bubbling its way around the arcade, an old-fashioned candy store nestled amidst the supporting columns, and, to keep everything toasty in the winter, "heat trees." The lobby, such as it is, consists of the elevator banks, and no more. Carrying his philosophy of fun into the elevators, Kaufman installed walls of illuminated Arabic numbers, and commissioned Morton Subotonick to write electronic music for the elevators. None

of that Muzak jazz here. And to please neighbors in taller buildings, the roof sports brightly painted mechanical equipment and a sculpture of a World War I biplane. (When the architects went to the Building Department, approval for the plane on the roof was originally denied. "You can't put a landing strip there," they were told. "You've got to get approval from the CAB.")

Kaufman's innovations have led to expenses in his buildings that the average management does not have to pay. Unlike most office buildings, for instance, this one invites people to "brown bag" their lunches in the lobby, and thus its maintenance workers have to carry away empty lunch bags, benches have to be painted regularly because they are used, and guards have to be reprogrammed to make visitors feel like welcome guests instead of intruders. The urban amenities that Kaufman provides were not legislated, they were given in the spirit that a builder owes something more to the city than his "bottom line."

9 West Fifty-seventh Street   1972

Between Fifth Avenue and the Avenue of the Americas
Skidmore, Owings & Merrill, Architects

New York's first sloping-front office building is a variation on a travertine Parsons table.

New York's two sloping-front office buildings arrived within the same year, one on Forty-second Street (1114 Avenue of the Americas), and this one on Fifty-seventh Street. Both buildings were designed by the same firm, but this one has more elegance, more panache. It is essentially a setback building, but instead of filling the allowable envelope of space with a right-angled, ziggurat building, architect Gordon Bunshaft designed a building that gracefully slopes up

to its tower in one unbroken line. The space is the same, only the effect is different.

Since 9 West Fifty-seventh Street was built midblock, it did break the line of the street. This effect was assailed by some urban planners and architectural critics, despite the diversity and a certain tension it brought to the block. An uncontested contribution was to passing pedestrians—instead of a fifty-story setback tower rising on 40 percent of the site with a dead plaza before it, the building almost comes to the building line. A treat is the playful sculpture of a "9" on Fifty-seventh Street. Designed by Ivan Chermayeff, it is there as much out of good-natured spirit as to tell the building's address.

Two great structures with sloping fronts preceded 9 West Fifty-seventh Street. The first was the Eiffel Tower, an intricate lattice of iron. The second was Chicago's First National Bank Building (1969; C. F. Murphy Associates), with clearly delineated columns that seem disassociated from the building itself. In neither structure was there any attempt to mask the reality of the structural components. At 9 West Fifty-seventh Street there is no obvious grid of posts and lintels on the 200-foot-long southern and northern facades, nothing but sheer walls of glass that seem suspended flush with the legs of the travertine enframement. The eastern and western facades set a different tone; there the glass curtain wall is set into the frame of travertine, pairs of X-bracings brazenly announcing that something has to keep the thing together. If you are looking for the lintels, they are to be found. The stone subtly reflects the window-spandrel configuration—slabs of

231

stone that are set vertically into the facade reflect the height of the windows; where they are placed horizontally, they reflect the girders.

The sloping front provides floors of different square footage, which makes renting easier, but this design must be the bane of the status-seeking office renter—there are no prestigious corner offices.

1 Liberty Plaza   1972

Broadway, between Liberty and Cortlandt streets
Skidmore, Owings & Merrill, Architects

The configuration of the flanged steel spandrels will not allow flames to rise but instead forces them outward.

The steel for the supporting frame of a high-rise building must be protected from flames and intense heat. Otherwise, just as with iron, the heat could result in structural damage and conceivably lead to the building's collapse. In 1968, engineers at United States Steel proved in tests that flanged spandrels of steel with fire-proofing on the outer faces of the top and bottom rims as well as fireproofing between the spandrels and the girders could protect the frame. The configuration of the flanged spandrels will not allow flames to rise, but instead forces them outward. Thus, the steel facade plays the role of the protector of the frame, fulfilling the same function as any other fire-retardant facade. What it means is that the steel you see is not the supporting frame, but a facade that protects and reflects the frame.

This building has a clear span from its core to its exterior,

232

made possible by vertical trusses in the core coupled to the exterior columns for wind resistance. Huge girders were used to support the floors from the core to the facade as well as for the outside frame. This is reflected in the spandrels, which are about 6¼ feet high, or about the same height as the windows.

The 772-foot-high building seems to have greater bulk than that allowed by the building code. What the City Planning Commission said was that U.S. Steel, the building's sponsor, could build one building on one site to the total allowable building gross of two sites combined, which explains the bulk as well as the little park south of the building, across Liberty Street. This park theoretically continues a bank of open area from Chase Manhattan Plaza to the World Trade Center.

The building that stood on this site previously was Ernest Flagg's second Singer Tower, the world's tallest building in 1908 and everyone's idea of the way a great Beaux Arts skyscraper should look. Unfortunately, the old phenomenon of "tearing down and building up" cost a jewel from the "strangest crown that ever a city wore," as H. G. Wells described the skyline. The Singer Tower's destruction, however, brought one more record into the lexicon of trivia collectors—it was the tallest building ever to be demolished.

One Liberty Plaza continues the new phenomenon of numbering a building according to its own artificial plaza, instead of numbering it by street. The building's address should really be 85 Liberty Street or 165 Broadway, which would make the building easier to find in the scheme of things.

Elmer Holmes Bobst Library   1973

New York University, southeast corner of Washington Square South (West Fourth Street) and La Guardia Place
Philip Johnson; P. J. and Richard Foster, Architects

A great cube, 150 feet high with a twelve-story-high court rising within, faced in redstone to continue the red-brick tradition of Washington Square.

New York University President James Hester embarked on an ambitious building program in the 1960s for New York's largest private university, with architect Philip Johnson charged with creating the master plan. One of the goals was to create a library to do for NYU what Low Library had done for Columbia—set the tone for the buildings to come and act as the university's focal point. Before it could happen, variances had to be granted by the City and approval given by the local community planning board. The community was reluctant in general to let NYU "take over" Washington Square as its campus, and adamant about allowing no building 150 feet high to cast its shadow on the southeast corner of the square. A 1950s ordinance protected the very light with which the local board was concerned. The law stipulated that the cornice line on the south side of the square could not be higher than 60 feet, yet the university's proposal called for a building two-and-a-half times that height.

After seven years of bargaining, NYU would have a monumental piece of sculpture for its library, a great cube, 150 feet high, its facade clad in Longmeadow redstone. Within is one of the city's great interior spaces, a 100-foot-square, twelve-story-high court that rises the full 150-foot height, with the stacks and reading rooms arranged around the shell. To relieve the towering space and bring harmony to the whole, Johnson incorporated chevronlike stairways that dominate the south side of the court, with their gold-anodized aluminum balcony railings providing delicate decoration. For the design of the black, gray, and white marble floor, Johnson went back to Palladio's design for the piazza in front of the church of San Giorgia Maggiore in Venice. For the design of the elevator walls, which have a woven, textured look of silver cylinders on a bronze background, Johnson went back to Johnson, and you get a different sense of déjà vu. This *is* a Philip Johnson–designed building, and the

234

elevator walls resemble those of the Seagram Building and the New York State Theater. Sometimes the strange sensation can come over you that you are in the right elevator but the wrong building.

The library was a daring stroke that has proved a harbinger of NYU's increased stature as a major urban university. Unfortunately, in an ill-considered use of space, the university has added platform tennis courts to the roof of the library, creating an unfinished look to the roofline and breaking its dramatic horizontality.

55 Water Street   1973

Between Old Slip and Coenties Slip
Emery Roth & Sons, Architects

The largest privately built office building in the world.

You might not believe it to look at it, but this fifty-three-story office building and its annex have rentable floor space that adds up to 3.2 million square feet, making 55 Water Street the largest privately built office building in the world. (The Pentagon, built by the federal government, is the largest, and the Merchandise Mart in Chicago, with about 4 million square feet, combines both offices and storage facilities in one building.)

In New York only the World Trade Towers have more rentable space, with almost 4 million square feet apiece; the

Empire State Building has only 2.17 million square feet; and the infamous Equitable Building boasted only 1.2 million square feet.

Fifty-five Water Street was given this bulk by New York City's Office of Lower Manhattan Development in exchange for some amenities. Its management, for instance, is responsible for the care and maintenance of New Jeannette Park; there is a rooftop esplanade atop the annex's third story terrace that is open to the public and may be reached by an outside escalator separating the annex from the tower; and the space occupied by the Downtown Branch of the Whitney Museum has been donated by the management.

The facade of 55 Water Street is a drab expression of contemporary commercial architecture, quite a contrast with the treasure trove of Federal and Greek Revival commercial buildings from the early 1800s that graced this stretch of Water Street until the 1960s. They were "progressed" to death on behalf of bland behemoths like this one. One distinction this building shares with the World Trade Center and Rockefeller Center—it, too, has its own zip code, 10041.

Waterside Houses   **1974**

East of the FDR Drive, between Twenty-fifth and Thirtieth streets
Davis, Brody & Associates, Architects

Proof that subsidized housing need not be anonymous slabs but can have strength and grace and visual diversity.

Davis, Brody & Associates are among the first wave of architects to break away from "City Housing Modern," the anonymous slabs that have characterized municipal housing for twenty years, houses that city planners planned but which are hardly more enlightened in their aesthetics than the dumbbell apartments they usually replace.

Here, built out over the East River on two thousand concrete pilings that go down 80 feet to bedrock, is Waterside, proof that subsidized housing need not be the mean kind of housing projects that are a debasement of Le Corbusier's Radiant City.

As you approach these buildings by the stairs that lead up to the plaza you will experience a certain earth-mother quality about them, amazonian, but with a seductive softness nevertheless. So much of their appeal lies in their staggered massing, with different sets of floors cantilevered out, others recessed, and no two sets doing the same thing in the same building. There is both strength and grace, and it all creates tremendous visual diversity, a sense of being offered a third dimension where most buildings offer only two.

Of the four apartment towers at Waterside, the northern, at thirty-one stories, is the shortest. Its financing was arranged with the federal government, which provided a low-cost mortgage to New York City. Three towers are thirty-seven stories each, and all were sponsored under New York State's Mitchell-Lama Act. This law allows tax-exempt bonds to be sold, with the proceeds going to limited-profit housing companies which in turn erect the buildings.

Built as they are, sequestered over the East River with the highway blocking easy access to the rest of Manhattan, Waterside disproved the axiom "population follows transportation." A special bus route was created—an extension of the M16—to act as a link between Waterside and the "mainland." In addition to the four apartment towers, low-lying service buildings supply such services as a supermarket, florist, restaurant, etc. (The United Nations International School, in a building designed by Harrison & Abramovitz, is at the south end.)

Other Davis/Brody buildings, many with the staggered massing and large (6½-by-8-inch) bricks that distinguish Waterside, include East Midtown Plaza, just a few blocks away on Twenty-third Street between Second and First avenues, the Ruppert and Yorkville Towers on Second Avenue in the low nineties, Cathedral Parkway Houses on Cathedral Parkway (110th Street) between Columbus and Amsterdam avenues, and Riverbend, on the Harlem River at Fifth Avenue and 145th Street.

World Trade Towers   1974

Between Vesey and Liberty streets, west of
Church Street
Minoru Yamasaki & Associates and Emery Roth
& Sons, Architects; Skilling, Helle, Christiansen,
Robertson, Structural Engineers

The two sculpturally rectilinear towers each rise 1,350 feet without the usual skeleton of steel that you would expect. New York's tallest buildings, the towers are tied for second place among the world's tallest.

The effect that the World Trade Towers had on the skyline was dramatic, even overwhelming. The two 110-story towers rise from 80-foot-high lancet windows, the towers' closely spaced aluminum facing projecting an image that seems more radiator than building. But the solid, monolithic look of the

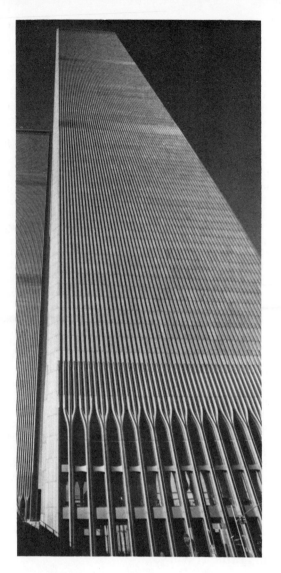

piers alternating with 22-inch-wide windows provides the hint of a technological breakthrough.

If you had witnessed the construction of the towers, you would not have seen the traditional, twentieth-century steel frame. Instead you would have seen the cores of the buildings rising first (they now house elevator shafts but then housed derricks). Just one step behind the cores came the walls, erected in prefabricated panels, the columns and spandrels welded together in modules two windows wide by two or three high. Once the walls and cores had climbed a few stories, they were linked by prefabricated 13-by-60-foot sections of floor framing. Each section consisted of the plenum between floors and ceilings (the conduits were added later), as well as lengthwise steel trusses for bracing. Crossbeams traverse the towers at every other floor. The result of this inno-

vative building system is a variation on a load-bearing wall, with unobstructed 60-foot spaces from the elevator banks to the outside walls.

Another revolution is the elevators: each tower, like Gaul, is divided into three parts; each part has a skylobby, the upper two reached by express elevators where a transfer is made to local elevators. By operating express and local service, the elevators do vertically what the subway does horizontally, while resolving the loss of rentable space on the lower floors (it was an old law that the higher the building the more space had to be given over to elevator banks on the lower floors).

The World Trade Center's more than 10 million square feet of space was created by the Port Authority of New York and New Jersey to bring together the business and government agencies involved in international trade. What that much space did to the real-estate market, of course, was to glut it. The towers alone, each over 200 by 200 square feet, provide 7.9 million square feet of rentable floor space. That is the equivalent of about fifty 200-by-800-foot blocks, or roughly the area of the blocks bounded by Thirty-fourth and Fifty-ninth streets between the Avenue of the Americas and Eighth Avenue.

For one of the city's most spectacular views, go to the observation deck. As you see planes flying below you, you will have the feeling that you too are in a plane, one that has magically stalled over the city, providing an undreamed-of panorama.

Olympic Tower   1975

645 Fifth Avenue, at Fifty-first Street
Skidmore, Owings & Merrill, Architects

An experiment in zoning—get retail stores, apartments, and pedestrian amenities written into the deal, and give greater bulk in exchange.

The cries of anguish over the future of Fifth Avenue could be clearly heard by the end of the 1960s. "Buildings to the building line," New Yorkers chanted. "Fifth Avenue for the shoppers," they placarded. "No more banks and airline offices," they petitioned. They did it because the disurbaniza-

tion of Fifth Avenue had already set in, and the coming of the General Motors Building, Fifth Avenue's first anonymous slab set back from its sunken plaza, sealed their resolve.

The Office of Midtown Planning and Development, city planners and architects who work for the City, realized that nothing but more GM Buildings would result from the economic reality of the then-current zoning laws, so they did the only reasonable thing—they changed the laws. The planners would encourage builders to bring their buildings to the building line, they would encourage the maintenance of Fifth Avenue as the prime shopping area of New York, they would even encourage residential living on the avenue again, and they would do it by offering greater bulk in exchange.

The first two floors of Olympic Tower are filled with some of the glossiest stores in town, and its seventeen floors of offices are 100 percent rented. Its thirty floors of cooperative apartments are practically all sold, with purchase prices averaging $200,000, a remarkable achievement since there has not been any residential living in this neighborhood since its days as Vanderbilt Alley. And it's all done behind a chic, blank facade that does not tell you where living spaces begin and working spaces leave off.

Only the entrances are segregated. To reach the apartments, one enters the smallish lobby on Fifty-first Street, a lobby through which, it is said, more Vuitton bags pass per capita than anywhere else in New York City. To reach the offices, one enters the block-through pedestrian arcade that runs from Fifty-first to Fifty-second streets. This "amenity," provided by the builder, was another exchange for building bulk, and so far it seems to have benefited only the builder. Despite the discreet signs on its marquees (they are there by legislative fiat), which say OPEN TO THE PUBLIC, 7 A.M. TO 12 P.M., hardly anybody seems to realize that "Olympic Place," as it is euphemistically called, is not just a nice entrance to Olympic Tower but is intended as a vest-pocket park, like Paley Park, and is indeed meant to be used by the public. So far, Olympic Tower is little more than a shaft.

Galleria 1975

117 East Fifty-seventh Street, between Park and
Lexington avenues
David Kenneth Specter and Philip Birnbaum,
Architects

*The experiment in zoning continued, this time resulting in a
schizoid building, part granite and glass, part brown brick
and glass.*

The same concern for an interesting and varied blockfront,
the same concern for pedestrians trying to get from street to
street without going around the block, the same concern for
integrating residential living with commercial office space,
in short the same concern that led to the City's changing the
zoning law, which led to Olympic Tower, led to the Galleria.
Since the Galleria is on the periphery of the office world, not
in the heart of it, more space could be devoted to apartments.
Instead of fewer than two apartment floors to every commercial floor, there are more than three apartment floors (thirty-
eight) for every commercial floor (twelve), and three of those
twelve floors are given over to a private health club.

The Galleria's appearance is almost schizoid, divided
between its Fifty-seventh Street entrance and its body. Its
entrance, which is likewise in two parts, is a granite and
glass, 90-foot-high atrium, a mini, and not terribly successful,
Ford Foundation. Through the glass doors and down twelve
steps, through the atrium and down some more steps, you'll
find the elevators to the offices and health club. Through the
atrium and up ten steps, you'll find doors leading to Fifty-
eighth Street, cleverly unmarked—unless you already knew
about the midblock connection you would never venture
there. This ninety-foot-high arcade is exuberant in its mag-
nanimity, but unfortunately this generous space is not one to
linger in. It is a space that neither takes your breath away nor
makes you feel comfortable. It is cold granite and clear glass,
and the few pitiful plants only add to the mausoleum quality
(granted, one terrace, Hanging-Garden-of-Babylon-style, is
bedecked with plants).

To the east of the "main entrance" is an awning and
steps leading up to the lobby of the apartments, safely removed from the public area. In fact, a "pedestrian bridge"

vaults the space over the lower lobby. Leather chesterfield sofas and Oriental carpets lend an air of old-world elegance to the lobby, and a fascinating tapestry of raw silk hangs from the east wall, a tapestry which when seen from the lower level looks like a fabric-shop display.

The entrance bears no resemblance to its tower, which is a conventional brown brick and glass building, only with "wintergardens," or enclosed balconies, on every other floor on the south facade of the building. The floors, which only measure about 80 by 112 feet, contain an average of eight apartments—four studios, three one-bedrooms, and one two-bedroom. What is unconventional is the top, a quadriplex that had been custom-built for Stewart Mott, with 7,500 square feet of terrace space for his "farm." His 2,000 tons of soil created a structural monster, making the fifty-five-story Galleria the tallest building in the city with a frame of poured-in-place concrete.

Roosevelt Island   1976

In the East River, roughly between Fiftieth and Eighty-sixth streets
Philip Johnson and John Burgee, Master Plan;
Johansen & Bhavnani and Sert, Jackson & Associates, Architects

A splendid bit of town planning for Manhattan's "other island," with a Main Street (literally) that creates sequential vistas and buildings that provide spectacular views.

Until its recent development as a new town, Roosevelt Island's existence was overlooked. It went through various ownerships, and names, including Varcken (Hog) Island, because swine herds were kept there, and Blackwell Island, because in 1685 it was owned by Robert Blackwell. In 1828 the City bought the island as a site for a penitentiary, and by mid-century a workhouse and orphanage were there, safely sequestered from the city. In the twentieth century, municipal hospitals were built on the island, and a little ferry would buck the mean East River tides from the foot of Seventy-eighth Street to link Manhattan with the island. Because of its municipal role, the island was named Welfare Island in 1914. It was only a matter of time, however, until somebody realized there were almost two miles of neglected real estate just off Manhattan's gold coast.

A first step in upgrading the island's image was the traditional name change: Welfare Island became Roosevelt

242

Island. Its master plan called for the island to be divided into three parts. Southtown was to have the necessary accouterments, including schools, hotels, offices, shops, etc. The center was to be a park. Apartments would be in Northtown. As a French magazine extolled its virtues, the island would be ringed by *la promenade, la circulation automobile* would be prohibited, and the *vues panoramiques sur Manhattan* would be *magnifique*. What has evolved is a splendid bit of town planning, with a Main Street that is purposely angled to create sequential vistas. The ambience created on Main Street is almost that of a ski town, or a new suburb of a medium-sized city.

Much of the massing of the U-shaped buildings is staggered, with wings as high as twenty stories on the spine of the island and rooflines that step down to the waterfront. The population of the island's 2,145 apartments runs the socioeconomic gamut, with low- and moderate-income housing overlooking Queens, and the middle- and upper-income housing overlooking Manhattan. A one-bedroom apartment in the luxurious Rivercross, which offers "Manhattan's most incredible co-op values" (Roosevelt Island is legally part of New York County, or Manhattan), carries an estimated monthly maintenance of $596.59, but included is an "all year swim/health club in the building."

The island is reached by an aerial tramway that opened in 1976, and will be linked to an extension of the subway by 1982. The question is, what do you do if you're cooking curry one night and you run out of cumin? Roosevelt Islanders say "Well, you plan ahead." Many who live there love it.

Its boosters promoted it as Manhattan's "other island." To many New Yorkers, however, it's just a nice place to visit.

One United Nations Plaza   1976

Northwest corner, First Avenue and Forty-fourth Street
Kevin Roche & John Dinkeloo Associates, Architects

Instead of setbacks or even "slopebacks," there are "slantbacks," with no hint that behind the taut skin is a combined hotel and office complex.

The United Nations Secretariat started the glass-wall movement in New York. Here, almost precisely a quarter of a century later, is the building that in the eyes of many represents the apotheosis of the style, as taut a glass skin as ever hugged a steel frame. The thirty-nine-story building provides no hint from its delicate grid of aluminum framing and blue-green reflective glass that the tower's first twenty-six floors house offices, that the twenty-seventh floor houses the Turtle Bay Tennis and Swim Club, and that the balance of the building is a hotel with tennis courts on its top floor.

This is New York's first building to combine office and hotel functions. It was built by the quasipublic UN Devel-

opment Corporation, a nonprofit organization that provides office space for the UN. The corporation's charter precludes its erecting any building taller than the UN Secretariat, so this one stopped at 505 feet, about 2 feet shorter than the Secretariat. One United Nations Plaza makes a bold statement about what a large building can accomplish by coming out to the building line. Instead of setbacks, there are "slantbacks," with two 45-degree planes on the north facade, and a slantout on the southeast corner that angles up. And angling down, extended over the street to create a covered pedestrian walkway, is a canopy that is an extension of the delicate curtain wall.

No neon announces the hotel's presence, no splavish Miami Beach awnings welcome conventioneers in search of a hot time in the old town tonight. Instead, tucked inconspicuously on Forty-fourth Street is a hotel lobby that is so petite it seems hardly large enough to accommodate the needs of the patrons in a 288-room hotel, but its functionalism is elegantly clear. And if you are someone in need of complete security, your bullet-proof limousine can pull up into an enclosed driveway that provides direct access to an elevator, so you never have to pass through the lobby at all.

When viewed from afar, say the FDR Drive in the twenties, One United Nations Plaza shimmers in the sun, like an oasis that is in reality a mirage. Fortunately, it is no mirage, and like all oases, its coolness is refreshing.

Manhattan Plaza   **1977**

Between Ninth and Tenth avenues, Forty-second
to Forty-third streets
David Todd & Associates, Architects

*A housing project that could have been a financial and
sociological disaster is instead a haven for performing artists.*

Plans were set in motion during Mayor Lindsay's administration in the 1960s to upgrade the Chelsea/Clinton area. A
new convention center, hotel, and housing project were all
planned as vital requirements for the area's renaissance, with
the new institutions, it was hoped, setting off a ripple effect.
Of the three, only the housing project has been built, and its
denouement was never dreamed of by its creators.

Manhattan Plaza was designed as housing for the upper
middle class. The one- and two-bedroom and studio apartments were built in two balconied buildings, one forty-five
stories high, the other forty-six, with amenities like squash
courts, tennis courts, and an Olympic-size swimming pool as
enticements. It was a nice idea, but unmarketable. Nobody
who could afford the rent was willing to pay it and live in
Clinton with the sleazy raffishness of Eighth Avenue only a
block away.

The City picked up the $90 million mortgage and was
stuck with two red-brick elephants. So great was the despair

that the eventuality of opening the buildings as a low-income development was considered. Clinton residents protested, claiming that the neighborhood would never be able to stage a comeback. On went the light bulb. Stretching a mile north from nearby Times Square is the greatest concentration of concert halls and legitimate and experimental theaters in the hemisphere. Two miles south are Greenwich Village and the East Village, with their nightclubs, jazz clubs, and even more experimental theater. Clearly, these 1,688 apartments were in the center of the performing-arts capital.

With about 80 percent of those in Actors Equity earning less than $5,000 a year, subsidized housing for performing artists seemed long overdue. The decision was made to rent 70 percent of the apartments to performing artists, with the understanding that the rent would be 25 percent of their yearly gross income. If an actor has a job this year paying $500 a week, his monthly rent is $500. If next year he is unemployed, his rent for the same apartment is one week's unemployment benefits. With this kind of security, the tenants are freed to concern themselves with other things than a roof over their heads. The rest of the apartments are about evenly divided among senior citizens who lived in the Chelsea/Clinton area, many of them retired performing artists themselves, and Chelsea/Clinton residents who had been living in substandard housing.

Where there might have been a disaster there are instead performing artists practicing their arts.

Citicorp Center
1977

Lexington Avenue between Fifty-third and Fifty-fourth streets, and east to Third Avenue on Fifty-fourth Street
Hugh Stubbins and Emery Roth & Sons, Architects

The city's most dramatic new skyscraper, its first great soaring thing since the RCA Building. The tower hardly begins until it is 127 feet up and doesn't stop until its trapezoidal roof pierces the sky 915 feet in the air.

The drama of Citicorp is everywhere within it and around it and away from it. The world's eighth-tallest building and midtown's third-tallest is entirely supported on four 127-foot-high super columns, or stilts. They are centered at the midpoints of the square tower, not at its corners, so where most buildings are, Citicorp is not. All four corners of the building are cantilevered on a steel frame, with a bracing system of diagonal steel chevrons on its perimeter that draws wind pressure away from the corners and down to the four columns. Except for its four stilts, the only link with the tower for its first 127 feet is the sheer wall of aluminum which houses the elevator shafts.

Tucked within the northwest corner of the open space created by the building's overhang is St. Peter's Lutheran Church, a chamfered cube of granite, like the rock upon which St. Peter said he would build the church. The former St. Peter's had stood on the southeast corner of Fifty-fourth Street and Lexington Avenue since 1904. Its congregation wanted to stay put, and was delighted to be part of Citicorp Center provided the church could maintain its own identity and remain at street level. St. Peter's agreed to sell its property to Citicorp and enter into a cooperative arrangement, the proceeds going into the construction of a new church. And so the idea of a great tower on stilts was born, with St. Peter's standing in its lee.

With one quadrant of the open space occupied by St. Peter's, a 9,000-square-foot sunken plaza was created for the second quadrant, on Fifty-third Street and Lexington Avenue. Here is a sunken plaza that works. With entrances to the building's concourse level and the IND subway, it works because it leads somewhere. Perched under the other half of the tower and extending east of it, a seven-story building houses a three-story complex of stores and restaurants, four stories of offices, and the way into the building, and it is all built around a multileveled skylit atrium. The view of the tower through its roof alone is worth the trip. Here is a place with a purpose and a vitality that are so often lacking in other interior urban spaces or midblock "amenities," a place that, like a London arcade, is filled with good things to buy, and, like a town square or piazza, is an elegant place to relax in.

The tower has none of the usual stage set for its lobby, nothing grandiose or pretentious. Banks of elevators are integrated into the public area, with the banks on two levels. Only odd-numbered floors are served from the street level, only even-numbered floors from the concourse level. Just as mysterious as the odd-and-even numbering system are the actions of the elevators themselves, which sometimes come to a full stop although nobody is getting on or off. Or so it seems. These are double-decked elevators, with one cab atop another, one set designed to stop at odd floors within a certain range, the other set designed to stop at even floors within the same range. (Local service is provided within each range, so if a passenger gets on at an even-numbered floor, he may get off at an odd-numbered floor.)

When the building was originally planned, its architect, Hugh Stubbins, hoped that the City would extend the special Fifth Avenue mixed-use zoning legislation to Lexington Avenue. Apartments were planned for the trapezoidal top, with each apartment given a terrace that would face south as part of the setback design. The City said no to the zoning variance, but Citicorp said yes to the trapezoidal top. Since it faced south, toward the sun, a solar-energy plant was planned for it, but later scrapped. Nevertheless, New York was given a break from the hegemony of the "flat tops."

The building's facade is a perfectly smooth skin of natural-colored, bright aluminum, banded with a double-glazed reflective glass, a facade that might be the ultimate statement of the International Style. Unlike some 1960s buildings, this facade is bright and cheerful, and reflects so much light that it is bruited that trees and bushes that have lain dormant in neighboring back yards are taking on new life. It is also a facade that reflects the colors of the sky. When viewed from the west at sunset, its silvered roseate hues stand out sharply against a dark sky, its shape a great soaring thing.

Glossary

abacus: the topmost member of a capital; the slab can be square, round, indented, etc.; it usually supports the architrave.

antefix: a vertical ornament at the eaves of a building that masks rows of joints in the roof; usually a leaflike ornament.

anthemion: a stylized honeysuckle motif; especially popular during the Greek Revival.

architrave: a lintel that spans the abacuses; the lowest part of an entablature.

Art Deco: the sleek "modernity" of the Jazz Age; geometric forms predominated, with Aztec and Egyptian art frequently incorporated; name derived from l'Exposition des Arts Decoratifs, a decorative-arts show held in Paris in 1925.

balustrade: a railing supported by closely spaced short pillars, or balusters; often found atop neo-classical buildings.

batter: to incline a wall from the perpendicular so that it slopes backward, often to create an illusion of height.

boss: decorative carving at the intersection of the ribs in a ceiling, usually found in Gothic architecture; bosses can depict people, animals, crests, floral patterns, etc., and are often painted and gilded.

bracket: a support that projects from a wall.

brownstone: Triassic sandstone with deposits of iron ore which give the stone a distinctive chocolate color; favored material for rowhouse facades in the last half of nineteenth century.

campanile: a bell tower.

cantilever: a structural member that projects horizontally from a vertical member and is supported by one end only.

capital: the uppermost set, or cap, of a column, pillar, pilaster, etc.

caryatid: a female figure that acts as a pier, usually supporting an entablature.

cast iron: molten iron that is cast in molds; cast-iron buildings had skeletons of cast-iron posts and lintels that heralded the advent of skyscraper design.

choragic monument: a small, decorative structure, usually round and supported by columns; erected in Ancient Greece to commemorate the victory of the leader of a chorus (hence, "choragic") in the competitive Dionysian choral dances.

classical: usually the style of Ancient Greece or Rome, including the five orders of architecture (Doric, Ionic, Corinthian, Tuscan, and Composite), decoration (egg and dart, fret, dentil, balustrade, rustication, etc.) and balanced form (usually divided into a beginning, middle, and end, or, in musical terms, the theme's introduction, development, and recapitulation).

colonnade: *a free-standing row of regularly spaced columns that supports an entablature or a roof.*

colossal column: *any column that is higher than one story.*

column: *a supporting pier in compression that is usually divided into three parts—base, shaft, and capital.*

console: *a decorative bracket, usually in the shape of a scroll.*

Corinthian: *of the five orders of classical architecture, these columns have the slenderest shafts and most elaborate capitals, decorated with acanthus leaves and buds.*

cornice: *horizontal molding that projects from a wall; used to define the terminal point, especially the roof, but often placed at midwall for composition.*

curtain wall: *a wall that does not support the building but hangs off the frame, like a curtain.*

deadlight: *round pieces of glass, about the size of silver dollars, set into the pavement to light the basement below; also called vault lights.*

dentil: *a band of toothlike rectangular blocks usually found in the lower section of a cornice (denticulated).*

Doric: *the least ornamented, most austere of the classical orders.*

egg and dart: *a classical pattern where egg-shaped elements alternate with dartlike arrows that are usually pointed down.*

embrasure: *the openings from which defenders would fire on attackers from the crenelated molding of a medieval fortress.*

entablature: *the horizontal structural lintel that sits atop the columns but below the pediment; usually divided into three parts—from bottom to top, the architrave, frieze, and cornice.*

escutcheon: *an ornamental shield that bears a coat of arms or initials.*

exedra: *a semicircular outdoor bench with a high back.*

fanlight: *a transom window that is usually semicircular and fitted with fanlike ribs.*

Federal: *the Americanization of the Georgian classical tradition in the decorative arts, 1790–1830.*

fenestration: *the design and organization of a building's windows.*

flèche: *a small steeple often found atop the transept of a Gothic church.*

Flemish bond brickwork: *a pattern where the sides of the bricks alternate both horizontally and vertically with the ends of the bricks.*

fluted: *concave grooves in the shaft of a column.*

Francis I: *a transitional style in French architecture that linked the Gothic with the Renaissance; named for Francis I, King of France (1515–1547), the monarch who made the Loire Valley "Château Row."*

fret: *linked, geometric ornamental patterns that are usually right-angled and often emanate from swastikas.*

frieze: *a horizontal member in a classical entablature that is flanked by the architrave below and the cornice above; often decorated.*

Georgian: the period in architecture in the United States dated by the first three English Georges, 1714–Independence; this classical style was derived from Andrea Palladio.

Gothic Revival: a Romantic revival of the Gothic style of architecture, reaching New York in about 1840 and continuing in its design stage for about fifteen years.

Greek Revival: the first of the great nineteenth-century eclecticisms; this Romantic approach to architecture added Greek trim to and increased the scale of domestic buildings, and created religious and commercial buildings in the temple image; about 1830–1845.

hexastyle: a portico with six columns.

International Style: volume that is geometrically bounded with absolute regularity and minimal decoration, synthesized by the aphorism "less is more"; begun in Germany during the 1920s, it is characterized by the use of industrial materials, glass, concrete, and steel.

Ionic: the classical order that is lighter than the Doric, not as elaborate as the Corinthian; the Ionic capital is characterized by four sets of volutes, or a pair of ram's horns per facade, with the egg-and-dart motif linking them.

Italianate: the mid-nineteenth-century style inspired by the Italian Renaissance.

lancet: the narrow, sharply pointed arches of the early English Gothic.

lintel: the horizontal, load-bearing member that links posts; often used above a window or a door.

lunette: a semicircular window or opening, often modeled after a crescent moon.

mansard roof: the roof of an attic story that is set back at an angle or a convex slope, often with dormer or bull's-eye windows poking out of it; named for François Mansart, French architect (1598–1666).

metope: the panels in a Doric frieze that alternate with triglyphs; they are sometimes decorated.

Moorish Revival: a short-lived eclecticism inspired by the Byzantine; it flowered in the 1870s.

mullion: in contemporary architecture, a vertical member that separates windows, often acting as tracks for window-washing gondolas.

oriel: a bay window that is cantilevered from a facade; sometimes more than one story high.

Palladian: modeled after the designs of the Italian architect, Andrea Palladio, 1508–1580; a pattern characterized by a round-headed window flanked by lower, square-headed windows; also, the name used to describe the neo-classical Georgian style.

parterre: ornamental flower beds.

pediment: in classical architecture, the triangular gable above a portico or wall that is often filled with sculpture; in Renaissance and Georgian decoration, variations that were pointed, curved, and broken topped doors, windows, highboys, etc.

peristyle: a colonnade on the periphery of a building.

pilaster: a flat pillar (often reflecting the form of a column), *which is not free-standing but projects from a wall.*

porte cochere: *a driveway that often leads to an inner court but that can arc through a building.*

portico: *a porch that is supported by columns and usually topped by a pediment.*

quoin, also known as coign and coin: *blocks with recessed joints set into a masonry wall at the corner (from the French, coin) of a building, often alternating sides with ends.*

reveal: *the side wall between an outer wall and a window- or doorframe in an arch.*

Romanesque: *the style of architecture characterized by Roman, or round-headed, arches, thick load-bearing walls, and barrel vaults; prevalent in Europe during the ninth to eleventh centuries.*

rostral column: *a triumphal column decorated with the bows of ships.*

rustication: *cut stone with deeply recessed joints, creating an appearance of great strength in a wall; favored for the lower third of neo-classical buildings.*

sgraffito: *wall or ceiling decoration that is achieved by scratching through one colored layer of plaster to reveal a second colored layer.*

spandrel: *in contemporary architecture, the panel between windows in a vertical row.*

stoop: *a short flight of steps leading to a platform and the front door of a private home or a tenement house; from the Dutch stoep, or step.*

stringcourse: *a horizontal band of masonry that is usually of a different material or color than the wall it rings.*

terra cotta: *baked clay—literally, "baked earth"—that is usually reddish-brown but can be almost any color; since it is baked in a mold, the same decorative motif can be stamped out and repeated on the facade of a building; also, an ideal fire retardant.*

torchère: *usually a three- or four-footed stand that supports a source for illumination; the style is usually Renaissance, but it can be Greek, Egyptian, etc.*

tracery: *in Gothic architecture, the curvilinear frames for glass within the upper part of a window.*

triforium: *in medieval church architecture, an arcaded gallery formed above the nave arcade and below the clerestory.*

triglyph: *the rectangular block in a Doric frieze that is divided into three vertical elements, or shanks, between the grooves.*

voussoir: *a structural wedge-shaped stone that forms part of an arch.*

ziggurat: *originally, an Assyrian or Babylonian temple tower in which each story was set back from and smaller than the one below it; used today to describe buildings whose bulk is set back and diminishes in cubic area the higher the building.*

Books for Further Reading

AIA Guide to New York City, by Norval White and Elliot Willensky. Revised edition, Macmillan, New York, 1978. The best and most complete one-volume guide to the architecture of New York's five boroughs today.

Cast-Iron Architecture in New York, by Margot Gayle. Dover Publications, New York, 1974. A photo-history, with text by a maven.

Classic New York, by Ada Louise Huxtable. Anchor Books, Garden City, N.Y., 1964. Georgian gentility to Greek elegance.

The *Columbia Historical Portrait of New York,* by John Kouwenhoven. First printed, 1953, by Doubleday; reprinted, Icon Editions, Harper & Row, New York, 1972. The best one-volume graphic history of the city.

Darkness and Daylight; or Lights and Shadows of New York Life, by Mrs. Helen Campbell, Col. Thomas W. Knox, and Inspector Thomas Byrnes. A. D. Worthington, Hartford, 1892. More darkness than daylight.

The *Epic of New York City,* by Edward Robb Ellis. Coward-McCann, New York, 1966. A most readable narrative history.

History Preserved: A Guide to New York City Landmarks and Historic Districts, by Harmon H. Goldstone and Martha Dalrymple. Simon & Schuster, New York, 1974. Good armchair reading.

The *Iconography of Manhattan Island,* by I. N. Phelps Stokes. Reprinted, Arno Press, New York, 1967. Everything you ever wanted to know about Manhattan Island, 1498–1909; in six volumes, this is the bible.

King's Handbook of New York City, by Moses King. Moses King, Boston, 1892. A treasury of pictures and words.

King's Views of New York, 1896–1915, compiled by Moses King. Reissued by Benjamin Blom, New York, 1974, Views.

Lights and Shadows of New York Life; or, the Sights and Sensations of the Great City, by James D. McCabe, Jr., 1872; reprinted, Farrar, Straus and Giroux, New York, 1970. How both halves lived.

Lost New York, by Nathan Silver. In many editions; first published by Houghton Mifflin, Boston, 1967. Responsible in large part for the awakening to the need for landmark preservation.

Mirror for Gotham, by Bayrd Still. New York University Press, New York, 1956. The city as seen by contemporaries from Dutch days to the 1950s, collected by and with text by one of the masters of urban history.

New York City Guide, Federal Writers' Project. Originally published, 1939; reprinted by Octagon Books, New York, 1970. The 1930s.

Old New York in Early Photographs 1853–1901, by Mary
Black. Dover Publications, New York, 1973. Photos from
the New-York Historical Society.
Rider's New York City, by Fremont Rider. Second edition,
the Macmillan Company, New York, 1924. The Jazz Age.

Walking Tours

These six walking tours are designed around essential New York buildings that cluster together. The routes have been intentionally plotted, and detours have been made, to include the greatest number of important structures. Naturally not every interesting building along a route is included, only those that are described in the book.

Depending on your pace and interest in exploration, each tour should take about three hours. The ideal way to take the tours is to read about the buildings along the route before setting out, and to refresh your memory at the sites. Page numbers for descriptions of these buildings can be found in the index. An asterisk after a building's name indicates that the building does not have its own entry, but is mentioned in the text under the heading of another building.

Convenient subway stations at the beginning and end of each tour are indicated by light gray balloons; a boldface letter or number indicates full-time service; all other letters or numbers indicate part-time service.

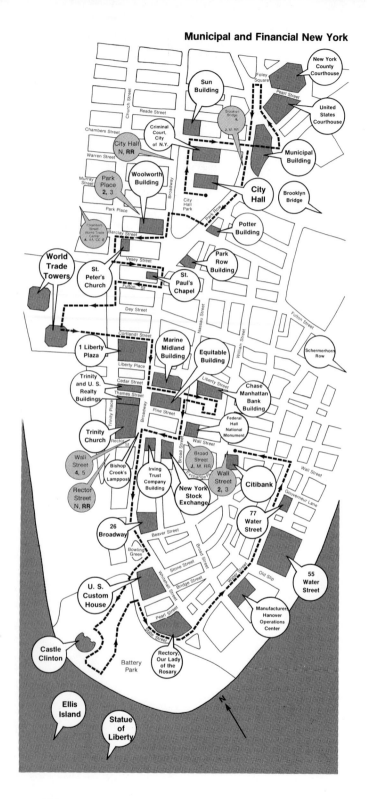

Greenwich Village

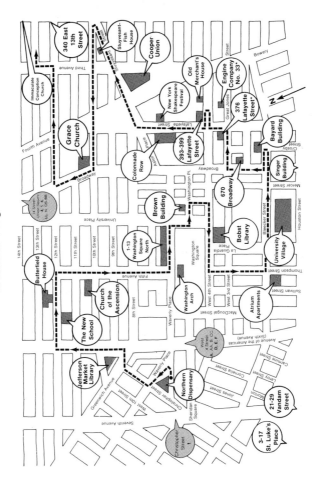

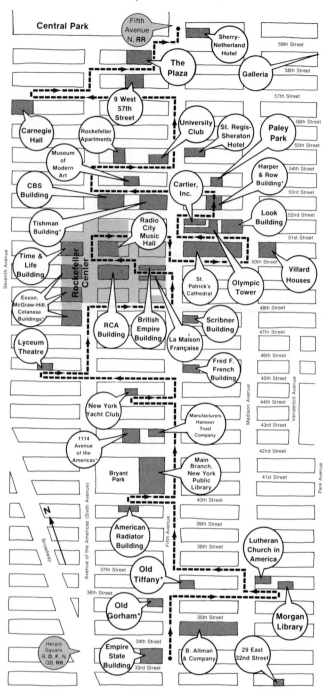

Fifth Avenue

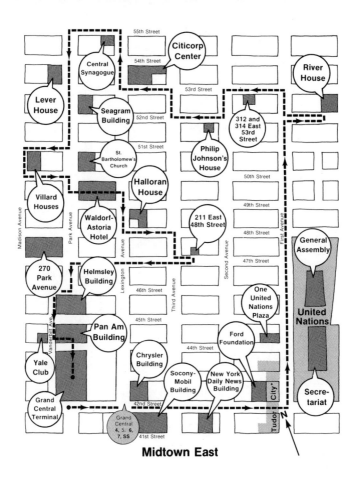

Midtown East

West Side

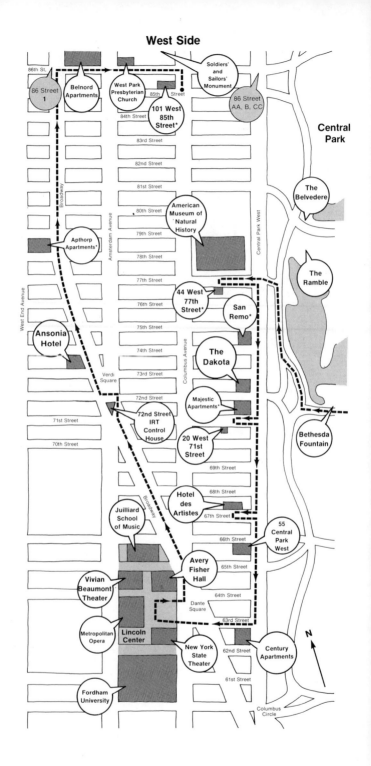

86th St.

86 Street 1

Belnord Apartments

West Park Presbyterian Church

85th Street

101 West 85th Street*

84th Street

83rd Street

82nd Street

81st Street

80th Street

79th Street

78th Street

77th Street

76th Street

75th Street

74th Street

Verdi Square

73rd Street

72nd Street

71st Street

70th Street

69th Street

68th Street

67th Street

66th Street

65th Street

64th Street

63rd Street

62nd Street

61st Street

Soldiers' and Sailors' Monument

86 Street AA, B, CC

Central Park

The Belvedere

American Museum of Natural History

The Ramble

44 West 77th Street*

San Remo*

Ansonia Hotel

The Dakota

72nd Street IRT Control House

Majestic Apartments*

Bethesda Fountain

20 West 71st Street

Juilliard School of Music

Hotel des Artistes

55 Central Park West

Avery Fisher Hall

Vivian Beaumont Theater

Metropolitan Opera

Lincoln Center

Dante Square

New York State Theater

Century Apartments

Fordham University

Broadway

Amsterdam Avenue

West End Avenue

Columbus Avenue

Central Park West

Columbus Circle

N

260

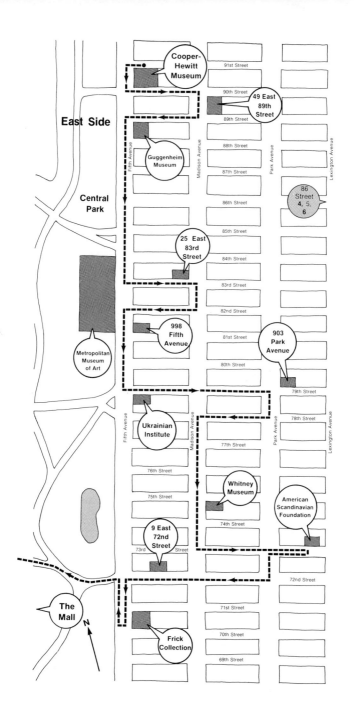

East Side

Central Park

Cooper-Hewitt Museum

49 East 89th Street

Guggenheim Museum

86 Street 4, 5, 6

25 East 83rd Street

998 Fifth Avenue

903 Park Avenue

Metropolitan Museum of Art

Ukrainian Institute

Whitney Museum

American Scandinavian Foundation

9 East 72nd Street

Frick Collection

The Mall

N

Fifth Avenue

Madison Avenue

Park Avenue

Lexington Avenue

91st Street
90th Street
89th Street
88th Street
87th Street
86th Street
85th Street
84th Street
83rd Street
82nd Street
81st Street
80th Street
79th Street
78th Street
77th Street
76th Street
75th Street
74th Street
73rd Street
72nd Street
71st Street
70th Street
69th Street

Index

Buildings known by their numbered street addresses are indexed under the street name: Fifth Avenue, No. 998; Eighty-ninth Street, No. 49 East; Liberty Plaza, No. 1.

Page numbers in *italics* indicate the main entry for a building or an architectural definition.